P9-CRL-727

MY JOURNEY

My Journey

A MEMOIR

OLIVIA CHOW

HarperCollins*PublishersLtd*

Dear Tiara,

Thank you for joining me on my journey.

Keep working for change.

Olivia Chow

My Journey

Published by HarperCollins Publishers Ltd

First edition

All photos courtesy of the author except where otherwise noted.

HarperCollins Publishers Ltd
2 Bloor Street East, 20th Floor
Toronto, Ontario, Canada
M4W 1A8

www.harpercollins.ca

Library and Archives Canada Cataloguing in Publication
information is available upon request

ISBN 978-1-44342-829-3

Printed and bound in the United States of America
RRD 9 8 7 6 5 4 3 2 1

For Beatrice and Solace,
in loving memory of their Grandpa Jack

CONTENTS

PROLOGUE

I follow the sun as it begins to rise over Toronto, and I start running east, along College Street. In black shorts and T-shirt, I jog by university students with backpacks heading to their classes, nurses and doctors in their whites entering the hospitals, cyclists in the bike lanes. My iPod is playing Jesse Cook, Latin guitar music I used to listen to with Jack Layton, my late husband, while we watched sunsets and danced on our back porch. Soon I cross Jarvis Street, not far from the high school I attended when I came to Canada.

Farther along, I run by Allan Gardens, a park with a Victorian greenhouse I used to visit as a teenager. I cherished the glass-walled conservatory's earthy damp smell and the warmth and quiet of the place. In those days, I lived with my parents in the St. James Town neighbourhood, just up the street on Sherbourne. My dad still lives there, and I wonder if I could get him to come out later for a walk in the park and to visit the nineteenth-century Gothic Revival churches, St. Peter's Anglican and St. Andrew's Evangelical Lutheran. They were designed by architect Henry Langley, who also designed the Toronto Chinese Baptist Church that my dad still attends weekly in Chinatown.

I run north on Parliament Street, then east again on Winchester Street, past elegant front yards full of hostas, cheerful black-eyed Susans and feathery reed grasses yielding to the breeze.

I am almost at Jack's final resting place, the Necropolis cemetery in Cabbagetown. I run past the Necropolis Chapel—also designed by Langley—and wonder whether I should pause and step inside. Maybe another day. I stop procrastinating, run through the gates and get there. To the spot where Jack's ashes are buried under a headstone of pink granite I ordered from Quebec and which is also the base for the bronze sculpture I created in the year after his death. Within seconds of entering the cemetery, I see Jack's smiling face staring at me. Perhaps I captured his likeness too well, because he looks so much like his joyful and cheerful self, and yet he is not moving. When he was alive, Jack was always in motion, always bursting with energy.

I fuss around the headstone with the little garden I planted, pulling out weeds, checking the plants. Is the bamboo growing too tall? Are the white mums still flowering? Should I add more of the purple lavender that Jack's mom so adores?

As I bid my farewell, I see a fellow with a camera taking a photo of the bronze sculpture. Of Jack.

My iPod is playing "Stand by Me," one of Jack's favourites, and I feel a deep sadness. I am sprinting now because I know that if I can absorb this sadness in the next few minutes, it will pass and soon I will be able to listen to the same song without the sorrow. I know I can slowly strip the sadness from all the songs, all the full moons, the scents, sights, light and sounds that all remind me so much of Jack—and then return to them as just the beautiful memories they are.

As I run, I reflect on how blessed my life has been. I turn my gaze towards the sky and I think of words from the Book of Job—words that helped me as I struggled to regain the balance in my life and understand the past few years.

"Have you entered into the springs of the sea, or walked in the recesses of the deep? Have the gates of death been revealed to you, or have you seen the gates of deep darkness? Have you comprehended the expanse of the earth? Where is the way to the dwelling of light, and where is the place of darkness?"

Accepting the mysteries of life and death and living in the moment help me contain the sadness of loss. And I think, instead of "stand by me," perhaps on my next run, my stepson, Mike, will "run by me." He has been training to do a half-marathon, something his dad always wanted to do but never found the time to train for.

Jack was a swimmer. Later on, I must take our grandchildren, Beatrice and Solace, for a swim. Maybe bring them and their mother, my stepdaughter, Sarah, to the big pool at the Central YMCA just north of College Street where I am now headed, running westward.

My sprint is fuelled by a change of tune and tempo on my iPod: Jimi Hendrix is playing "Crosstown Traffic" and then "Valleys of Neptune." In all my years with Jack, I could never figure out why he liked Hendrix. But now that Jack is gone, I can appreciate the soulful angst—I get it now.

I pass the College Street subway entrance and jog by as people stream in—it's rush hour, and they will be packed like sardines. Maybe soon the Toronto Transit Commission will have to take a page from Japan and hire staff to cram more people into the overfilled cars.

Maybe there is a reason why I am gradually listening less to my Arcade Fire and Adele in favour of the music of the sixties that Jack so loved. The sixties, a period of hope and optimism, when Canada had governments that believed in "caring and sharing." When the Canada Pension Plan and medicare—programs that are the essence of our country—were born.

In the last blocks of my five-kilometre run, I listen to the words of the Youngbloods' song "Get Together," sung at Jack's funeral, and smile at its call to love one another. Such a beautiful thought. I think of Jack's last message: Love is better than anger.

Canadians are generous; we believe we can create a fair and balanced society. So how can we come together to form a government that reflects our values? How can we persuade government to invest in children and public transit and to help generate good jobs so that no one is left behind? Jack and I always asked those questions, and sought the answers. I still do.

This gets me thinking about all the calls and meetings on today's agenda. I am running south on Huron Street, towards the house where I have lived for years—so many happy years with Jack. I need to open the door for a caregiver who helps look after my elderly mother. So I pick up speed and run home.

As I write these words, I realize that I have used the present tense, as I so often do when I speak. My first language is Cantonese, and in Chinese languages there is no past or future tense, just a sort of infinite tense. Jack is now part of that infinite tense. But I live in the present tense, and the stories in this book are my stories. Stories from the journey that has brought me here today. My journey, so far.

CHAPTER 1

Blue Pool Road

Naughty, spoiled, rebellious and lazy, I was a terrible student. I actually managed to fail Grade 3.

Father's Day, 2013. I am celebrating with my father and mother at the Dim Sum King Seafood Restaurant, in the heart of Toronto's Chinatown, this day packed with happy, chattering families.

I help my father, Wilson Wai Sun Chow, now suffering from dementia, while my mother, Ho Sze Chow, picks dishes of dumplings and ducks' feet from the passing carts, shouts greetings to friends and urges us all to eat everything in sight. We are an ocean, a continent, a half-century away from Father's Day in my first home, in Hong Kong, on Blue Pool Road in the community of Happy Valley. That magical name seems straight out of a children's book—the kind I devoured as a little girl.

There was then a dark and unsettling side to my life, and only when I was older did I fully grasp the cause. But as a child I was able to counter this mysterious black menace by creating my own world, one bathed in light. I convinced myself that I led a charmed life, marked by play, books and toys. And chocolates.

When my father, a highly respected school superintendent, made official visits to schools, he would be showered with gifts—usually luxurious gifts of chocolates. Boxes of them, tins filled with them, all colour-coded. Thin silver paper housed square or rectangular solid chocolates, while fine gold paper encased circular chocolates—nutty on the outside, creamy on the inside. These chocolates were fit for a princess, and because I was the centre of my father's universe, they were bestowed upon me. The sight or smell of chocolates still brings back memories of Hong Kong.

My father was a very talented, artistic and well-read man who chose to name me, he later admitted, for the olive colour of my skin at birth and also for a royal character in Shakespeare's *Twelfth Night*.

As elsewhere in Hong Kong in those days, where you lived reflected your class and status. Working-class people lived in overcrowded tenements at the bottom of the mountain, where the smog would settle. The rich lived at the top of the mountain, in spacious residences where cool breezes freshened the air and where the views were spectacular.

The Chow family lived halfway up the mountain—in the middle between those two extremes—and we were, indeed, firmly middle class. My father earned a good salary as a senior public servant, and my mother worked as an elementary school teacher, so we had a very comfortable family income. And we enjoyed a comfortable life, with a roomy apartment and a live-in housekeeper who did all the cooking and cleaning. Ours was a tight-knit community because most of the people living in the apartment complex were professionals, civil servants or educators like my mother and father. Every apartment was the same, with the housekeeper's living quarters right behind the kitchen and the laundry room.

Our household then seemed to revolve around me. But the Chow family tree was much more complicated than just father, mother and little Olivia.

My mother has had an extremely hard life, and in talking to her about my own journey as I wrote this book, I have learned more about hers. She lost her own mother to dysentery during the Japanese invasion of China that started in 1937 and lasted until Japan's surrender in 1945. My grandfather Ho, a silk merchant with five other wives and families to support, had disappeared to escape the invaders. When my maternal grandmother died, my mother was just thirteen years old. She had no money to bury her mother and was left to take care of herself and her two younger brothers, Ah Sing and Ah Ball. My mother survived by smuggling sugar, soap and oil, using a boat between Zhongshan and Macau.

This was a dangerous time. Japanese soldiers would come every night to look for "flower girls" to rape. My mother and other girls would hide in a mountain of hay at the back of a storage area while Japanese soldiers stabbed into the hay with bayonets to flush them out. She tells of smudging coal on her face so, if she was found, she would look horrific to the soldiers.

My mother's older sister had gone to another part of Guangdong, Qujiang, and later on my mother took her two brothers there, a dangerous trip through the occupied territory. Qujiang was the headquarters of the regional Chinese army, which had retreated there to escape the Japanese invaders. My mother joined the army and was teaching singing when she met Chow Nam Shang, a soldier whom she later married.

A year later, the Japanese planned to invade the area and again my mother fled, this time with her new husband. They had to hide in a ditch to escape the advancing Japanese army. Those were awful times, as on countless occasions my mother witnessed Japanese soldiers shooting indiscriminately. But again, she survived.

After the invasion, my mother and her husband settled in Guangzhou, where she gave birth to my brother Yu Ching Chow, later known as Andre. In the late 1940s, when my brother was about a year old, his father was killed by the Communists, in action during the civil war.

Seeking a better life, my mother, a young widow, returned to Hong Kong with Andre and married her second husband: my father, Wai Sun Chow. He was the sixth of ten children, the son of a domineering mother. His father had died when my dad was quite young, and there was no father figure in his life. My father and mother had known each other during their school years and, in the beginning at least, they got along well.

My mother loved Andre dearly and sacrificed a great deal for him. And at first my father accepted his stepson. Andre has an early memory of his mother and stepfather walking somewhere with him. "They were holding my hands, one on each side," he remembers.

But family peace and solidarity did not last. In my teenage years, after we had left for Canada, I would learn why. My mother revealed to me that while my father was married to her, he had maintained another household, with a woman called Lau, and they had a daughter, perhaps my age. And there was also a son, but the paternity of that child was very much contested by my father.

I have to say, in my father's defence, that most successful men in Hong Kong, even today, have a mistress. It was and is like a badge of honour. And polygamy—prevalent in China for thousands of years—

was only one generation back. My own maternal grandfather, remember, had six wives.

Amid all this turmoil at home, my mother gave birth to another son. The infant was just days old and still in the hospital when he became listless and developed a fever. A few days later, he died. My mother believed that the medical staff were tardy in detecting her son's symptoms and that the treatment had been inadequate. The hospital later claimed that the baby's blood type and my mother's were mismatched, and the cruel consequence was that my mother's immune system attacked her own infant's red blood cells in utero. The loss of his newborn son must have been devastating to my father and may also explain his choice of my name: at the beginning of *Twelfth Night*, Olivia is grief-stricken at the loss of her only brother.

Just as my mother bore the brunt of my father's anger, my brother Andre would come to suffer from his indifference and vindictiveness. The relationship between father and stepson had been good in the early years, but somehow things went sour—perhaps because my father had no room in his affections for anyone but me.

My father also beat my brother, mostly by kicking him. While I was writing this book in the summer of 2013, Andre told me that he would apply red dye to his skin after these beatings to draw attention to his injuries and to ensure that the bruises were visible to all—and especially to my mother. To alleviate her sorrow and as a form of escape, my mother became briefly addicted to the ancient Chinese game of mah-jong. She would go out to play all day and return home just before my father came back from work. So my brother was mostly alone after school.

My brother fed me and took care of me when my mother was out at her games. He was doing triple duty—as my brother and caregiver, as son and as my mother's protector in her battles against my father. The situation was so tense at home that Andre suffered from constant stomach problems caused by stress and was often sick with a host of illnesses—smallpox, sores and hepatitis A among them.

When I was two and my brother was twelve, we moved to Blue Pool Road and into an apartment much bigger and more prestigious than the one we had before. My dad didn't want his new middle-class neighbours to know about my brother, so even though Andre did well at school, my father would not allow him to continue his studies and insisted that he learn a trade—tuning pianos. My brother was a gifted pianist who had perfect pitch and he should have been encouraged in his music lessons, not elbowed into an apprenticeship. Of course he declined. My mother, naturally, objected to this harsh treatment of her son and persuaded friends to take in Andre. Only twelve then, he was shunted from one home to another, three in all.

Later on, when my brother finished high school, he wanted to go to university. As civil servants, my parents were entitled to send their children to study in England at very low cost. But my father refused to support the application. My mother had to borrow a lot of money from friends to send Andre to the United States to study electrical engineering. She went back to school and earned advanced certification so she could make more money teaching, enabling her to fund her son's education while paying back all her loans. Eventually, Andre won a scholarship in the United States, but my mother was burdened with these debts for years—all because of my father's inexplicable hostility to Andre.

What was there not to love about Andre? Ten years older than me, he was studious, meticulous, patient, obedient—everything I was not. My ideal brother treated his toys with care while I abused mine.

My brother had reason to be bitter, but he put aside his own treatment at the hands of my father. By his actions, he let me know: you, my little sister, are the apple of my eye. Until he left home, he would meet my school bus and give me a piggyback ride up the hill so I wouldn't have to walk. He would let me pull his hair and he played with me all the time. We went to the park on weekends and always had ice cream. He spoiled me and gave me any treats I wanted. He was my playmate and protector. One of the few crystal-clear memories I have of my early childhood was Andre's departure from Blue Pool Road. I can see him still, going out the door with his luggage and looking back at me as I wept and screamed for him to stay. Although he would return for weekend visits, he no longer lived with us. It felt as though my guardian angel had abandoned me.

A troubled man, my father had many blind spots, and my mother had a fiery temper.

Here was the source of the mysterious darkness I alluded to earlier. Our apartment in Happy Valley was a combat zone, and the combatants were my mother and father. I didn't know then what they fought about, but I can speculate now. The newborn son they had to bury and whose fault it was that he died. The stepson my father at first accepted and then rejected. My behaviour and performance at school. My father's jealousy, my mother's suspicions and her discovery of my father's other family.

A man who lived one floor above us was an amateur photographer, but my father became hostile when the man took some pictures of my mother and me. I was too young to recognize these early signs of his paranoia. He was jealous, too, of my mother's many friends in the building.

As for my mother's suspicions, it turns out that they were well founded. I never discovered the existence of my father's other family until many years later, but my mother certainly faced that hard truth back in Hong Kong.

The eviction of Andre ratcheted up the clashes between my parents. Had my father not been so threatened by my mother's affection for her son, had he not been so jealous and insecure, he could have embraced Andre as his own son. But he could not.

I still have powerful childhood memories of loud and violent arguments between my parents. My father beat my mother on many occasions, and my mother would throw things at him, or wield a knife to protect herself. (Fortunately, she never used it.) When I was in Grade 3—the year I failed—my mother once leaned out on the balcony and yelled that she would die soon because my father was going to kill her. While this drama unfolded, I hid under my desk and pulled in my bamboo chair.

Was I traumatized by these events? Perhaps. I have a powerful ability to shut out unwelcome noise, and I used it then. But is this ability innate, part of my makeup? Or was it a survival skill, something hard won through years of practice? I honestly don't know.

My father and mother were then in their late thirties, and that pattern of raised voices continues to this day, when both are in their late eighties. Still married, they have been separated for more than thirty years. My father still lives in the apartment in St. James Town that we moved to shortly after we immigrated to Toronto more than forty years ago, and my mother lives with me in my Victorian semi-detached house in downtown Toronto. I would love to have my father under the same roof, but I know what would happen. Our house would once again become a battleground.

After Andre left, I was the only child.

I had started kindergarten when I was just three and a half years old (this is still the norm in Hong Kong). Rosary Hill, a two-kilometre bus ride up the mountain, was a brand-new Catholic school started up by the Dominican Fathers. Neither of my parents was religious; their hopes for my education had drawn them to enrol me in this parochial school. I was the daughter of a senior educator and a teacher, and both were convinced that I would excel there. I proved them wrong. Naughty, spoiled, rebellious and lazy, I was a terrible student. I actually managed to fail Grade 3.

At that point, I was taken out of the hands of the Dominican Fathers and sent to the Maryknoll Sisters. This American order of Catholic teaching nuns had established themselves in Hong Kong in 1925 and set high academic standards for the teaching of girls. As it happened, in addition to their main Convent School in Kowloon, Hong Kong, they ran a neighbourhood school in Happy Valley, right across the street from our place on Blue Pool Road.

The Sisters were well educated, tough and kind, and they did their best to teach me. But I just picked up where I had left off at Rosary Hill and became the hellion of the school. Later, in my early teens, after I had discovered self-discipline, I excelled in class and even skipped Grade 8. But during those early years, I was a teacher's worst nightmare. Obsessed with play, I was the leader of the pack in the schoolyard. And in the classroom, I was the one organizing arsenals of paper folded into hard little Vs—missiles to be launched via elastic bands at other kids' heads when our teachers' backs were turned.

Every morning before class, dressed neatly in my blue and white school uniform, I went straight for the swings in the playground. I would skip, run and immerse myself in my make-believe world, one that books had helped me construct. Despite being a defiant student, I had learned to read when I was very young, and I consumed huge numbers of novels: Chinese romances by Chiung Yao, the martial arts novels of Gu Long and Jin Yong, and weekly kung fu magazines. At night, long after I had been sent to bed, I would read books under the covers using a flashlight and escape into my imagined world—one fed not just by books but by Chinese soap operas on the radio and my favourite TV shows and movies filled with drama, adventure and the heroics of Lassie, Batman and the characters on *Mission: Impossible*.

Every evening after dinner, it seemed, my father would say, "Why don't you go up to the rooftop and play with your friends?"

"But what about my homework?" I might reply. "I have to do some writing."

My mother and father played good cop/bad cop in this scenario, with my mother telling me, "Ollie, do your homework!" and my father indulging me. "Oh, don't worry about it. I'll write it for you" was his standard response.

"But you don't have the same handwriting as I do," I would counter.

"You'll never get away with it" was my mother's admonishment to the two of us.

"I'll use my left hand, and no one will be able to tell," my father would say, and so it was settled.

This all seemed perfectly normal to me, and I took full advantage. But my teacher eventually noticed that I wasn't actually doing the homework myself, and I got a detention. My father was doubly upset. It was unacceptable that the daughter of the school superintendent should be given a detention. He could not see that the detention was well deserved, or that he was the cause. By indulging me and meddling with my homework, he jeopardized both his career and my schooling.

My father was an educated, creative and talented man who sang Western opera in his spare time and who regularly performed on radio and with Hong Kong opera companies. Yet he had such a blind spot where I was concerned, and I was always prepared to take advantage of it.

My fantasy world didn't disappear when the sun came up. I had a bunk bed and I would hang curtains from the upper bunk to create a stage so my friends and I could put on elaborate dramas. No doubt influenced by what I was reading and watching, I stuck with an abiding theme—impossible rescues, with me as the invincible superhero.

Another stage was the rooftop of our apartment complex, a series of three interconnected four-storey buildings with a common roof. This was our playground, and what a vast and wonderful play space it was, filled with hiding spots—behind water tanks, under the various staircases. Up here, with friends who lived in the complex, we played catch and tag and hide-and-seek.

My constant companion was Ah Qui, a babysitter whose only job was to play with me, do my homework with me and be a "good influence." Our housekeeper was older and adept at cooking and taking care of the house, but she was definitely not a playmate for me. My mother had actually enrolled Ah Qui in my English classes to help me learn, but instead of studying at home we mostly listened to Chinese soap operas on the little radio I got for my seventh birthday. When my mother hid that radio, we listened to the big family radio in the living room. And when my mother pulled the plug on that one, we started exploring the neighbourhood and getting into endless trouble, for we were both fearless, high-energy types.

Living out superhero fantasies was exhilarating for both of us. One time when I was about ten years old, I climbed a very high rooftop antenna, which was a deliciously scary but reckless thing to do. Ah Qui was older than me and should have restrained me, but she did not. Neighbours saw me and dutifully informed my parents. The ultimate adventure was the day that Ah Qui tried to teach me how to climb the building—from our third-floor balcony to the one above us—using water pipes and the bars that secured the balconies. She had climbed up to visit her friend on the fourth floor, so why couldn't her ten-year-old charge do the same? There was one minor detail she had ignored: if she slipped, she would fall three storeys and break her neck. And the same fate awaited me if I lost my grip. We were caught in the act, and our days as a Dynamic Duo came to an end. Ah Qui was sent packing.

I was once again on my own, and I remained obsessed with play. I had plenty of playmates at school and in the complex—including my best friend, Rosalind But, another high-spirited girl. Unlike me, though, she excelled in school and at piano. And, as my father's over-indulged only child, I certainly had all the toys I needed. At my birthday parties, the presents would roll out: the teddy bear, the furry Bugs Bunny that said "What's up, doc?" when you pulled the string on his back, the James Bond peashooter (which stung many a victim), the wooden sword, the electric train, the remote-controlled tank that I deployed to bulldoze the Lego houses I had just finished building. All perfect for an adventure-seeking tomboy. I had a dollhouse, too, and I occasionally moved the furniture around.

On weekends, my mom and dad and I would often go to the beach with my dad's brother and his six children. We would swim, play catch, build sandcastles and dream. My mother and father had many friends in Hong Kong and they all had children my age, so we were constantly playing.

~

My childhood was marked by light and dark, by times of pure joy and other times of almost unbearable tension at home.

I recall the dread I felt whenever I was asked as a child to make an impossible choice. From time to time, my parents would ask me: If we separate, which of us would you choose to live with? My father doted on me and let me do whatever I wanted, while my mother was the disciplinarian. But I loved them both.

We had many wonderful moments as a family when I was little, like the days at the beach, and parties and celebrations. I had many friends—all of them more diligent than me in their studies. Virtually all little children in Happy Valley took piano lessons, and the expectation was that we would all do well in school.

I did not meet those expectations. My piano lessons lasted less than a year. At school, I was punished time and again for acting out. I'd get the strap—those were the days when corporal punishment was normal—or I'd be made to put my back to a wall with my knees bent. The aim was to make my thighs burn, but I was in terrific shape from all my running in games of tag. My attitude was, "Bring it on!" I was rebellious, restless, difficult—and a supreme embarrassment to my educator parents. In a class of thirty-five, I would habitually come in thirty-fourth—because I was not paying attention, did not study or do homework and just did not care. It's amazing that I failed only one grade.

My dad thought I was doing poorly because I was lonely, so he bought me a dog—a little terrier I called Bella—to keep me company. She was a wonderful pet, but she met a sad fate on the road and was replaced by another terrier, also called Bella. This second Bella was impossible—constantly barking, disobedient, frenetic. She chewed everything in sight and was soon banished from the household. And then came Ah Woo (which means "grey" or "dark" in Cantonese). I did many drawings of Ah Woo. I captured his curling tail, his dark sensitive eyes and his stubby legs with hair almost to the floor. I even captured his sweet and attentive face. Ah Woo followed me everywhere and would quietly sit by me through good times or bad. We also had hamsters, fishes, birds and, at one time, two turtles.

And when the miniature zoo failed to have the desired effect, and the hamsters were threatening to take over the apartment, my father started hiring tutors. Every few months, a new one would appear and try to make me focus on my studies. They mostly quit because I was impossible to teach, and I would make their lives hell, hiding their umbrellas, ignoring my schoolbooks and disobeying them.

By Grade 6, when I was ten, I was on the brink of being tossed out of school. But then a remarkable young woman entered my life—Sophia, my new tutor. She had been educated by the Maryknoll nuns, and she embodied the selflessness that was central to their faith. And somehow, she had faith in me. Sophia connected with me through her patience, her love and her understanding of what I was going through at home. That connection was a turning point.

By now I finally clued in that I would have to pull up my socks and behave or else I would get kicked out of the school and lose many of my friends. I would also have to face the humiliation and boredom of travelling for an hour each day to another school. After my mother read me the riot act, and with the gentle encouragement of Sophia, I ditched Batman, *Mission: Impossible*, Lassie, the countless Walt Disney movies and the Chinese variety show "Happy Tonight." Ditto the romances, fantasy novels and superhero comics. I snapped out of my make-believe world, and I squarely faced reality. Finally, and for the first time in my life, I studied. I applied myself to work as I had applied myself to play.

My dad got into the act, too, and purchased the Hong Kong version of *Coles Notes* for me—shortcuts to help me make up for lost time. Within six months, I had passed all my exams and had high enough marks that I was promoted to Form One, meaning that I could now proceed to junior secondary school.

~~~

When he was fourteen, my brother had taken up Wing Chun, a Chinese martial art later made popular by the movie *Ip Man*, about the Wing Chun kung fu grand master (who taught Bruce Lee, among others). No doubt Andre started learning it in order to protect my mother. On and off, Andre practised Wing Chun for more than six years, and he became more and more confident. Whenever Andre came home to visit, he would show off his latest Wing Chun move. I was totally mesmerized and would often beg him to teach me a few moves. He knew he could tackle my father if he had to. And my father seemed to know it too. Every time Andre came home on weekends, my father was too wary of him to strike my mother.

After such beginnings, I am amazed that my brother turned out strong and well. Andre got a degree in electrical engineering and held down good-paying jobs all his life. After a successful career in New York as the chief financial officer of a fashion company, he's now semi-retired and works part-time. He's also a talented photographer—he took my very first campaign photo when I ran for school trustee almost thirty years ago. We both have two grandchildren, and even though he has a lot of buried anger, he was able to manage it through meditation—he is a vegan Buddhist.

This lovely, gentle man managed to rise above my father's ill treatment. One of my dreams is to have him retire to Canada so we can meditate and travel together.

"I want to learn judo, ballet and guitar," I said to my mother when I was thirteen, "but I can only take two after-school activities, not three. What should I take?"

"Judo and guitar," my mother advised.
~~~

"Ballet," said my father. "Definitely not judo, because you are enough of a tomboy already."

My mother had a reason for picking judo. As she told my father, "She can defend herself in future against men who want to take advantage of her."

So I signed up for guitar lessons—and judo. Three months later, my mother invited me to practise on my father. We all cheered when I was able to "throw" my dad to the ground.

But then it was my turn to be thrown and have my world turned upside down. My father announced that we were leaving Hong Kong.

Meanwhile, the Cultural Revolution was raging in Mainland China, bringing upheaval and bombings to Hong Kong. I was barely aware of the 1967 riots, but my parents were alarmed. I vaguely remember a bomb that was planted in our neighbourhood. Those riots had been accompanied by drought, made worse when China cut off the flow of water from the mainland. There were severe water restrictions, and people went days without water. Anxiety about the future of Hong Kong was widespread.

Finally, my father embraced the hope that if he took early retirement and made a new start somewhere else, family tensions would subside. Vast numbers of people were leaving Hong Kong, and we would ride that wave. (Andre had preceded us; he was by then studying at an American university.) My dad wanted a clean slate, and a better future for his daughter.

Soon I was saying farewell to all my friends, my dog Ah Woo and my comfortable middle-class life on Blue Pool Road in Happy Valley. The Chow family was being uprooted. Our destination was Canada and the city with the largest Chinese-speaking community in that country. Toronto.

CHAPTER 2

St. James Town

An immigrant to a new land is always looking for home, in whatever form. For me, home—our apartment in St. James Town—was a place marked by angst and sometimes violence. So I sought a sense of belonging elsewhere.

Saltine crackers with peanut butter on top.

This became my comfort food, an after-school snack, soon after I arrived in Toronto from Hong Kong in the summer of 1970, at the age of thirteen. I can't remember where I picked up this habit—certainly not from my mother, who found Canadian food bland and who had no interest in venturing into a new cuisine. But just as the sight and smell of chocolates bring back memories of my Hong Kong childhood, the sight and smell of peanut butter conjure up my teenage years in Toronto.

In the Chinese calendar, 1970 was the Year of the Dog, and I sorely missed mine. My beloved Ah Woo was given away to relatives when we left Hong Kong, relatives who passed him on to other relatives, after which Ah Woo's trail goes cold. I don't know what happened to him. I know only that when I arrived in Canada at the age of thirteen, I felt an overwhelming sadness. I was Woo-less.

I don't really remember our departure from Hong Kong. I look at a photograph of thirteen-year-old Olivia taken at the airport, and she looks like a bored teenager, but I'm sure I was anything but bored. I don't recall much of the flight either—except for a memorable moment when fire broke out on the left wing and we were forced to stop over for a day in Anchorage, Alaska.

I can't say that I suffered much from culture shock when we first arrived, beyond enduring the usual teenage angst about where I fit in and belonged. There were large numbers of Chinese Canadians in Toronto, which is, in part, why my father and mother had chosen that city. I am so grateful for the many Chinese Canadians I befriended at this time who eased me into school and this new life in a new country. I had friends who looked like me.

My mother spoke very little English, but my father spoke fluent English and I had studied English in school. I had another advantage when orienting to this new world: I had grown up watching Batman, Bugs Bunny, Mr. Ed and the delightful Road Runner and the less than aptly named Wile E. Coyote.

Home on our arrival was a house at 124 Kendal Avenue in the Annex neighbourhood of Toronto, where many grand old Victorian homes had been converted into rooming houses and flats. We occupied the third floor. Downstairs lived the Mah family, whose children had been born in Canada and who knew the ropes. In Hong Kong I had been the bold and audacious leader of the pack, but in this new environment, I went through a period of shyness and held myself back. I would steel myself and sometimes go downstairs and watch hockey with the Mah kids and marvel at the speed of the game.

When winter came that year, I would often take the subway to city hall and skate under the arches at Nathan Phillips Square—built just five years before the Chow family came to Canada. I think I fell fifty times the first time I put on skates; I came home black and blue. But like all immigrants to a new country, and all teenagers, I wanted to fit in. Knowing how to skate seemed a quintessentially Canadian skill, and it was the first one I acquired. Others would follow: wilderness survival skills, backwoods hiking, whitewater paddling and long-distance cycling.

Not long after we had settled in Toronto, our family moved to the newly built high-rise neighbourhood of St. James Town, just south of Rosedale, Toronto's most affluent neighbourhood. St. James Town consists of nineteen high-rise apartment buildings comprising some seven thousand units—all set on a relatively tiny patch of land, of thirty-two acres. We lived on the eighth floor of an apartment building. Our apartment was standard issue: wood parquet floors, a galley kitchen, a balcony with a view of a parking lot and a swimming pool. Our building was only a few years old and still had a shine to it. Densely populated St. James Town was a magnet for newcomers from all over the world, and our building was no different.

I was still the tomboy who used to arm-wrestle the boys and sometimes win. One thing I did not do was bring my friends home, for home—more than ever—was a tempestuous place.

The move to Canada was supposed to give us a wonderful new life, but, like many immigrants, we experienced setbacks and shocks. My father, the former school superintendent, and my mother, the former teacher, suffered a perilous decline in both income and status.

At first, the only work my mother could find was as a seamstress in what can only be called a sweatshop. I worked there, too, for several months, sewing decorative buttons onto blue jeans (as was then the fashion). Then my mother worked as a maid and later in the laundry department of a hotel near city hall. The first job was tough, the second one tougher. The basement laundry at the Delta Chelsea Hotel was noisy and damp, and although my mother worked quickly, as the job demanded, she was unable to avoid the scorn of her supervisor, who was unfair and likely a racist to boot. There were many stations in the laundry—dropping sheets and towels into the machines, hauling laundry out, drying the linen, folding it. Taking out the wet and heavy just-washed linen was the hardest task, and one that often fell to my mother. From working in all that humidity for decades, my mother developed arthritis, which worsened as she aged.

When she finally retired at the age of sixty-five, after all those years of toil, my mother's pension was a lump sum of just over three thousand dollars. Later, in my political life, I would come to understand the importance of a good pension plan so that seniors can retire in dignity. My mother's own story would become a powerful motivating force.

I wish I could report that when my mother finished her gruelling shift she found respite at home, but there was none. My father could not find a job teaching, though he was qualified and spoke English well. There wasn't much work for him as a substitute teacher, and when he did get called in, he found it difficult to control the classroom; he complained that Canadian students were not as obedient as those in Hong Kong. He tried pursuing a master's degree, but it didn't seem to make any difference. He lasted a year delivering Chinese food at low pay. Then he worked for a few months as a taxi driver, but found he couldn't understand the rapid-fire dispatch orders. He worked occasionally as a labourer, but he never found a niche or made much money, so he was increasingly frustrated and bitter.

Worse was the violence. My father had been beating my mother even before I was born, but these beatings now escalated as new strains and pressures rocked them both. My father had been managing his life quite well in Hong Kong despite the irrational anger that darkened the home front. But now, in that eighth-floor apartment in St. James Town, faced with disappointment and shame, his fury boiled over. The paranoia that had emerged back in Hong Kong now manifested itself in new and terrible ways. Again, my mother bore the brunt.

One night, when she was asleep, he hit my mother's head with a lamp and left an awful gash. It's a wonder he didn't kill her. He was neither athletic nor tall (just five foot seven), but he was strong when he was in a state. So many times when we were living in that St. James Town apartment, I put myself between my warring parents or pulled my father off when he was battering my mother. One time I almost lost control: I grabbed a lamp and had it raised, intending to hit him. Something stayed my hand.

This may seem strange but I have to say: my father was otherwise a wonderful and generous father, always kind to me and nurturing. I eventually managed to separate the quintessentially decent man from his sometimes quintessentially indecent behaviour. He did unforgivable things to my mother and my brother. I was in my late thirties and early forties when I was finally able to forgive him. It took me that long to discover what state of grace is—it's achieving the peace and freedom of living in the moment, and not allowing past wrongs to colour the present.

Even as he struggled with his demons, my father remained creative. Music was his one solace. He has composed music for hundreds of songs, using biblical passages or poems in both Chinese and English—the romantic poetry of Byron was his favourite. For years he was in the church choir at the Toronto Chinese Baptist Church and he was happiest when he was performing and composing. When Jack and I were married, my father composed a beautiful song for our wedding, using the words of the poem "Friendship" by Elizabeth Jennings, which has themes of gentleness, respect, trust and awe.

But my father's creative impulse, while vibrant, could not subdue or soften the anger and emotion roiling inside him. One day I had the idea of secretly recording what he was saying in hopes that when his ravings were played back to him, he would fathom, finally, how ill he was. But he was too far gone to be helped in this way.

I rarely brought friends home lest they see for themselves the yelling, the nonsensical mumblings of my father and the depressing environment in our apartment. But on the few occasions that I did invite friends over, my father would follow them back to their own homes and try to befriend them along the way. He would stay at their houses and refuse to leave. Needless to say, this was supremely embarrassing to me as a teenager.

This was a period in my life of great loneliness and great shame. For us, no help was forthcoming. I did try speaking to someone in the guidance department at Jarvis Collegiate, where I was then a student, but that got me nowhere. My mother could not speak English, so she couldn't seek help either. Like so many immigrant families, we were on our own in a new land with no relatives or friends to help us.

My father finally had a mental breakdown and landed in a psychiatric ward. He was totally paranoid, imagining that people were trying to poison or drug him. Various doctors posed different theories about what was wrong before they decided on electroshock treatments and medication that profoundly affected his ability to function normally.

I think back to those times and I wonder how differently things might have gone for my parents had there been comprehensive support, counselling and psychological help—beyond what my father got in a hospital when the crisis point had already been reached. The isolation that we felt as a family is something I have never forgotten. Later, as an immigrant support worker who became engaged with the community socially and politically, I did all I could to propose and enable organizations such as Chinese Family Life Services of Metro Toronto and the Hong Fook Mental Health Association so that people in my father's shoes would have access to a wide range of mental health supports. My own experience within an immigrant family had stamped me, and when I became an elected official, I did all I could to change patterns and to find solutions.

In those teenage years, I was longing for some sort of escape, but there was none to be had. My mother had gone from having a housekeeper in Hong Kong to being a maid in a Toronto hotel. My father, meanwhile, had struggled in vain to find a good job and couldn't handle the stress. So life was hard. But one summer, when I was sixteen, I saw an opportunity to escape. I saw an ad calling for a junior forest ranger. Against the wishes of my parents (my mother, especially, was horrified at the idea), I went up north to work in the wilderness for the summer—planting trees, clearing and cleaning portage routes and campgrounds—for five dollars a day.

From Toronto I took an eleven-hour bus ride over a thousand kilometres northwest to Wawa—the town at the east end of Lake Superior famous for its twenty-two-foot-long Canada goose monument alongside the Trans-Canada Highway. I then travelled many more kilometres to a wilderness camp not far from Lake Superior. I was in the company of other girls my age and a cook—an eccentric old fellow who used to feed pancakes to the black bears that hung around the camp. My experience with the ranger program was a turning point in my life, as it has been for thousands of other youth. (I'm sad to report that the Province of Ontario announced in the summer of 2013 that it was selling the camps and closing the residential junior forest ranger program that had been going strong since 1944.)

This camp would lead to other camps in other summers, church camps run by the Toronto Chinese Baptist Church, or Outward Bound courses. In one, I spent three days alone on an island. Another saw me rappel down a cliff. I was picking up useful skills—how to navigate in the forest, how to survive in the bush and how to paddle a canoe, at first on a lake and then down rapids, Class I and up to Class III, the truly challenging ones.

Up north I fell madly, passionately in love—with the Canadian wilderness. During my first years in Toronto, when I was deeply involved with the Toronto Chinese Baptist Church, I had read a great deal about the Promised Land. And here it was. When I was in the North I felt in touch with the divine, and that connection has endured.

From never seeing stars in the middle of Toronto, I was suddenly seeing millions of them, plus northern lights, and watching beautiful sunsets and admiring the magnificent colours in the Canadian Shield. Even the blackflies, horseflies, deer flies, sandflies and mosquitoes seemed lovely to me. Though bitten, I was smitten.

This was a life-changing experience. I came to appreciate nature. I came to have a sense of Canada—of being a Canadian. I came to understand those words we sing in our anthem—the true North, strong and free.

I also came to acquire a sense of the infinite—of being part of something huge and powerful, pure and beautiful, this vast land with its boreal forest, its Great Lakes and thousands of pristine rivers. I came to understand that there was a powerful force bigger than me, bigger than my family problems. I found a sense of peace and belonging I had never felt before. And I began a lifelong love affair with the wilderness.

And it wasn't just tranquility I loved. One summer, on one of my canoe trips, we encountered a massive storm. I sat under a rock cliff and watched the approaching thunderclouds. The sky darkened, the wind picked up speed and howled. The power of the wind, the rain and the lake mesmerized me for hours. I marvelled at the smallness of my being in the face of such immense force and put my own problems in proper perspective.

An immigrant to a new land is always looking for home, in whatever form. For me, home—our apartment in St. James Town—was a place marked by angst and sometimes violence. So I sought a sense of belonging elsewhere.

School, for one. Jarvis Collegiate dates from 1807 and is the oldest secondary school in Toronto. Conn Smythe, the long-time owner of the Toronto Maple Leafs, went to Jarvis, as did newspaper magnate Roy Thomson and author Ernest Thompson Seton.

I owe that old school a great deal. They took a little immigrant kid and made her feel loved. The school had an interesting mix of students—some the born-in-Canada sons and daughters of immigrants; some kids like me, "just off the boat"; and some the offspring of elite Rosedale families with expectations of rigorous academic standards. There were also a few kids from a low-income area called Regent Park.

My mind was really opened at Jarvis, and it was there that I began to acquire true self-discipline by taking challenging math courses (triple math, we called it) and physics. After skipping Grade 8, I had come to the school primed to study, and study I did. I was getting perfect marks in physics, and once I became accustomed to those marks, nothing less would do. The bar had been set. Besides, by now I had acquired pure discipline, and that was a good thing, for I had the Hong Kong kids who got 100 per cent in math breathing down my neck.

But while I was excelling in math and physics (where discipline helped) and art (which came naturally to me), English remained a hurdle. Pronunciation, especially, was hard in the beginning. I would slide down low in my seat so my English teacher would not ask me to read aloud. One day I was asked to read from *To Kill a Mockingbird*, a book I still adore. But that day was a disaster. I stumbled, turned beet red and could not wait for the ordeal to end.

I had some close friends during those first few years in Canada, but not many since I remained shy. I desperately wanted to fit in, so I joined the basketball team and the track team, specializing in the hurdles and sprints but not distinguishing myself in either. Bell-bottom jeans were all the rage then, but I had no money. So I took the jeans I already had, opened them up with scissors and inserted a piece of denim before sewing them up again. The result looked strange and actually set me apart—not what I had had in mind. But this was one measure of my desperation.

The real connection came through my teachers, some of them quite gifted. One was a demanding and innovative English teacher who would invite some of his students to his farm property for weekend retreats, where we would discuss at greater length the novels we were reading. This was in the early seventies, and though this practice would be absolutely forbidden now, I found it was a fabulous way to delve deeper into literature, and it opened up a whole new world for me.

Books like Orwell's *Animal Farm* and Golding's *Lord of the Flies* got me thinking: Are we born evil, or not? Are we born good, or not? Who wins when the two collide? The villain in Orwell's satire issues a commandment that reads, "All animals are equal, but some animals are more equal than others." Really?

By the time I was in Grade 12, I was reading Dostoevsky's *Notes from Underground* and *Crime and Punishment* and went about inserting lines from T. S. Eliot's poem "The Hollow Men" into my paintings. I am eternally grateful to that English teacher. He was kind and shy but demanding—the hardest-marking teacher I had ever encountered. A 70 from him was a good mark. He challenged us and pushed us to think hard. He introduced me to more work by the existentialists (Camus, Kafka, Kierkegaard), and another world opened up for me.

Art was my other great passion. My father had been artistically inclined, and from childhood on, I was always drawing. In fact my father had moved our family from the Annex neighbourhood to St. James Town so I could attend a high school that taught art. My father was functioning well enough in those days, and by the little bit of supply teaching he had done and by asking questions, he had learned where his daughter could study art.

I was active in the school's art club, and my paintings were hung in the corridors. I was also learning to do Chinese brush painting, and every Saturday morning I would take life drawing classes at Central Tech high school. Art was a passion of mine and, soon enough, a paying proposition. Money was tight at home, so I always had part-time jobs. For a few years I worked two or three shifts a week as a cashier at the Shoppers Drug Mart at Bloor and Spadina, in midtown Toronto. But I was also working for an artist with an entrepreneurial bent. This fellow employed men who knocked on doors around Toronto selling "original art" out of vans. In fact, he had about eight ink-drawing designs (Toronto City Hall, the Rideau Canal and Parliament Hill, a sailboat, a farm), which he would reproduce via a silkscreen process; I would then lay overtop a fresh coat of watercolour. Presto—original art.

During my last year of high school, my family needed more money—we could barely survive on my mother's income. Though we watched every penny and worked hard for every dollar, I knew I needed a job that paid better than what I was earning as a cashier. At first I tried my hand at telephone soliciting—selling newspaper and magazine subscriptions. I was good at this, but I thought I could earn even more working in a restaurant.

That's where the Old Fish Market Restaurant (since closed) came into play. I started working there as a hostess, and in 1975, when I was of drinking age, I became a waitress. I had no idea of the names of beers and cocktails, nor did I know how to open a bottle of wine. I would learn to perfect the task over the next five years. My job as a waitress and hostess taught me how to approach people warmly, people of all sorts, and how to defuse any kind of problem. I had been a shy student in high school and did not socialize a lot. This job forced me to be outgoing. I had to put on a smile and greet customers—even when the kitchen was a torrent of yelling and screaming.

In many ways, it was a perfect job for me. I was a little manic and hyperkinetic, I was high-energy and I had spent too much of my childhood playing. Now it was time for work. The restaurant was downtown, by the St. Lawrence Market, and close to the theatres, so it was always busy. The key was to be calm in the face of chaos. Anyone wanting to learn how to multi-task should consider being a server, at least for a time. In later years, when I became involved in politics, I was able to draw on this experience.

On the other hand, there was stress in waiting on tables. I would have what those who have worked in the restaurant business call "waiter dreams," in which the anxieties of serving play out. My own waiter dream had to do with how to fillet a whole rainbow trout—an item on the menu at the Old Fish Market. Trout tastes amazing, but this fish has to be cooked just right. Overcooked, it loses the flavour, but if it's undercooked, the meat won't come off the bones. When filleting tableside, cutting off the head looks terrible, but retaining the head while deboning requires skill—surgical precision, really—owing to fragile bones immediately behind the fish's head. When my task was done well and elegantly, I would get good tips and satisfaction; when I did it badly, I worried that customers would choke on the fine bones. In my dream, perfection always eluded me.

By Grade 13, I knew I had to get top marks if I hoped to enter a top-tier post-secondary institution such as the University of Toronto. My father's inability to control his nonsensical, loud mumblings was making it impossible to study at home, so I moved out and shared an apartment with a boyfriend.

I should explain that ours was a platonic relationship. All through high school, I had male friends, but at the time I was a fundamentalist Christian and I insisted on certain rules. No sex before marriage was one of them. As a seventeen-year-old, I was very strict about this. In this older student's house, we slept separately—so even my mother had no objections to my new living arrangement. The relationship, though chaste, was romantic, at least at the outset. This fellow had walked into the drugstore where I worked one day and began reciting a beautiful Chinese poem to me (his BA was in Chinese literature, and he was pursuing his MA in poetry at U of T). He was a quiet, thoughtful, considerate man with no particular ambitions—which seemed ideal to me at the time.

An added bonus was that his place was like a sanctuary—quiet and free of turmoil. Again it seemed ideal. But unfortunately, I am easily bored, and I soon became restless with our relationship. After a year, I ended it, citing our different temperaments. I was competitive and didn't want to waste one moment of my life, whereas he was content with a slower pace, and accomplishments mattered less to him. By that time, though, I had been accepted to the University of Toronto and was back living at home in St. James Town.

I loved the process of learning, and one of my favourite places on campus was the tranquil neo-Gothic library at Emmanuel College, with its stunning stone-framed arched windows and its gorgeously ornate carved-wood ceiling—so unlike the modern, oppressive concrete of the Robarts Library on the same campus.

I devoured my courses in philosophy and religion. Then a devout Christian, I was obsessed with the question that if God is all-loving and good, why does he allow evil to exist? What does free will mean, and what role do prayers play? How does art intersect with worship? What other forms of worship are practised by other religions and how do those practices relate to their gods? I set out to find the answers and took six courses instead of five (as full-time students were allowed to do). I skipped the first-year introductory courses and went right into Emil Fackenheim's Philosophy of Religion, John Meagher's various courses on theology and the New Testament, and Arthur Gibson's study of Ingmar Bergman and especially his "Silence of God" trilogy of films. I was a seeker looking for answers in the New Testament and in the films of Bergman (I bought all the screenplays and pored over the dialogue).

And just as music was solace to my father, art was solace to me. Although I was intellectually satisfied and challenged by my university professors, I wanted to explore my creativity and engage my hands as well as my brain, so while still studying part-time at

U of T, I took sculpture courses at the Ontario College of Art from 1976 to 1978. The last year of my academic life, 1978–79, I spent at the University of Guelph (because it had an excellent sculpture department), and I graduated from there with an honours BA in fine arts. At one point I had my own darkroom while I studied photography. Sculpting remains to this day a great source of pleasure to me. In my early twenties, I was a sculptor with a studio, with lots of clients. I made eagles in flight, polar bears, horses, deer, beavers and even cats. Hundreds of these sculptures were cast from my originals and sold in hotel shops.

I absolutely love clay. I love how the clay changes right before my eyes and how the act of sculpting links my brain and my hands. I love the feel of wet clay. When, many years later, I sculpted the face of my late husband, Jack Layton, there existed in my head a map of what he looked like when he was smiling. My challenge was to make the transfer so that the image in my head was reflected perfectly in the hardening clay.

As a young artist, I did a series of drawings, sculptures of children dying of famine, a large oil painting of a mother desperately trying to breastfeed her child when no milk was forthcoming, a big relief of a hungry child staring at the viewer and seeking a response. I didn't just create realistic pieces, though. Some were abstract—beings bursting into the open. One remains in the basement because Jack found it too disturbing to look at.

In a way, I am always sculpting, as both artist and politician. I work with clay, of course, when I create a piece of art. But as an elected official, I work as part of a team—reaching out to the biggest possible art mob and taking the clay we find around us before trying to make something better with it. Each act of shaping—the one a solo activity, the other inherently collective—complements the other. It seems I need both.

~~~

Trying to live the motto of Love Thy Neighbour, while I was still at university I was also volunteering at Toronto East General Hospital's crisis centre and participating fully at the Toronto Chinese Baptist Church. Sleep? Who needed sleep?

I was nineteen when I worked as a volunteer counsellor in the crisis intervention unit at the hospital, in 1976. I had a desk in a room right beside the intake desk in the emergency department. As patients came in, I would be notified if attempted suicide was suspected. Overdosing on pills or wrist slashing were the methods of choice.

These attempted suicides would occur mostly after office hours, when the psychiatrists had gone home. My job was to assess what kind of support the patients needed. Why did they want to end their lives? What was the trigger? Did they have any support network? Were they emotionally balanced? Was this a call for help and, if so, what kind? If they went home, would they make another suicide attempt? Should they be asked to stay in the hospital to be monitored even though they were medically cleared to leave?

The best time to connect with these patients is the moment when they regain consciousness and discover that they are still living. This is when they are at their most vulnerable, most open, most eager to connect with a live human being, and this is when I would do my assessment.

My shift at the hospital was usually in the evening, sometimes starting at midnight and continuing almost to morning. I often did the holiday shifts. People feel their loneliness most acutely when others are celebrating—Christmas, Valentine's Day, Saturday nights.

When I wasn't seeing patients, I was answering the unit's crisis hotline. In one such call, a man who had already overdosed just
~~~

wanted to talk to someone. He was middle-aged, lonely, with no one to love, and he had made a decision to end his life. I tried to persuade him to give me an address so an ambulance could be dispatched, but he was starting to slur his words and I could tell he would soon become unconscious. No matter how hard I tried to persuade him otherwise, he said there was nothing in this life worth living for and that no one would care whether he lived or died. We were trying to trace the call, but back in the mid-seventies this took a long time, and I desperately needed to keep him on the line.

Someone had committed suicide while on the line with one of my fellow volunteers. The emotional trauma was too severe and she was no longer able to work in the unit. I couldn't bear the prospect of the same thing happening to me.

As I frantically tried to engage this man, I heard a dog barking in the background. I asked the man to tell me the name of the dog, her breed and age. I asked him if he loved his dog.

"Oh yes," he replied. "My dog is my companion. She's the only friend I've got."

"After you die," I said, "who will take care of her? Will she be taken to the humane society and destroyed?" I then told him about the dog I grew up with, Ah Woo, and how important he had been in my life. And how, when I came to Canada, I had to leave my dog behind and was heartbroken.

"Why don't you tell me where you live," I said, "so I or someone can come over to pick up your dog? I will care for her."

After a long silence, he gave me his address. I then gave it to a colleague and an ambulance was dispatched. We continued our chat about what his dog meant to him, and how and when he got her, until, finally, I heard a knock on his door. I have never felt such relief.

During the two years I volunteered at the hospital, I encountered men who had lost their purpose in life when they retired and teenagers whose lovers had left them or who were conflicted about their sexual identity. I came across lonely souls who felt abandoned by the world. Some drank too much or took too many painkillers to dull their emotional pain and were not yet ready to take their own lives. For others, their suicide attempts were actually desperate cries for help or attention.

And then there were those who failed in their attempts because they were discovered earlier than they had expected and who would attempt again the minute they left the hospital. I came across one such young man, who was so tired of his life he refused to speak. His silence was a manifestation of his determined will to die.

But in my experience at the hospital, I was mostly successful in connecting even with hardcore cases. If they can get help, even in their darkest moments, there's a good chance they will choose to live.

Through my experience in the crisis unit, I discovered not just the deep satisfaction that comes with helping others but also my ability to connect and empathize—and, above all, to instill a sense of hope.

While I was able to empathize with others and dispense advice, I could have been a candidate for the help line myself. At that time in my life, I was drawn to the wrong kind of men.

For a time when I was seventeen, I lived, as I mentioned, with a man whose only sin was to lack ambition—a sin that led me to end the relationship. After that, I began courting disaster.

The next man was a bruiser—literally. He was much bigger than me, a former marine with a black belt in karate, and twice he came close to killing me. I was choked and punched in the face, and yet, the first time he beat me, I made excuses for him. *And* the second time . . . he was drunk and he did apologize, after all. It took me more than a year of black eyes and bruises to leave that relationship. And I never sought help or called the police.

The next man seemed gentle enough, but when we ended the relationship he was enraged, and he lashed out physically. He hit me, but this time I was the stronger one: I hit him back and I called the police, but I never did lay charges.

The pattern is so familiar, regardless of background, ethnic origin or education level. Male-against-female violence is rooted in a desire to possess, dominate and control. Women in every culture are so often encouraged—or encourage themselves—to believe "just love him a bit more and all will be fine. Just don't provoke. Be more obedient, or do a better job of taking care of him, and all will be well." This imbalance of power causes untold suffering and even death.

How could I have been drawn to these men, and why did I stay with them? Why did I put myself at risk? I had been a crisis counsellor, I had seen the patterns, and I had seen how children who had witnessed violence (and I was certainly one of them) had themselves become involved in abusive relationships. Yet I, like so many others, believed, "Love him enough and he will change." I may have subconsciously thought that physical violence is normal, or perhaps I lacked the self-confidence to leave these abusers sooner. Perhaps I felt my mother had suffered abuse because she herself was somehow to blame; perhaps I felt that if she had been more submissive, my father would not have abused her, and we would have enjoyed harmony in our home.

Years later, and after much reading and research, I taught several courses part-time in George Brown College's Assaulted Women's and Children's Counsellor/Advocate Program, aimed in part at survivors of abuse who had committed their lives to helping others. I worked with students to help them understand the underlying causes of male violence, and I taught them how to build confidence, develop power and find solutions for themselves and for the people they might get involved with in the future. As well, I worked with them to explore why women who endure racial bias are also the most poverty-stricken in our city, in our country and around the globe. I assigned books that developed intellectual understanding along with films (such as Spike Lee's *She's Gotta Have It*) to explore rape, dominance and the ingrained double standard that governs the sexual behaviour of young men and women.

At the same time, I taught a course in feminist political action and community development. I would ask students to identify one area that they wanted to change in their lives. Often they said they wanted to establish or provide more funding for a women's shelter; sometimes the goal was to create more childcare spaces, or provide more counselling for children to help them overcome their cycle of violence and poverty. And as I taught, I also learned to appreciate the vital importance of achieving true equality for women in the political sphere. Understanding weakness becomes a source of strength.

The key is to empower, to turn helplessness and despair into a quest for political action. I was beginning to wake up.

CHAPTER 3

Political Awakening

There is a Cantonese word, guo, *meaning "the hand that stirs." Starting in 1979, I started stirring the pot. Many, many pots. But the first pot stirred had to do with the boat people.*

In the spring of 2013, as I was writing this book, I indulged in a Sunday tradition—one that had become almost sacred to the Chow family from the moment we arrived in Canada forty-three years earlier. I dropped my father off at the Toronto Chinese Baptist Church so he could take in the morning service, to be followed by a family brunch at our favourite dim sum restaurant, around the corner on Dundas Street.

Located in the heart of Toronto's Chinatown, that church played an important role in my life when I was a teenager. "Our home and sanctuary," the church's website reads, and for many years that was true for me. A red brick edifice with white pointing, this handsome but understated church dates from 1880. There are now many Chinese Baptist churches in Toronto, but this one is the mother of them all.

In my earlier life, I was questing for community. When I was still feeling like a newcomer to both the city of Toronto and the country of Canada, this church on Beverley Street was my community centre. It was the place where I came to know about the power of unconditional love. It was the place where I was baptized and where I worshipped. Through the youth fellowship—the Gideons—that church created in me a sense of belonging.

Here I learned hymns and Bible stories and felt the connectedness that comes with being in a choir and hitting the right note. My friends Betty Chee, Wendy Chan and Ann Ling and I were the Four Altos in the choir. (Truth be told, I don't sing well.) Here I learned the joys of working co-operatively. I learned at that church to speak in public, to teach a Sunday school class and chair a meeting, to head up a group at a summer camp. At the church, I was the de facto publisher and editor of an in-house magazine called *Image*, and I decided which articles and poems would be printed and how much editing was required.

I learned teamwork and skills that would serve me well later on when I waded into political waters, first as a school trustee, then as city councillor and then as a member of Parliament.

Reverend Andrew Wong and his wife, Linda Wong, presided over the church. They were good and honest, loving and caring people who led by example. And I was a totally dedicated member of the congregation. On weekends, my life revolved around the church. Friday night was choir practice, Saturday afternoon was dedicated to "fellowship," Sunday meant teaching Sunday school, attending the service and partaking in the lunch that followed. The church helped me understand the power of the collective. I felt the pull of the congregation and the yearning to proselytize. To bring others into the fold, I would invite all my classmates and friends to join me at church.

When I stand on the steps of Toronto Chinese Baptist Church, I can look across to Grange Park. For me, church and park are connected—yet disconnected. The first political rally I ever attended took place in that park, in 1979. The plight of the Vietnamese boat people had brought several hundred citizens to that park, including me—a still-shy young woman who, if she read a newspaper at all, went straight to the arts section and ignored the rest. But my friends had alerted me and others in my community to the travesty that was then taking place on the seas off Southeast Asia.

That rally on that rain-soaked day sparked in me a slow politicizing process that led me to ask hard questions of my church: Why the focus on a distant heaven when there was so much to do here and now on earth? The Lord's Prayer said, "Thy kingdom come, thy will be done, on earth as it is in heaven." To me that meant that God's dominion has arrived and that we are called to "give new life to the broken-hearted. Share our bread with the hungry. Bring the poor, the outcasts, to our house. When we see them naked, clothe them . . ." (my take on Isaiah 57–58). Isn't the true call of Christians to "love our neighbours as ourselves"?

If so, why spend so much time saving souls when saving lives—by rescuing them, feeding them, clothing them, sheltering them—was at least as important? What place does social justice occupy in the long list of my Christian church priorities if Jesus's mission was to "to bring good news to the poor," according to his first teaching as recorded in the Gospel of Luke? If the oppressed are drifting and starving in broken boats, should we not do everything we can to free them?

I knew that if I was to be true to my faith, and to my life priorities, I had to act now so that those who are most vulnerable are protected. Rather than being the last in line to be served, they should be the first.

~

I was born in the Year of the Rooster in the Chinese zodiac calendar. I put as much faith in what that portends as I do in astrological forecasts—which is to say, no faith at all. But if you're curious to know how those of us born under the rooster sign are characterized, here it is: we are said to be talkative, outspoken, motivated, hard-working, confident, multi-talented and healthy types who enjoy hiking and swimming. All of that, I would say, holds true for me. But we are also said to be vain and boastful; I will leave it to readers of this book to be the judge of that.

When I arrived in Canada at the age of thirteen, I went through a period of shyness that was not at all in keeping with the bold girl who grew up in Hong Kong and who was clearly leader of the gang in playgrounds. And there's no hint of shyness in me now, as my friends and political foes will attest. But during my teenage years, new language and culture and adolescent awkwardness combined to usher in a period of reserve.

Winnie Ng and Dr. Joseph Wong were two individuals who were a major influence on drawing me into political activism in the late seventies. Winnie has been active in the labour movement all her adult life and now teaches courses in social justice at Ryerson University. But in 1977, a group she belonged to, Chinese Canadians for Mutual Advancement, hired me as a summer student to work as part of a team producing a documentary slide show about the history of the Chinese in Canada.

At our first meeting, I was joined by a young filmmaker named Nancy Tong—another immigrant from Hong Kong who had also been educated by the Maryknoll nuns. Nancy would become my best friend. I was nineteen years old and a student at the Ontario College of Art; my task was to do research and create graphics—some of which were used in the slide show. While Nancy supplied the structure, the narrative and the texts, I helped with the visuals. For the first time, both of us learned about the history of Chinese Canadians and the injustice they had experienced.

For Nancy and for me, this was the dawning of our political awareness as we came to understand the power of systemic racism. Both of us were art students at the time, and this project opened up our eyes and showed us how art and social justice can meld. Art is not just for art's sake. Art can also foster social and political awareness.

Still, my political awakening happened slowly.

Winnie recalls that I was more reticent then. She assumed this owed something to my artistic temperament. Still, she saw my potential. Joseph Wong likewise remembers me then as having few to no political bones in my body—at least in the beginning. I struck him as very young, with few ideas on social justice. But through action, we all learned along the way. By *action*, I mean the rally in the park and a host of other activities that would mobilize the Chinese-Canadian community during the years and decades to come.

There is a Cantonese word, *guo*, meaning "the hand that stirs." Starting in 1979, Joseph, Winnie and I and a great many others started stirring the pot. Many, many pots. But the first pot stirred had to do with the boat people.

"The Vietnamese boat people" was an umbrella term for the more than one million refugees who fled the war-torn countries of Vietnam, Cambodia and Laos in the late seventies. They left their homelands in waves, at first because some of them had supported the South Vietnam–US alliance during the war against North Vietnam. The victorious Communist government was now exacting its revenge, sending countless Vietnamese to prison or labour camps. Then a second wave of ethnic Chinese fled during the Sino-Vietnamese War of 1979 when they, too, faced expulsion or forced labour. These refugees set out in leaky fishing boats in hopes that once in international waters, help might be forthcoming.

Sometimes it was, sometimes it wasn't. These desperate people had bribed government officials (the going rate was five to six ounces of gold per citizen) and then had to pay smugglers who packed them into barely seaworthy boats. Once at sea, the refugees were vulnerable to pirates who often raped the female passengers, tossed some passengers overboard and pillaged their possessions. Many drowned. The United Nations High Commission for Refugees put the number of deaths at between two hundred thousand and four hundred thousand.

Refuge seekers put themselves at the mercy of passing ships in the South China Sea. At first, both refuge and mercy were shown. Men, women and children were picked up and then dropped off at ports in Japan, Singapore and Taiwan. But governments there, wary of being overwhelmed by refugees, began to insist that refugee claimants present guarantees that Western countries would offer them permanent resettlement. For its part, the no-nonsense government of Malaysia warned that Indo-Chinese refugees deposited on its shores would be shot. At that point, humanitarian help at sea dried up. In one case, bad weather drove a ship with ninety-three refugees aboard onto a reef off an island in Vietnamese waters where soldiers used artillery, machine-gun fire and mortars to kill all but eight of them. Many such atrocities reached the Western press, and as awareness grew, so did outrage.

Dr. Joseph Wong, a family doctor, remembers going home after a day at his medical clinic and heading for the back of the bus so he could weep without being noticed. Nothing was being done to help these people. Finally, Joseph met with a small group that included his wife, Christine, and Winnie Ng. They formed an organization, the Toronto Interagency Project for Southeast Asian Refugees, and they joined forces with Operation Lifeline, a refugee sponsorship group led by Howard Adelman, a philosophy professor at York University. Eventually, the Canadian government responded. More than a hundred thousand refugees landed in this country, an extraordinary achievement.

For me and for many others, the starting point for getting the Canadian government, Canadian citizens and Canadian churches, synagogues and temples involved in sponsoring refugees was that rally in Grange Park. Cleverly, Dr. Wong had arranged for a child of ten to address the rally. The boy's family, the Luongs, had set out in one of those overcrowded boats, and of his twenty-five relations aboard, only seven survived the ordeal. Having someone describe social injustice is one thing; hearing from an actual victim of such injustice is quite another.

Sponsorship took off—because of all the publicity, because of the sheer number of victims, because of the staggering cruelty. And also because Canadians were being praised around the world for our generosity: on a per capita basis, no country took in more refugees than Canada. Sophocles once said, "Kindness begets kindness." Widely circulated stories of Canadian generosity only served to encourage more Canadians to be more generous as they saw the goodness in themselves.

"Many people became full-time volunteers," Joseph Wong remembers. "Sponsorship spread like wildfire. I have not seen anything like it since."

All these dispossessed families needed help settling in. I got a job in immigrant services at WoodGreen Community Services and started working with Vietnamese refugees and Chinese immigrants. Typically, sponsor families looked after them for one year, but at the end of that year they were expected to manage on their own. I was profoundly affected by their suffering. This was a humanitarian crisis on a level I had not seen before, yet these new Canadians valiantly struggled to move forward in life. I organized all sorts of classes for them—cooking, income tax, badminton, swimming, English as a second language—and I advocated for them in every way I could.

But it wasn't enough, not nearly enough. I remember one time being at the church for Saturday-afternoon fellowship and hymn singing. Through the window I spotted a homeless man, and I wondered: What's our response to *his* plight? The church choir would sing at the nearby Scott Mission (it has offered food, clothing and shelter to the poor and the homeless since 1941) in hopes of "saving" these people. But what does *saving* mean? Where was the justice? I was now having debates with elders at my church about other religions, about how the Bible should be interpreted and about the church's response to social injustice. I wanted to retain my faith but felt that I needed to find another spiritual home and to seek out another place where people of similar beliefs were gathered to worship.

One day I saw on the front page of the *Toronto Star* a sculpture of a female in the form of a crucifix. The sculpture was hugely controversial, for how dare a church put this female crucifix in front of the altar? Intrigued, I went to a Sunday service at the Bloor Street United Church, and here I learned from Reverend Clifford Elliott the power of mercy and forgiveness, and a feminine aspect of Christianity that was being ignored by the traditional male-dominated churches. I learned that the crucifix does not represent justice alone, and that equally important are the concepts of love and grace. This inspirational sculpture and message spoke to me, so I stayed and became a member of the United Church.

In the meantime, I could see a change in how I viewed the world.

Winnie Ng puts it this way. "We all need time to connect the dots. When you started working for WoodGreen Community Services, the personal became political. We all became stirrers of pots."

Winnie Ng, Dr. Joseph Wong, Olivia Chow: we were all born in Hong Kong, where no political dissent was allowed. As Joseph says, "You listened, you obeyed." Canada wasn't like that. The boat people issue taught us what was possible if we took a stand, if we educated ourselves, if we organized and strategized, if we garnered media interest and mobilized public opinion. The refugee issue was our training ground. And when, a few months later, CTV ran a program titled "Campus Giveaway" suggesting that Asian kids were pushing out other students in Canadian universities . . . or years later, when a deputy mayor in the suburban city of Markham suggested that "everything is going Chinese," implying that an influx of Asians had somehow damaged the social fabric of her community . . . or when resolution to the longstanding Chinese head tax issue looked to be stalled, we knew how to proceed.

We stirred the pot.

By this time, I had changed. The artist became an activist—and then she got political.

CHAPTER 4

The Two Dans

I learned from Dan Leckie that a key ingredient of success is to bring diversity together—whether you are gardening, cooking a good meal or getting things done politically.

The first time I saw Dan Heap was in the pouring rain at Grange Park in Toronto. There he stood, bearded and rumpled, his bicycle close by.

Hundreds of people had assembled there in 1979 to protest the plight of the Vietnamese boat people. The gathering at the park was meant to raise awareness of their situation and to goad the Canadian government into action. But what was a city alderman, as Dan Heap then was, doing here? He was a social justice advocate and an ordained Anglican priest who believed that compassion does not end at constituency borders. He was calling on Canadians to offer these refugees sanctuary.

As a Christian, I was there out of a love-thy-neighbour sense of compassion. It struck me then that if this man cared enough to come out in the rain to speak for the dispossessed, he must be all right.

One year later, at the end of 1980, Dan was running as a federal candidate for the New Democratic Party in the Spadina riding. (Now called Trinity-Spadina, it's the seat I would represent many years later.) Dan wanted to honour his commitment to the large number of Chinese constituents, and was looking for a Chinese-speaking assistant. Dr. Joseph Wong, who had introduced me to community activism, now played a hand in the next phase of my political life.

Joseph asked Dan to seek me out. So late one evening, Dan came by WoodGreen Community Services, where I was organizing a large group of volunteers stuffing fundraising letters into envelopes. He asked if I would join his campaign team. Soon after, I became one of his constituency assistants. I moved into the basement of a house one street away from the office and literally spent all my waking hours at the office.

Thus was I drawn into the maw of politics.

Dan Heap was a sincere man who practised politics with a particular style. He was dedicated to giving voice to the voiceless and to social justice—and these goals would later become my goals, too. Many of the issues that Dan embraced—poverty, homelessness, the peace movement, immigration matters, social housing—were ones that I would later embrace as an elected official. I admired Dan and his wife, Alice, for the way they lived their lives, offering their own home as a base of operations (and free bunk) for young people who fought the good fight. When it came time to sell their home in Kensington Market, they sold it at much below market value to a community organization that was helping refugees. And Dan was co-founder, in the late nineties, of the Toronto Disaster Relief Committee, which for more than a decade waged a vigorous campaign on behalf of the homeless.

I can see Dan now: he's wearing flat shoes (no fancy loafers for him), black jeans, a white shirt in need of pressing, and over it a tweed jacket with patches at the elbows.

What I loved about Dan Heap was his integrity, his bravery and his passion. He was a worker-priest and an authentic man. When he had first been elected as an alderman in 1971, he made a joyous promise during his victory party: "We're going to organize the ward!" He didn't mean organize so he could stay in power; he meant organize to give neighbourhoods a say in issues that mattered to them. The Italians in his riding, the Portuguese, the working people who lived south of Bloor Street, all loved him because he knew how hard it was to make a living. And the affluent folks in the Annex north of Bloor likewise loved him because many of them embraced his work on peace and disarmament.

We ran his constituency office in Toronto much like a community drop-in centre. And Dan wasn't the sort of politician who filled his constituency newsletters with fluff. Ours were substantial, with stories about the anti-war movement and cruise missile testing, immigrant workers who were being exploited in the garment industry, and the union of unemployed workers.

Dan Heap would talk to the press if necessary, but he preferred the direct route to get his message across. But as his assistant, I often talked to reporters. I would get so outraged about some injustice inflicted on immigrants that I would pick up the phone and call a journalist so I could shine a spotlight on the issue at hand.

I also realized that very few Chinese Canadians, or any other new immigrants in the riding, had any idea what their member of Parliament did—or could do—for them. So I wrote a weekly column in a local newspaper and I had a weekly radio show on CHIN so I could explain the intricacies of immigration policies and other federal issues such as unemployment insurance (as it was then called), pension and income tax. I had already established a good working relationship with a few journalists when I was at WoodGreen Community Services, and now these contacts came in handy. Dan was the immigration policy critic for the NDP in the House of Commons, and I had to know immigration law inside and out. His passions lay more towards peace and disarmament and oppression in Central America, while I was drawn—in no small part because of my background—towards the plight of immigrants.

When government-sanctioned death squads began operating in Central America, and the United States refused to accept refugees fleeing the violence, many of those desperate people looked to come north to Canada. And suddenly Dan Heap's personal passion and mine intersected. We did not want to see these Chilean and Salvadoran refugees deported back to face death squads.

So Dan Heap mounted a campaign. We worked with progressive lawyers and Latin American groups in Toronto to pressure the federal government to establish a special program. We called on lawyers, law students and legal workers at the Law Union of Ontario (whose offices were in Dan's riding) to help. Many progressive immigration lawyers would figure largely in this campaign. So would smart, young and dynamic law students at the University of Toronto. Together, we'd frame the policy and draft the right questions. Dan Heap would then pose those questions in the House of Commons.

We won. It was incredibly rewarding to see the relief on the faces of many of these Latin American refugees. They were now safe and no longer had to live in fear of deportation to face torture, beatings or even death. I went to many of their joyous, colourful and exuberant dances to celebrate this victory, and to fundraise to help sponsor others to Canada. Through a program that allowed these refugees to stay, Canada admitted some sixteen thousand people from war-torn Central America between 1982 and 1987.

I was learning the ropes, all manner of ropes. My goal was to get Dan re-elected and to change policy at the federal level using tactics and strategies I was learning at the community level.

~

Around this time, friendships and allegiances were forming that would have a powerful influence on my political and personal life.

On the very day that Dan Heap became the MP for Spadina, he hired Dan Leckie as his executive assistant, based in Toronto. Leckie had a Heap-like beard and a Heapian approach to fashion. If I close my eyes now, I can conjure Dan Leckie: open shirt, no tie, rumpled brown jeans, nothing matching, and his bicycle nearby. Dan Leckie rarely dressed up, even for formal events when he was later a city councillor, and on the rare occasion when he put on a tuxedo, he would refuse the limousine service offered by the city. ("No thanks," he would say. "I'm going to ride." Even if that meant cycling in a tux.) And if Dan Leckie is doing anything in my little daydream, it is this: he's making a list. This is where the two Dans part ways. Dan Heap needed help with structure and organization; Dan Leckie was supremely organized and a master strategist. He was, quite simply, brilliant.

Before becoming Dan Heap's assistant, Leckie had been a school trustee and chair of the Toronto Board of Education. During those early years on the board, Dan had been an integral part of a group of pioneers who included Gordon Cressy, Bob Spencer, Doug Barr and others. This young and dynamic group of trustees and educators helped usher in progressive urban reforms—such as the working group on multiculturalism and a ban on corporal punishment—that changed the course of urban education in Canada. Following that stint, Dan was a special assistant to Mayor John Sewell. Later on, he became Jack Layton's executive assistant and then a city councillor between 1994 and 1997.

How he came to work with Jack is a story in itself. Dan Leckie, you must understand, was a free spirit. After Dan Heap won his second term, in 1984, Dan Leckie took a year off and went to Italy with his Italian-born wife. Money, career, ambition: none of that factored in his life. His intention in going to Italy was to drink wine, visit art galleries and maybe admire the gardens there—for he was passionate and very knowledgeable about backyard agriculture.

I knew from working with Dan and from his capable work with John Sewell that he was a perfect fit for Jack. "You have to hire Dan Leckie," I told Jack one day, and I told him why. I described Dan as a much-loved man and a systematic thinker with good politics.

"Okay, I'm interested enough to meet him," Jack replied. "I'll check him out."

"Well, it'll have to be on the phone," I said. "He's in Italy."

But on the phone, it wasn't Jack who interviewed Dan. It was Dan who interviewed Jack. Dan set down a long list of conditions under which he would work for Jack, and these had nothing to do with wages and hours. I repeat: Dan cared little for money, and he worked around the clock. One condition was that Jack not call a press conference for the next six months. What Dan had observed was Jack then being ruled by passion and instinct and a tendency to lead the parade before the parade had properly formed. Jack immediately saw how smart and sensible this man was, and he hired him before that phone chat had ended.

For as long as Jack and I knew Dan (in my case, seventeen years), he was an integral part of our lives. Holidays often meant whitewater canoeing on northern Canadian rivers where the safe custom for Jack and me was to park the canoes in order to scout the rapids: the idea is to map out a route so you can run the rapids while avoiding rocks, ledges and impossibly high standing waves. In more challenging rapids, we would portage our gear ahead and run the rapids with empty canoes. This accomplished two things: if we did capsize in the rapids, at least we wouldn't lose our gear downriver, and it's a lot easier to run rapids with a lighter, more manoeuvrable canoe. And such scouting and planning reduced the likelihood of dumping.

Dan Leckie took a different approach. He did love to plan ahead, but sometimes he would run through the highest and most dangerous water, come what may. He did not look like a lean, hard-muscled type at all, and in fact (Dan, you know this was so) he was a little plump—but he was strong. I have pictures in that ramshackle family photo album of mine and there he is, parked on a massive rock with a smile on his face while a northern river, in this case the Missinaibi (it flows into James Bay), courses wildly behind him.

Dan had an MA in education, but that hardly mattered. You need only have conversed with him for a few minutes to know that the man was extraordinarily well read—and had the sharpest wit. He was a humble man, and a deep thinker and visionary. He once said, "Politicians come and go and so do political initiatives, but once you engage citizens and empower them to make a difference and embed the policy structurally into the administration, the changes will last and stand for a long time because they are rooted in the community." I never forgot that.

In his early days as school trustee, then chairman of the school board, these were a few of Dan's causes: heritage languages, parental empowerment, neighbourhood schools, and putting an end to streaming (which sorted students into academic, general and basic levels). Many of these issues were ones that I would embrace as I continued my own political trajectory from trustee to councillor to member of Parliament. On all these matters, Dan Leckie was way ahead of the curve.

Dan Leckie was a great friend to cycling in the city. In fact, both Dans were inner-city bike riders long before that became popular. When Jack Layton was a Toronto city councillor in the eighties and chairing the Toronto City Cycling Committee, Dan Leckie was active behind the scenes, and when Dan himself became a councillor a decade later, he chaired the same committee.

Dan brought to the constituency office his flare as a writer (which is rare in political circles) and his optimism (which was contagious). He grew his own vegetables and herbs at home, and he was the kind of gardener who always found something to be thankful for: if the beans didn't flourish, well at least he had lettuce. And if the garden didn't produce a bumper crop, or some of the political campaigns faltered, it wasn't because the effort wasn't there, and anyway, at least many involved in the campaign learned from the process and emerged stronger and better prepared to make changes in the future.

Dan also understood the importance of diverse opinions. Just as a healthy, vibrant garden or ecosystem requires diversity, he believed it was important to have different political voices at the table. I learned from him that a key ingredient of success is to bring diversity together—whether you are gardening, cooking a meal or getting things done politically. Just as different plants can complement each other, or diverse spicing can work in harmony (think of the combination of salty, sweet and sour in Thai food), so too can varying and opposing political voices, ideas and opinions work together for the common good. And if one plant fails, or one political idea falters, progress will be made if there are others there to take their place.

Needless to say, Dan Leckie was both a very good chef and a very good organic gardener. I learned much from him politically, and I later learned to love and know gardening. Today my greatest extravagance is spending money on my garden to make it beautiful. One regret: I never figured out how to cook well. Perhaps one day soon.

Dan Leckie was Jack's best man at our wedding in 1988, and when Dan died tragically of a brain aneurysm ten years later, at just forty-eight years of age, Jack and I were overwhelmed with grief.

At five o'clock one Tuesday morning in May of 1998, Dan was in the midst of writing a list (what else) when he was felled. He was taken to hospital, but he never regained consciousness. Jack and I rushed to the hospital, but there was nothing to do but wait. So loved was he at city hall that many of his friends and colleagues held a meditation circle, hoping that their energy, their good wishes and their prayers could somehow reach him. Six days later, on May 30, Dan died.

Jack and I organized a visitation at the community centre on Cecil Street, right around the corner from our house on Huron. We put up huge photos on tall panels depicting scenes from Dan's life so that people could walk through the places where he had been and write down reflections on how they had shared their lives with him. Dan at the school board, Dan at city hall, Dan on a bicycle, Dan in a canoe.

A few days later, I helped put together a memorial tribute in the Brigantine Room at Harbourfront Centre, where Jack somehow managed to deliver a eulogy for his best friend. Gordon Cressy, then the president of the United Way of Toronto, talked about Dan's contribution to the education of Toronto's children. Then the singer and composer David Wall sang "Danny Boy," whereupon everyone just lost it. At the end, everyone's spirits were lifted by an idea that had come from Dan's children, Patrick and Tina, then in their late teens. Their notion was that everyone present would hold up multicoloured ribbons that would connect all of us and signal our interdependence through our generosity of spirit.

Dan Leckie's death marked the end of an era. The Heap years, as I sometimes refer to them, were about more than inspiration. This period constituted my political training school. The two Dans were my mentors, but especially Dan Leckie.

I learned from Dan Leckie how campaigns are run and how to approach public policy in a strategic way. At Dan Heap's office, we focused on three key concerns: on jobs and protecting the garment industry, on peace and on a matter that I can perhaps be forgiven for taking personally—immigration and the Chinese head tax.

A legendary figure, Dan Leckie played a transformative role on the left of the political spectrum. He wasn't interested in yelling about what was wrong; he focused on where he could move things forward to advance change and social justice. Through Jack Layton's office, Dan Leckie developed many groundbreaking initiatives that put Toronto on the map in terms of health, education and the environment. Bring Back the Don (a task force aimed at reviving the then heavily polluted Don River), the Toronto Atmospheric Fund (a revolving loan fund to help reduce climate change), the AIDS Defence Plan—that was Dan Leckie.

Dan was Jack's political soulmate when Jack was a city councillor. It was Dan who encouraged Jack to seek election as chair of the Toronto Board of Health, a position that Jack took on just as the AIDS epidemic was emerging.

Dan taught me that good political leaders are a conduit between the people and public services, and that the best public policy decisions come through three streams: political leadership, professional public administrators and citizen engagement. Politicians and public servants are the employees of the people. Their job is to act in the people's best interests. The people must be constantly engaged to understand what's going on. It's called participatory democracy.

CHAPTER 5

Into the Fray

My question as a newly minted school trustee was this:
What was going on, or not going on, in schools that would lead "average, normal kids" to stalk and savagely beat a man because of his perceived sexual orientation?

I was twenty-eight years old and I had never been so scared in my life. I stood on a community centre stage in downtown Toronto and before some three hundred people made the case for my election as school trustee. I remember what I talked about, as I explained why I wanted to serve my community: I talked about value. The value of helping underprivileged children overcome barriers so they could get a better education. The value of heritage language classes to help second-generation children communicate with their parents in their mother tongue, allowing for the parental involvement that has been shown to improve academic performance. The value of curriculum that is relevant to students' lives and gets them engaged. The value of ensuring that no one fell through the cracks.

From the outset, I was focused on helping students who were struggling, often the immigrant kids and the gay kids and the poor kids—the young people who had no say. As far as I could see, they were all outside, and I wanted to do everything in my power to bring them inside—to *include* them. The problem was that I had little to no power: I had to get elected first.

I wasn't the typical candidate for trustee—I didn't have kids, I was younger than most, and I was probably the first would-be trustee in Toronto to have flunked out of Grade 3. I had studied religion and philosophy at university and trained to be an artist—I had never thought about having a career in politics. Jack Layton had written in his high school yearbook that he aimed to be prime minister one day. But there was no road to Damascus moment for me, no sudden realization that running for office was what I was meant to do. My entry into politics occurred organically, as I saw an opportunity to make a difference in the lives of others.

I had prepared for my speech as well as I could and I had packed the place with as many friends and supporters as I could muster. To fund posters and a modest campaign, I had taken out a personal bank loan. I had even taken one lesson with a speech coach, a professional actor. Stand straight, he told me, feet shoulder-width apart. Relax your shoulders. Think of a beautiful scene to calm your mind. Be natural with your arms and don't rock back and forth. All the advice did help, but still my heart was in my mouth.

I was taking a big chance with this run for office. I had left my job with Dan Heap to become a school trustee's assistant, but I had to resign from that position in order to run as a trustee myself. That meant I had no income.

So I was racked by nerves—but I believed I was ready for the job of trustee. I had grown up listening to my mother talking about teaching young children, and how some of them had no room in their homes to do homework, or they simply had no time since they were expected to tend brothers and sisters or help in their parents' shops. I listened to my father talking about the schools he had inspected and what curriculum should be standardized. In the Chow apartment on Blue Pool Road in Hong Kong, education was the subject of dinner conversation and debate. In Canada, my own experiences as a high school student at Jarvis and Central Tech had shown me where the system needed to be improved.

And while I was new to public speaking, I was no newcomer to the Toronto political scene. For the past four years, I had participated on different election campaigns, and worked for MP Dan Heap and then as an assistant for progressive school trustees Joan Doiron and Bob Spencer. And I had been mentored by former school trustee Dan Leckie as well as by Joan and Bob, so I was surrounded by talented, experienced people who wanted to make a difference and who knew how to make things happen.

I also knew exactly what the job entailed: trustees presided over the primary and secondary schools and oversaw school board budgets, policies, personnel decisions, the use of school buildings and facilities, maintenance, relations with the community and matters concerning educational programs and curricula. I can do this, I told myself. I can contribute. I was a first-generation immigrant, and the issues of the day were vitally important to me.

My speech in the community centre that day in the spring of 1985 went well, and I had a great campaign as part of a progressive slate of candidates that included Joan Doiron and me for the board of education, and two men for city council—Dale Martin and a guy by the name of Jack Layton. All four of us won in the election in November that year, by a wide margin. My career in public office was under way.

~~~
~~~

Although our slate had won in downtown Toronto, progressive trustees were in the minority in the new school board and faced strong opposition for any challenge to the status quo. But that didn't hold me back—I was determined to proceed in my first term on the board with the issues I held dear. Heritage languages, for instance.

When I was in high school, I was struck by the fact that some of my Chinese-Canadian classmates who were born in Canada had difficulty communicating with their parents, who had been born in China. That meant their parents weren't able to get fully involved in their schooling, and it also meant these second-generation students were not fully able to connect to their own heritage and culture.

I knew instinctively—and research bore me out—how crucially important the mother tongue was for our increasingly multicultural population. Furthermore, being able to speak other languages enhances intellectual capacity, and is an advantage for all students, regardless of their mother tongue. But in those days, there were few options in the school system for languages other than English and French, so students who wanted to study their parents' mother tongue had to take special classes, after school or on weekends. And for most children of immigrants, that seemed like a form of punishment as they saw other children playing games or sports while they had to study their parents' first language. As well, parents care more about education when their children learn the parents' first language at school. I began to make headway on this issue when the advantages for all became clear: one being that the children of English-speaking parents could acquire, say, Spanish or Mandarin, a big asset in a changing world. Gradually, international languages were integrated into the regular curriculum, and today, more than fifty-five languages are offered in Toronto's schools.

Another issue I began to tackle in my first term was "destreaming," an effort to counter the practice of streaming students, based on the educators' expectations, into three levels of schooling: advanced, general and basic. Many immigrant kids from poorer families ended up in "general and basic levels" schools, where they learned useful trades but were not challenged intellectually and had few incentives or opportunities to proceed with higher education and realize their potential. At the same time, kids from middle-class and wealthy neighbourhoods tended to be streamed into advanced-level schools.

I understood that divide, for I had seen it unfold all around me. I was fortunate to be able to attend Jarvis Collegiate, an advanced-level school, but it was wealthy kids from the affluent Rosedale neighbourhood who made up the majority of the student population, not my neighbours in St. James Town, which was much closer to the school than was Rosedale. At Jarvis, the curriculum and academic standards were markedly different from Central Tech (a general/advanced-level school, where I had studied art in the evening) or Castle Frank Secondary School (a basic-level school located between Rosedale and St. James Town).

How did students get streamed into the general and basic schools? And who were these students? Some of them had learning disabilities, or a genuine aptitude and appetite for the trades and education on offer. But many were streamed simply because they were the children of new immigrants and were seen as having few prospects. Some came from families where they were expected to work as much as possible and as young as legally allowed to contribute to the family income. For some kids, if your English wasn't very good and you had just arrived in the country, you were streamed into a basic-level school where little would be expected of you. Some of these kids who could not yet speak English were plunked into special education classes. Learning wasn't the problem; a new language was.

Other students, from troubled, poorer families, struggled through Grades 7 and 8 and had much of their future determined for them when they, too, were streamed into a basic program. And a larger percentage of these students dropped out of school even before they turned sixteen owing to boredom, low expectations and an uninspiring curriculum.

From my personal experience—and again, research bore me out—I knew that streaming students early on in their educational careers just limited their learning potential. It is difficult for some students to choose between being "good with their brains" (i.e., advanced level) or "good with their hands" (i.e., general technical level); for many, it may simply be too early for them to make that decision. But surely you can be good with *both* hands and brain?

I set out to educate parents and their children on the differences between the advanced, basic and general levels, and I set out to destream Grades 9 and 10 to enhance students' educational choices and academic performances.

Here was another ambition of mine: along with many others, I set out to reinvent Castle Frank Secondary, a basic-level school that had been suffering from declining enrolment. The school was not in my district, but I saw it as an academic institution crying out for help. Students here had a high dropout rate, the school's reputation was poor, and graduation certificates could not get students into a college to learn a trade or to university to get a degree. While I was pushing the school board and the provincial government to destream Grades 9 and 10, it struck me that if we could create a model school, we could demonstrate the benefits of destreaming. We could create what we would come to call the Ideal School. But that would have to wait until after the next election.

While I was getting to work on heritage languages and destreaming, another issue emerged that became a lightning rod for the board in my first few months as a trustee: intolerance and homophobia in schools. This issue had been brewing for years, but an ugly and tragic gay-bashing incident in a Toronto park a few months earlier had brought it to the fore.

In late June of 1985, five Toronto high school students celebrated the end of school by drinking beer, which was harmless enough. But they then concocted a plan to go to High Park—known as a gay hangout after dark—and, as the Ontario Supreme Court later heard, "beat up a fag" and "get money from a queer."

In the park, the boys came across Kenneth Zeller, a forty-year-old librarian and one much loved by his elementary school students. One of the boys tripped him, and Zeller then sprinted more than a hundred metres to his car. He did manage to get the driver's door open, but at that point he was set upon and beaten by fists and kicks around the head and chest for three long minutes. He didn't survive. Kenneth Zeller's body was found at midnight, when someone called an ambulance. The boys were found and arrested.

Each boy was charged with manslaughter and pleaded guilty, each boy wept on sentencing, each boy expressed to the judge regret over what he had done, and each boy was sentenced to nine years in prison.

What was most chilling was that these were young people who had graduated from a Toronto high school; their lawyer had described them all in court as "average, normal kids." So my question as a newly minted school trustee was this: What was going on, or not going on, in schools that would lead "average, normal kids" to stalk and savagely beat a man because of his perceived sexual orientation?

Several years before the Zeller murder, a Toronto Board of Education swim instructor had been fired, and although he was later reinstated, he believed that his sexual orientation was the cause of his dismissal. He had approached the board with a plan to teach about homophobia in the schools, but the board did not view this as a priority. That was about to change.

Alarmed by what I was seeing and hearing in the wake of the Zeller murder and determined to do something about it, I visited Toronto high schools and spoke to many gay and lesbian students. I encouraged them to talk about what was happening in their schools. I collected stories about how they were assaulted verbally and physically. Some had been humiliated and bullied to a point where they could not learn. Many of them went into smaller alternative schools, where they found shelter and understanding, but they were not able to return to their neighbourhood high school. I also heard stories of young gay and lesbian students who hadn't been able to handle the pressure and had taken their own lives. Suicide is all too common for victims of homophobia.

Joining me for many of these visits was Tim McCaskell, then employed by the board as a student worker (a student advocate who tries to ensure that board policy is actually student-friendly and inclusive). Tim was a contributor to *The Body Politic*, a monthly newspaper aimed at Canada's gay community. He also ran weekend programs sponsored by the Toronto Board of Education at Camp Kandalore, a rustic wilderness facility about a three-hour drive north of the city, where students would gather to talk about equality and how they could be empowered to overcome the discrimination that had touched their lives. They then became advocates in their own schools to help other students create an environment free of racism, sexism and homophobia.

Working together with Tim McCaskell, my assistant Sean Meagher and John Campey, a trustee's assistant (who would go on to become Toronto's first openly gay trustee in 1991), we produced a report documenting the stories that Tim and I had heard. I then made key recommendations to deal with homophobia in the school system: develop an anti-homophobic curriculum, train all staff to teach human rights and not discriminate, and change board human rights policy to include sexual orientation to ensure that no students or staff can be discriminated against because they are gay or lesbian.

Our report and recommendations generated a huge controversy, with fanatical evangelicals descending on board meetings and right-wing newspaper columnists seething with anger. They were convinced I was converting students to homosexuality just by talking about homophobia. Tim McCaskell had a good line to sum up the position of the more rabid opponents: "These school trustees are communists and they want to hand your kids over to the pedophiles."

Judi McLeod, a *Toronto Sun* education columnist who wrote from the far right perspective, set me in her sights: she raged against heritage language instruction and multiculturalism—issues that I embraced—and claimed I was pandering to gay voters. (A few years later, McLeod likened me to Nicolae Ceauşescu—the despotic leader of the Romanian Communist Party. McLeod called me Chowsescu because of a petition I was pushing to get to the bottom of a case involving a young black woman who had been shot in the back by Toronto police, and temporarily paralyzed. In October of 1989, twenty-three-year-old Sophia Cook—the mother of a two-and-a-half-year-old son—was the third black person to be shot by city police in a fifteen-month span. Cook had no history of criminal activity but had accepted a ride in a reportedly stolen car.)

One especially feisty opponent of my report was Reverend Ken Campbell, a Baptist minister from Milton, a small town west of Toronto, who decried what he called "the homosexual lifestyle"—as if sexual orientation was something one could turn on or off, like a light bulb. Reverend Campbell accused me of pushing this lifestyle onto students.

If the report had been our only weapon, we would have lost the battle. But I had something far more powerful—the students themselves. I had invited many of those who had told us their stories to speak to the school trustees and senior administrators about their horrific and heartbreaking stories of gay bashing and sexual harassment. Many trustees and directors of education had never heard directly from students about their pain and the discrimination inflicted upon them. For the first time, trustees and directors could put a human face to the issue—and that brought them face to face with a critical question: What can be done with a system that allowed students to endure such severe bullying?

The brave testimony of the students won over many of the school trustees who had previously opposed these measures. Trustees heard the students' heartbreaking accounts of the humiliation and physical and psychological abuse they had endured. Those stories cut through all the ideological rhetoric and won the day—a majority of the board voted in favour of the recommendations. Amendment followed amendment but finally, in April of 1986, the board published *Sexual Orientation: Homosexuality, Lesbianism, and Homophobia*. We had won, against the odds.

This groundbreaking document meant that sexual orientation would now be discussed in high school sex education classes and, further, that counselling services would be available to lesbian and gay youth. The Toronto Board of Education was the first school board in North America to adopt a curriculum that talked about sexual orientation. We also pledged to train all teachers and adopt policies to protect students.

But on one of my recommendations, I lost on a tie vote: the board would not agree to insert the words "sexual orientation" into its human rights code as grounds for preventing discrimination. Sometimes, however, you lose a battle but win a war. I threw my support behind NDP MPP Evelyn Gigantes's gay rights amendment to Bill 7, which sought to align Ontario's statutes with the new Canadian

Charter of Rights and Freedoms. Later that same year, 1986, the bill passed and the Ontario Human Rights Code was amended to ban discrimination or harassment on the basis of one's sexual orientation.

That moment in April of 1986 when the board moved forward on this vital issue was a very proud day for me. It was my first taste of victory as an elected politician. And what made the taste so sweet was that it wasn't my victory. It was the students'. I had helped them find their voice.

Gay and lesbian students were not the only ones facing discrimination and a difficult learning environment. Through surveys and polls, the Toronto Board of Education in those days was tracking students who were having trouble. A pattern emerged that Portuguese and black students were having more difficulties than other students and had a higher dropout rate.

I had become chair of the Race Relations Committee, and we strived to level the academic playing field through anti-racist education. Aside from working to destream Grades 9 and 10, we wanted to make sure that the curriculum was relevant to the lives of these students. As part of that effort, we held an Anti-Apartheid Conference, focused on South Africa and the imprisonment of Nelson Mandela, to bring anti-racist and equity lessons into the school system and to teach students the harm done by institutional racism. We intended these gatherings to continue every year until Nelson Mandela was freed from jail.

However, not all trustees believed that race policies some thirteen thousand kilometres away should be a focus of the Toronto school board, and in 1986 they voted to cancel all future anti-apartheid conferences. Many students were enraged, and so was I. John Campey came up with an effective strategy to turn these trustees around. P. W. Botha was then prime minister of South Africa, at a time when apartheid still formed a cornerstone of the government's rule, so John's idea was to create a poster with the headline "Botha Would Be Pleased" and, beneath that, the names and telephone numbers of all the trustees opposed to the conference. These flyers were widely distributed by students at the Queen's Park rally against apartheid that was about to welcome Bishop Desmond Tutu.

The next school board meeting was stormed by hundreds of outraged students. The vote, needless to say, was reversed.

A few years later, on June 19, 1990, not long after he was released after twenty-seven years in prison, Nelson Mandela came to Toronto and visited Central Tech High School. I was there. I remember how the building practically lifted off the ground with the cheering and the stomping of feet. Many of the students at that school are black, and just to see him mattered a great deal to them. There was an aura about the man. As I write this in midsummer of 2013, Nelson Mandela is gravely ill, and that truly distresses me. He was so gentle, so lacking in bitterness and so clear and determined in his quest for justice. Madiba, as he is affectionately known, has always been a hero of mine. And, by a serendipitous coincidence, his birthday is July 18, the same day as Jack Layton's.

In 1987, a year ahead of the next municipal elections, Jack Layton as a councillor and I as a trustee set out to craft a progressive vision for the city *and* for the education system. We brought together close to a hundred passionate and knowledgeable individuals and held a city summit.

Working with me on the education side were fellow progressive school trustees Pam McConnell, Tony Silipo and Penny Moss and a group of young, dynamic people. Working with me at the board of education level was my assistant, Sean Meagher, who had just graduated with a degree in philosophy from the University of Toronto. At heart, he's a natural, committed and passionate community organizer, and that's the kind of work he was doing for me as a part-time assistant receiving next to no pay. These days he heads up Public Interest, an organization with ten employees that offers outreach strategies to public sector and non-profit organizations. "I now get paid," he jokes with me, "for doing what I used to do for you when I was a student."

John Campey, who was to run as a trustee himself and served from 1991 to 1996, is today executive director of Social Planning Toronto. I had come to know him in the early eighties when we were both trustees' assistants. He was a creative guy, the master of the one-liner. And there was Katheryne Schulz, then a teenaged volunteer in my office, who went on to become a leading childcare activist and childhood education specialist, and is now completing her doctorate in sociology at the University of Toronto. Katheryne possessed rare passion, drive, tenacity and fearlessness. She was a table thumper, and I was not afraid to give her responsibility despite her youth.

Our City Summit produced two documents. "The Ideal School" was a roadmap to enhance education, and "Toronto: A New Vision" set out what a progressive city council would achieve once they formed the government in 1988. These two documents would become central in the minds of all progressive city councillors and school trustees for many years.

In the Ideal School vision, we saw the school as a community hub. Students would be given a nutritious breakfast (if their parents so wished), and after-school activities would be provided so there would be fewer latchkey kids and all students could benefit from more physical activity. Parents would be involved in the evening through parenting courses or English as a second language if needed.

Seniors would be able to enrol in continuing education to learn such things as tai chi, art and music. Literacy classes and childcare centres would also be based in the schools to reflect the board's fundamental belief in life-long learning. And of course the playing field, the gymnasium, the library and the classrooms would be opened to community groups for neighbourhood meetings, book clubs and sports clubs.

The Ideal School was a rallying cry in the 1988 election. I was re-elected as a school trustee by a wide margin—and, even more important, progressives were now in the majority on the school board.

So, armed with this vision of deep parental and student involvement, we led the charge to reinvent Castle Frank Secondary—then a basic-level school, looked down on by the students who were streamed there. We involved everyone—parents, students, teachers and school administrators—and we crafted for the school a different vision, one involving high expectations. We gave students more choices in Grades 9 and 10 so they did not have to decide which "levels" they want to enter until Grade 11 (when most turned sixteen).

We reviewed the curriculum, the hiring practices and all practices and policies around engaging students and parents. One of our goals was to ensure that the principal shared the vision and had the power to re-interview all existing staff and, if necessary, hire new ones who supported the model. The Ontario Principals' Council had a hard time accepting that the new concept might require a new principal. The Ontario Secondary School Teachers' Federation, for their part, didn't want existing teachers to have to reapply for their jobs. But we knew that if we kept all the existing staff, the culture of the school would remain the same and nothing would change. It took a few years before we won that battle. In the end, we got the very best principal—the best—a man named Barrie Sketchley (who is still the principal all these years later). And with him came the shift in culture and the new crop of teachers that could make the vision a reality.

With the support of students and parents, who had always thought of Castle Frank as a dead-end school, we renamed it Rosedale Heights Secondary School in 1990.

The provincial Conservative government of Mike Harris that came to power in the mid-nineties would later reverse our destreaming efforts. Yet Rosedale Heights has survived as a progressive arts school—one that *Maclean's* magazine in 2005 ranked one of the top ten schools in Canada. Ideal, indeed.

In every important initiative I had launched as a trustee, I had involved students and given them important roles to play. To me, this only made sense, as they were the key stakeholders. Our education system was for the students, yet they had no say. Hoping to empower students, I had started visiting student council presidents in my first term and urged them to get involved. A secondary school review was under way at the time, and the board was indeed reforming the system, but no one had bothered to poll the students. That's when young Katheryne Schulz surfaced. "How dare they?" was her response.

I heard directly from the student council presidents what some of the key issues were for students. And one thing was the high cost of public transit—critical transportation for students, since most of them are too young to drive and few of them have cars. Why, they asked, can adults and seniors buy transit passes, but not students? Emerging at the time was the Toronto Association of Student Councils, and some very smart council presidents were coming on board, people such as Noah Novogrodsky, at Northern Secondary, and Elisabeth Johnson, at Jarvis Collegiate. We started a student Metropass campaign, circulating a petition in all the high schools—standard stuff. Then students wrote a letter to the Toronto Transit Commission. No response whatsoever.

I brought the students together to brainstorm, and urged them to ask themselves: "What can we do to catch the public imagination?"

They came up with a brilliant strategy—the Let's Pay by Pennies campaign, where all the students in the city would pay their fare in pennies rather than using a ticket. We picked a date, then held a press conference one day after school to give the TTC a heads-up. The TTC freaked out! Paying by pennies would have jammed up everything. They *immediately* said, "Let's have a meeting."

The TTC proposed doing a study. Of course they were just buying time. Elisabeth was about to graduate, and she wanted this issue resolved while she was still student council president, so she persisted.

Phase two of the pressure campaign followed. Again, the students themselves came up with an effective strategy. The idea was to focus on those city councillors who occupied seats on the transit commission. Their phones began to ring off the hook as high school students and parents in their wards pushed for a student Metropass. Then came media coverage. And then came the student Metropass.

Students realized from this experience the power they possessed. And I managed to get approval for a Student Affairs Committee of the school board. This was a standing committee that included student council presidents as well as trustees and had its own staff, office, computer and budget. This committee was the forerunner of what we have today: elected student trustees who sit on the school board itself. Now every school board in Ontario includes one or two elected student trustees, who hold an annual conference. These students don't vote at board meetings, but they do speak to issues and they get the same background material that trustees get. They have a voice.

This all started in Toronto. It's about starting small and then putting in place structures that will endure long after their creators have moved on. Progress is possible when people are engaged and empowered.

~

With the student Metropass campaign, I had ventured beyond school board concerns to broader, city-wide concerns. I did the same thing with another issue that was important to all immigrants—a multilingual 911 emergency service.

Imagine what would happen if you dialed 911 (say your spouse has collapsed from a possible heart attack, or your kitchen is on fire) but you are capable only in a rudimentary way of speaking and comprehending English.

This was a question I began to ask myself in the late eighties. I kept hearing from front-line staff at Chinese Interpreter and Information Services that in multicultural, multilingual Toronto, dialing unilingual 911 was a serious problem for people who couldn't speak English. Many of these, like my mother, were female seniors who had spent the better part of their lives in the service industries and taking care of their families and hadn't had time to learn English. What if you can't say your address in English? Or you can't describe the actual problem? How can the dispatcher instruct you how to control the situation?

I went to all service providers, including immigrant service providers, and I asked: Check with the people you serve—do they have a problem with 911? It turned out they did, but petitions from various service groups to the police services board always met the same response: we can't afford it.

Finally the matter was studied by the Toronto Police Service, and the ensuing report showed that the 911 service would save both money *and* lives if dispatchers always knew precisely what the call was about. If, for example, dispatchers come to understand that the case involves someone who is not breathing, they can coach the caller in what to do while the ambulance or fire truck is en route. That's the life-saving part. The money-saving part derives from the dispatcher's knowing how to most efficiently deploy resources—because they know whether to send an ambulance or a fire truck in the first place.

So the system was changed. Here's how it works now in Toronto. You call 911 and you start speaking in Punjabi or Urdu or Cantonese or any other foreign language, and the dispatcher transfers the call to a company with a staff capable of speaking 144 languages. Their dispatcher, in turn, is trained to know which language is being spoken, and in seconds, someone speaking Punjabi, Urdu or Cantonese is on the line in a three-way conference call. When this system was instituted back in 1991, dialing 911 became a safer, more efficient and more valuable service, one that reflected the realities of modern Toronto.

This initiative was typical of the kinds of civic issues I was being drawn into, and it began to dawn on me that my days as a school trustee were numbered.

Things were pretty much on track in the Toronto school system, by then seen as one of the best in North America. An astonishingly cohesive collective had done what we had set out do—destreaming, Castle Frank Secondary, the Ideal School, student involvement, sexual orientation, heritage language. And those two campaigns—the student Metropass and 911—had moved me beyond the immediate concerns of a school board to the broader political arena. In the next municipal election, in 1991, I entered that arena. I ran for Metropolitan Toronto council.

Leaping into the fray by running for school board back in 1985 had set me on a course that changed my life. So did an encounter that year with a certain city councillor. His name was Jack Layton.

CHAPTER 6

"Four Nanoseconds"

Our wedding gift to each other—a bicycle built for two—says it all. The tandem bike was a metaphor and a symbol of our partnership. On it we were together, we were cycling, having fun and being a little outrageous. More important was that we were in step, in time, in rhythm—going in the same direction.

Four nanoseconds," Jack Layton would say in answer to anyone—from journalists to prime ministers to squeegee kids—who asked about our marriage. "It was love at first sight, and it only took me four nanoseconds to realize that Olivia was the love of my life."

Jack loved to embellish. He also loved to dress up.

One of my favourite photos of Jack was taken in the mid-eighties, around the time we met, and he's dressed up as William Lyon Mackenzie, the first mayor of Toronto and a hellraiser who was the leader of the Upper Canada Rebellion of 1837. Mackenzie died in 1861 and is buried at the historic Necropolis cemetery in Cabbagetown, just east and south of St. James Town. In his historical costume, as part of the Cabbagetown Festival, Jack would lead tours through the Necropolis, telling tales about some of the famous among the fifty thousand at rest there, great Torontonians such as George Brown, a Father of Confederation, and Ned Hanlan, a world rowing champion. And now, Jack himself.

I gaze at a black-and-white photo of Jack posed near the Gothic Revival gates of the Necropolis. He looks impossibly handsome (quite unlike W. L. Mackenzie, although Jack's trademark moustache lends an air of historical authenticity). In all the years we were together, Jack took off that moustache for just one weekend. He looked just as handsome without it, but he felt the moustache was part of his identity, and so he grew it back right away.

He thought of me as part of his identity as well. He actually told the *Toronto Star* back in 2005, "Olivia is fundamental to my life. She is woven into every minute, every second, of my existence." In that, I know, he wasn't embellishing, because I shared that feeling completely. Jack was just as fundamental to my life, just as woven into my existence.

Jack's essence, his spirit, and so many beautiful memories reside in me—in my heart and brain and being—and they will reside there until I die. When I think of John Gilbert "Jack" Layton and the twenty-six years we had together, I realize how extraordinarily lucky we were to have met, and to have had that time. Plain and simple, we were blessed.

One evening as I was working on this book, I pored over family albums while sitting at the massive table in my kitchen on Huron Street. Over in the corner of the room, the fat goldfish my mother insists on overfeeding swam awkwardly while the bubbler percolated away. Lager the cat (so named by my stepson, Mike, who loves beer) was up on the chair for a look-see. Meantime, Coco the cat (so named by my stepdaughter, Sarah, who loves chocolate) kept an eye on Lager while gazing up at the coppery brown pressed-tin ceiling. Dinner guests would arrive shortly, and takeout Indian food was warming in the oven.

Maybe your family photos are gathered neatly and digitally on CDs, sorted by date or theme. Mine are jammed willy-nilly into old three-ring binders that open with difficulty and, once open, refuse to close.

There was photo after photo of Jack in costume. For all the great events—Caribana, Hallowe'en, the Pride Parade. Jack in his wedding tux. Jack and I in our ceremonial Chinese robes, and in our matching Star Trek outfits. Jack wearing a pink wig . . . and sometimes, Jack wearing not very much at all. Jack in a top hat, wielding a wooden hammer as the auctioneer at a fundraising auction.

A fundraising auction brought Jack and me together, so I'm partial to them.

Some of us never meet the one person on the planet best suited as partner and soulmate. I was lucky enough to meet mine. Before then, I'd had lousy luck with men.

My luck and my life changed when I met Jack. We were amazingly compatible. He was so driven, just like me, yet so gentle and loving. I found myself wondering, "Is this for real? How is this possible?"

Jack had enough confidence that he was not possessive. Some men seek control. Jack didn't. He was completely at home with himself, and he never questioned the love that each of us felt for the other.

We would mark birthdays and Valentine's and Christmas with gifts, of course, but material things didn't matter. With us, it was all about what we could do together, what kind of change and what progress we could make. Our idea of a romantic evening often involved working on a political strategy or policy. Soulmates, indeed. And vacations weren't about five-star destinations but rather about what kind of joy we could experience together in our travels. Having said that, Jack picked out and bought me the first suit I ever owned and, as my Christmas present the year we met, he re-outfitted my entire wardrobe. He loved buying me clothes and jewellery—just as I loved picking out his suits and ties.

Through all the years we were together, Jack always attributed our meeting and the four nanoseconds to a charity auction in 1985. But he was no stranger to me. He was a rising star on Toronto city council, and we had met before, more than once. I had actually helped out on his municipal election campaign, and we had even discussed strategy over lunch, as I was then running for the first time as a candidate for school board. But the auction was a seminal moment—it certainly took us in a new direction. The location was the mall of the Village by the Grange, and the aim was to raise money from the Chinese community for Mount Sinai Hospital. My old friend and mentor Dr. Joseph Wong had organized the event. Jack was there as the celebrity auctioneer, trying to muster a response from the mostly Chinese crowd, and I was his interpreter and assistant.

On that hot summer night, I caught Jack's attention. He seemed dazzled, and we worked well as a team: we raised a lot of money that night. Something had clicked.

I was wearing a sexy off-the-shoulder dress, "a yellow number," as Jack would later tell it. He would remark, too, on my long dark hair. And he was looking pretty handsome that night, so there was a physical attraction—but nothing like love in four nanoseconds for me. It was when we had a meeting of the minds over dinner two weeks later, just after Jack's thirty-fifth birthday, that everything started to come together.

Jack was then renting the second floor of a house on Olive Avenue, just a few blocks away from Kendal Avenue where I first lived in Toronto. He had a deck and, over post-dinner gin and tonics, we talked for hours. Eight hours? Ten? I can't remember.

I learned that we came from different worlds, different continents, different cultures. Jack had upper-middle-class roots in Hudson, Quebec, where he'd been a leader, even as a student. And he came from a large, close and outgoing family.

That night we talked about politics, music, art, religion, spirituality, family, philosophy. I liked Kierkegaard and his thinking on faith, as did Jack, but he was drawn more to Hegel and his dialectical approach to politics (his screen saver at city hall featured the word *dialectics*). My mentor in philosophy was Emil Fackenheim at the University of Toronto, while Jack was a huge admirer of McGill University's Charles Taylor—a fellow Hegelian philosopher.

What I discovered that night was that our basic political philosophy was precisely the same: Give voice to those who have little power and seek to improve everyone's quality of life. Hold firm to the principle of fairness. Do the work collaboratively, but never back down. Or, to use Jack's words, "Don't let them tell you it can't be done." By collective action, we can achieve social justice and change the world.

That philosophy never changed. It was a guiding light through our life together, and is my guiding light today.

That night in 1985, the words just poured out of us. We found that for all our differences, we had a lot in common—mission in life, spirituality, books we liked to read, things we liked to do. Both of us had moved to Toronto in the same year: 1970. Both of us were fitness fanatics and we both made time for daily exercise, ideally outdoors. But we also both loved a party; we would both gravitate to the kitchen at a house party and we'd both be the last ones to leave. Neither of us worried much. Both of us had high energy and needed little sleep. We had it all covered. It was a magical night.

Next time we met, we went for a long lunch at La Raclette, a fondue restaurant, long since closed, on Queen Street West. And then we went swimming at the Sheraton Hotel. Swimming was a big thing for both of us—Jack had been a competitive swimmer in his youth and had played on McGill's water polo team. So was cycling. Jack and I discovered that we were both year-round cyclists and went everywhere on bikes.

A few days after that lunch and swim, I left for a three-week whitewater canoe trip with three friends. After that, I went to San Francisco with my mother to visit my brother and his family. Jack, meanwhile, had gone back to Hudson to visit his parents. Doris Layton remembers that weekend well: "Jack arrived and he couldn't wait to sit me down and say, 'Mom, I've met someone, and I'm in love. She is the most beautiful woman I have ever met. It's her eyes, Mom. She has the most beautiful eyes. I could spend my life just gazing into her eyes.'"

At lunch on her eighty-eighth birthday in 2013, Doris joked that Jack spent half his time on the phone that weekend—calling me in San Francisco—and racked up quite a phone bill. He also racked up quite a florist bill—by then, the long-stemmed red roses were coming fast and furious. And with the flowers came long-distance serenades; he would play his guitar to me over the phone. He later claimed that on one call, he got through to me intending to play Van Morrison's "Into the Mystic" (or was it "Moondance"?) only to find that I was playing the same song at my end. I really don't remember, but that was the story Jack loved to tell. He would have seen the coincidence, the pure serendipity, as proof: the heavens had interceded, and our coming together was meant to be. Beyond the fact that he was amazingly attractive and romantic, I was swept up by his energy, his exuberance—and his persistence. Who could resist?

In any case, I cut my holiday short to come back to Toronto, leaving my mother behind. I knew at that point that I loved Jack. He met me at the airport, and while I waited for the massive embrace, he sailed right past me. I had cut my hair short and he failed to recognize me. He soon made up for lost time.

Jack had booked a place for the night in Niagara Falls, a classically romantic location, where he laid on more roses and a bottle of champagne. I then borrowed a cottage, and Jack and I stayed there for a few days, on the edge of Frontenac Park north of Kingston. That weekend sealed the deal. We started talking about our future together.

By pure coincidence, before we met, we had both applied to move into a new co-op housing building called Hazelburn, at the corner of Dundas and Jarvis Streets in downtown Toronto, and we moved there later that year—to two separate apartments. My mother and I occupied a one-bedroom unit on the fifth floor; Jack and his two young children had a two-bedroom apartment on the tenth floor.

My mother did not warm to Jack at first: he wasn't a doctor or lawyer and he certainly wasn't Chinese. But Jack made a noble effort to learn some Cantonese. Much was made of his coming to dinner at our place one time and thanking my mother profusely for the wonderful meal. The story (which Jack was to embellish in his usual fashion, but which is essentially true) is that he got the tone wrong—and tone is everything in Cantonese. So instead of thanking her for the good meal, he thanked her instead for the good sex.

My mother and Jack were exact opposites: Jack always saw the positive and she always saw the negative. Yet they had one thing in common. Both were born in the Chinese Year of the Tiger—Jack in 1950, my mother in 1928. If you believe in this (as I've said, I take it with a grain of salt), those born under the tiger emblem are said to be born leaders, fearless and courageous and daring. Prone to selfishness at times and yet also capable of great generosity, they are confident, magnetic characters who will stand up for what they think is right and would rather lead than be led.

In any case, Jack and my mother were soon fast friends, and Jack's Cantonese improved enough that he could conduct himself quite handily at auctions—without a translator—and he was much sought after for this work in the Chinese community.

When my mother had friends over, Jack would drop lines of Cantonese into the conversation and crack everyone up. *"Yao mo gao cho"* (Are you nuts?), he would say, emulating my mother, and following up with her favourite insult in Cantonese, *"Chi sin nai mo no"* (Crazy, you have no brains).

Sometimes he goofed. One time, he meant to say "That's enough" to the heaps of food given to him by my mom, but he ended up saying "It's penis." Another time, on the street in Chinatown, he wanted me to look at a cute dog, but instead of *dog* he said, "Look at that penis." The mortified look on my mother's face was just priceless, and I did not stop laughing for three full minutes.

In Cantonese, *enough*, *dog* and *penis* (as well as *help* and *nine*) have the identical sound—*gau*; it's the tone that distinguishes meaning. There are six tones in Cantonese, and Jack would practise them regularly. After saying the word for penis a few times by mistake, whenever he wanted to crack us up, he would practise. "Nine. Dog. Penis. Enough. Help," he would say deliberately in Cantonese, pausing for effect, and then rapidly with dramatic exaggeration.

Jack's tone was often letter perfect, and it made my mother very happy that he was so entertaining to her friends. He won marks for that. She started taking him to Chinese restaurants, where he could order in perfect Cantonese, comment on how fresh and tasty the food was and impress all the servers. Or they would go off together to Chinatown to shop and Jack would exclaim loudly how cheap or expensive the produce was—cracking each other up as people reacted.

With my mother, Jack pushed the language button and the food button. Her job was to cook Chinese delicacies, and his job was to eat—

and enjoy—everything. Such a contract suited them both to a tee.

He would come down in the morning and cheerfully say in Cantonese, "Good morning, Mother. Everything smells delicious."

And she would glare at me. "You are a bad daughter," she'd say. "Why can't you be more like Jack?"

When I met Jack at that charity auction in 1985, he was thirty-five and the divorced father of two children, Mike and Sarah, then six and nine years old respectively. I was twenty-eight. When Jack and I became a couple, I found myself part of a wonderful family unit—one that included, along with the extended Layton clan, Jack's ex-wife, Sally Halford. But my entry really was effortless, like slipping into a refreshing lake on a hot summer's day.

From the start, I was on easy terms with Sally—in no small part because I had not been the cause of the breakup and I did not make any attempt to usurp her role as mother. Sally remained the disciplinarian for her children; I was more like a playful aunt (the one they told their secrets to) and a playmate for Mike and Sarah in those days, which was a great thing for all of us. Not having had siblings to play with in my own home as a child, I loved every moment of those times.

From the time Jack and I got together, the weekend visits from the kids were wonderful occasions, and it seems I was always part of everything they did. We would cook together (although I was never much of a cook). I would break out my paints and crayons and do crafts with them. Sarah and Mike also recall those days with terrific fondness.

"Olivia, remember how Mike and I did plays for you and Dad?" Sarah recalled not long ago. "We'd plan them in five minutes and grab every costume item we could find and do it. And you were our ideal audience. Jack and Olivia."

The plays that Sarah and Mike put on as kids were often their version of TV cooking shows and they were often staged in their bedroom, with a blanket hanging from an upper bunk bed serving as curtain and with pots and pans brought in from the kitchen as props. It was like the stage sets I had devised as a child when escaping into my fantasy world. But Mike and Sarah preferred the reality-show approach. Mike (now a Toronto city councillor) and Sarah (now human resources manager at the Stephen Lewis Foundation) were very close as children, and, happily, they remain so today.

Theirs was a childhood marked by play, with both Jack and me as playmates. We would all walk to the St. Lawrence Market to shop on a Saturday morning and then swim at the Sheraton Centre, which offered the incredible luxury of an outdoor pool heated in winter. Mike and Sarah swam like fish, and I can't say who had more fun—the kids or us. What could be better than a game of tag in the snow followed by a leap into warm water? We would throw pennies in the pool and dive in to get them. Catching Jack was another game, with Mike, Sarah and me teaming up.

Fun came in so many shapes: roller-skating at the Terrace had great appeal—and so did political rallies. Jack made everything fun. He was that rare human—genuinely happy most of the time. And he expressed it, all the time and right out loud. He was a great whistler, and he would walk down the street whistling wild, intricate tunes. Sarah and Mike used to cringe when this happy guy let forth on a crowded escalator at the Eaton Centre or on a subway car. "Stop it! Just stop whistling! You're embarrassing us!" they would cry—which just egged him on.

But when Sarah is walking her own daughter home from school, she'll start singing a song to her or whistling a little tune if she doesn't know the words. And she'll think of her dad.

~

Sarah has a vivid memory of Jack's last days: I was acting as gatekeeper—welcoming people he wanted to see, but keeping tabs on each person's time lest he get overly fatigued. She understands me so well. "That's the way you've always been, Olivia," says Sarah now. "It's one of the ways you cope with any stressful situation. You make lists, you like to be kept busy and organized. It's your personality. You never could keep still, whether the situation is stressful or not."

Actually, I could kick back and relax sometimes—with Jack, when we went away on canoe trips, for example. And when I was painting or sculpting, I could be still because the art demanded my focus. But, as Sarah says, I was never much of a put-my-feet-up person. Jack could sit on the dock at the cottage and chat to people about life for hours, but after a while, I would go swimming or paint a picture.

When Mike Layton was older and able to compare my relationship with Jack to how other couples seemed to operate, he would say, "You guys never fight. It's not normal!" In fact, Jack and I so seldom fought that I can pretty well remember the few times we did quarrel. One argument we had was on a whitewater canoe trip after we had been together for about a year. We were at the Madawaska Kanu Centre getting Jack trained for his first whitewater trip—on the Dumoine River, in western Quebec. The Dumoine is a serious, fast river, with lots of Class I to Class III rapids with descriptive names such as Canoe Eater, Log Jam and Big Steel. The final waterfall, called Ryan Chute, once featured thirty-five pairs of hobnail boots nailed into nearby trees as memorials to loggers who had drowned there.

I wanted to make sure that Jack took some proper whitewater paddling lessons so that when we were in the water he'd know what to do. As the more experienced paddler, I was in the stern, where the paddler has the most control, steers, and acts as the ship captain. I was trying to give Jack, who was in the bow, some instructions (draw left, pry right), but he didn't like to take orders. Neither do I, but this was an area where I had expertise and he didn't. We kept flipping because of the unevenness of our body weight—with his far greater weight in the front and not the reverse as it should have been. We were arguing; we were frustrated.

After an hour or two of this, we both looked at each other and said, "We're supposed to be having fun. We never fight! Something is wrong with this picture. So why don't we treat each other like friends, stop arguing who was right or wrong, stop worrying about who caused the canoe to flip and have fun instead?" We had lunch and then the afternoon was fine. Jack moved to the stern and I took the bow, where I still gave instructions. Before long, we were paddling in sync and nailing the rapids with some precision. Our instructor at the canoe camp, Rudy, also went to the Dumoine afterwards, and we hung out with him and had a grand time on our first canoe trip. Once Jack learned something, he had it. Whitewater paddling is all about reading the water, timing, speed and angle.

A good metaphor for politics.

Jack and I became the best of partners—whether in politics, on a tandem bike or in a canoe.

Sarah always called us the most connected people she had ever met, with a strong, loving relationship based on total respect. She told an interviewer not long after Jack died, "This wasn't a couple hanging on to each other for political purposes. These were two people who were just so connected on every possible level that even my mother says that Jack had found his match."

Key for all of us right from the beginning was to keep the family together and to avoid any question of divided loyalties. So Jack and I went to Sally's house for Hallowe'en and also on Christmas Eve, when we would stay over so the children would wake up on Christmas Day with their immediate family there for the opening of the stockings.

Sally had been Jack's high school sweetheart, and they had married when they were just twenty. The marriage ended after fourteen years, but Sally and Jack remained close. A friendship formed between her and me. She was at our wedding, where Mike and Sarah thanked their mom publicly. When she married Hedley Roy, I was the photographer at their wedding. And Sally was there with us during Jack's last days and at his funeral.

Sarah and Mike have always called me OC or Ollie or Olivia—and yet clearly I had assumed some sort of parental mantle in their eyes by virtue of my relationship with Jack. Sarah talks about having BBQs at her house, and how Jack and I would arrive later—after some community or political function. And some new friend or a friend of a friend would say, "Wow, Jack Layton and Olivia Chow are here." And Sarah would say to them, "Calm down. It's just my parents." Some nosy neighbours who noticed Sarah and I had different hair and skin colour asked me, "How come you don't have kids?" "I do have kids," I would reply. "I have Sarah and Mike."

Still, I was often asked, "Why did you not have your own children?"

Many women start families and balance them with careers. Others focus on children. Others decide not to have children and to put their energy into their work lives. These are choices most women didn't have until very recently, anywhere in the world—including Canada and Hong Kong. But now we do. And so I did have a choice. And since Jack already had two wonderful children, and I wanted to focus on my public life, there was no need for us to have another child. I have never regretted that choice, and I am glad it was mine to make. I am also eternally grateful for our wonderful and loving kids, Sarah and Mike.

Sally was the primary parent for Sarah and Mike, who stayed with us on weekends to play and study. This setup of shared parental responsibilities was ideal since it afforded more support for the children. I often thought I had the best of both worlds: a family with children and also time to work long hours for political change.

On the subject of children and housework, my cooking—particularly one memorable dish—is something that Sarah and Mike still tease me about even after all these years. Jack had high cholesterol, so we thought we should eat more fish than red meat. But the kids generally disliked fish—so what to do? Jack and I concocted a fish chili that we thought was truly wonderful, and we made a huge pot of it because we were quite proud of our creation. The kids politely had a few bites—then said they weren't hungry. This shows how well brought up they were, because Sarah says today that the fish chili was the most disgusting concoction she ever saw or tasted. Jack and I kept the fish chili in the freezer at our Hazelburn co-op for years, thinking we could one day tempt Sarah and Mike to try some more. Even now, I occasionally threaten them that as a special treat, one day I am going to do up a fabulous gourmet fish chili for them. Luckily for the kids (and for Jack and me), my mother, who is a wonderful cook, did most of the cooking in our household.

One of the unique and wonderful things about Jack was that his sense of fun and delight extended to the political process. Politics for us was something to be enjoyed—not a chore. It was a true passion. Jack had a vision for what the country needed. Even when he was leading the party with only a few seats in the House of Commons, he was tenacious. The quest for an apology from the government of Canada for the shameful treatment of aboriginals at residential schools was one example. Every time he met privately with the prime minister, Jack pushed that agenda (and Stephen Harper was gracious in acknowledging Jack's role in the apology when it finally came). It was the same with the NDP gains in Quebec. No one believed as he did that making Quebec a party stronghold was even possible. It took just eight years.

When I first met Jack, I loved him as a man and deeply admired his political philosophy and passionate commitment to building a better world, but I could also see his political weaknesses. When he first got involved in politics, he was very eager and aggressive, he didn't listen as well as he should have and he made assumptions—one being that he knew the answers. But over time, he grew into an extraordinarily effective politician. With Dan Leckie's help, Jack became much more of a team player and long-term strategist.

He also became a better human resources manager and developed very strong leadership skills. For a long time he saw only the good in people; he saw only strength, never weakness. This was both his own strength and his weakness. He opened himself up to disappointment when he chose to overlook the faults of others, but on the other hand, his believing in everyone inspired great loyalty. My work in the field of domestic violence and the violence my mother and I had both experienced greatly influenced Jack's political approach to this subject. He listened closely to tragic stories of women in a horrific cycle of violence and poverty. He listened and took action: he and I were both shaken to the core by the massacre of fourteen women at Montreal's École Polytechnique in 1989. Jack's response was to immediately ensure that he and other like-minded men took responsibility for ending violence against women, and together they started the now worldwide White Ribbon Campaign to speak out against men's violence against women. So Jack listened, and learned, and over the years developed a leadership style that inspired loyalty and respect from others.

As for my own flaws, I'm too impatient. There are times when I should wait, take a longer view. I multi-task well, but if I do that too much my focus can get scattered and I am easily distracted. So I work from two lists. One records all the matters I must attend to urgently. The other lists the longer-term projects that are critically important, with deadlines attached to them. I also rely on my staff, team and friends who provide a structure to keep my energy focused.

Our wedding gift to each other—a bicycle built for two—says it all. The tandem bike was a metaphor and a symbol of our partnership. On it we were together, we were cycling, having fun and being a little outrageous. More important was that we were in step, in time, in rhythm—going in the same direction. Working together, playing together, moving together. Forward, always forward, pursuing goals, making progress. Everything in our life was like that—right to the very end.

That tandem bicycle, though, had an inauspicious start. Jack was on it with Sarah just days before the wedding when the gear jammed—he slammed into a newspaper box and shattered his kneecap. "Yet another confrontation with the press!" he would joke. That bike was later stolen, so we bought another, and that one remains in my possession.

The groom at our wedding thus hobbled around on a cane with one leg in a cast. So at the beginning of our marriage, so at the end.

Though the tandem had an inauspicious start, our marriage did not: we had an amazingly perfect wedding day—an entire day, with three ceremonies.

We began July 9, 1988, with a morning ceremony in a meadow on Ward's Island (with my attendants and me being pulled across the harbour on a barge gaily decorated with white and pink balloons, silver streamers and windsock kites). I wore a classic white wedding dress made by a seamstress who was a neighbour of ours, while Jack wore a white suit. Some two hundred friends and family were there for the ceremony, officiated by two United Church ministers.

The ceremony on the Toronto Islands was followed by a huge banquet at the China International restaurant (now the Dim Sum King, our family favourite) in Chinatown with five hundred guests. For this occasion, I switched into a gorgeous red Chinese wedding dress.

"Hey, Olivia, great dress," guests said. "Did you get it from your mom?"

"Well," I said, "yes and no. Not from *my* mom, but from Jack's mom." Here was yet another magical aspect of our wedding. Jack's father, Bob, had been to Hong Kong many years before, when I was still a schoolgirl there. And he had bought this beautiful dress for Doris—not to wear, but for the fabric, because the embroidery was so magnificent and Doris was an expert in needlework. She tucked it away carefully in a drawer, and pulled it out, twenty years later, when Jack and I told her we were getting married. When I tried it on, it fit like a glove. "It was meant to be," said Doris. Jack wore a grey-silver tailor-made robe, and so we had just the right costumes for our wedding banquet.

Finally, the day ended with a traditional Chinese tea ceremony and "hug dance" in the north building of the St. Lawrence Market, along with nine hundred family members and friends. I had enlisted the folks at Shadowland Theatre—a theatrical troupe based on Ward's Island—to help me make paper cut-outs to hang from the ceiling at the market. They featured traditional Chinese calligraphy that spelled out "double happiness," plus scenes that many Torontonians would recognize, but there was one recurring motif: the bicycle. Pushed along by the music of Parachute Club and rapper Clifton Joseph, we danced until four in the morning.

Lorraine Segato, the lead vocalist with Parachute Club, also sang at Jack's funeral. After the funeral, she was quoted in *Maclean's* magazine describing the nature of my relationship with Jack, and, just as I still sometimes do, she occasionally slipped into the present tense—

as if Jack were still alive: "What you see is a couple engaged in each other's best good. The level of respect is so profound. They didn't agree on every issue, but they had the discussion. They were the embodiment of the equal, feminist relationship. It's not some political ideal. They're living it."

Among those who spoke at the tea ceremony was our friend John Campey, who said he looked forward to the day when lesbian and gay couples could celebrate their relationships with weddings like ours and enjoy the same legal recognition. It was a wonderful day for all of us when the City of Toronto allowed same-sex marriage in 2001, and then when they became legal across Canada in 2005, when Jack was leader of the NDP in Parliament.

In 2011, on the tenth anniversary of the first same-sex weddings, a reaffirmation ceremony was held for the first couples, performed by Brent Hawkes, the pastor of Metropolitan Community Church. It was to be the last year of Jack's life. Jack and I, too, reaffirmed our vows at that special ceremony, and every day we were together, we counted our blessings. We never ceased to marvel at the fact that we had found each other.

Jack was always able to express himself emotionally and he wrote beautiful letters, as people across the country discovered when he wrote his last message to Canadians. He never tired of writing loving and romantic letters to me. One that I kept from our courting days in the autumn of 1985 was a form of proposal that perfectly captured what we had come to mean to each other, what "together" meant and what "forever" meant. It was a declaration of the love, hope and optimism that were always central to Jack's being. I couldn't bring myself to look at that letter again until two years after he was gone.

I read it now—written in Jack's bold, confident handwriting—

and I see his passionate love of life and his love of me and of our life together. And his joy—joy that I was privileged to share, from the first four nanoseconds to the last.

Dear Olivia,

So many images have captured my mind that I wish I were a poet. I would weave the music of our love through the images that have made it real. I would speak of the great loves of history—for we are one of those. The world will know this in years to come. I would set your beauty against the strength I feel when we love; and your strength against the challenges that we are joining hands to confront: our strength.

I have said that I was searching for the mysterious, the mystic and profound sensations which can develop between a man and a woman. I have said that I wouldn't rest until I found these elusive goals . . .

You are a remarkable woman, Olivia. You have no jealousy, no pettiness: you are deeply wise, freshly childlike, endlessly energetic, unbelievably passionate, totally committed . . . I could go on forever. (I hope I will have that chance—I believe I will).

We know already, don't we. We <u>know</u>! There is no <u>doubt</u>—but there are fears, protocols, and obstacles. Some of these are very difficult, some are just silly. But they're there. You know, I have absolute certainty that these obstacles will be overcome: not "defeated" in a conflict; but submerged through understanding and love—not just ours of each other, but our love of those who are close to us. (When your mother said I was "stupid"—I felt so good because it showed that she will come to love me someday!)

What about the fears? I know you have moments, like I do, where an unexplainable "panic" sets in—only for a moment. Is this the feeling of the mountain climber—knowing that this is the ultimate mountain: halfway up a sheer vertical face, looking down and finding no heartbeat, with breathing stopped in momentary terror? Then the climber looks up, sees the goal, receives an immediate injection of confidence, overpowering optimism, a total sense of direction and purpose—the heart is suddenly racing, the breathing is fast, the excitement is total. Fear?!? Who's ever heard of it?! . . .

I love you, Olivia. I want us always to be together. God may have other plans though . . . and if so, we can cherish beautiful memories: But I've talked to him/her about this and I've seen the blueprints (they are the most amazing blueprints: gold and silver, pastel and oils) and they say Olivia and Jack, Jack and Olivia, Olivia and Jack, reflected in an infinitude of mirrors: the message is everywhere.

My love, I have never felt such a touch of love—your delicate, strong touch has reached through all fears, all doubts, and touched my soul.

Take my hand. I take your hand. We shall live forever, together. We can conquer all.

My dear, dear Olivia—

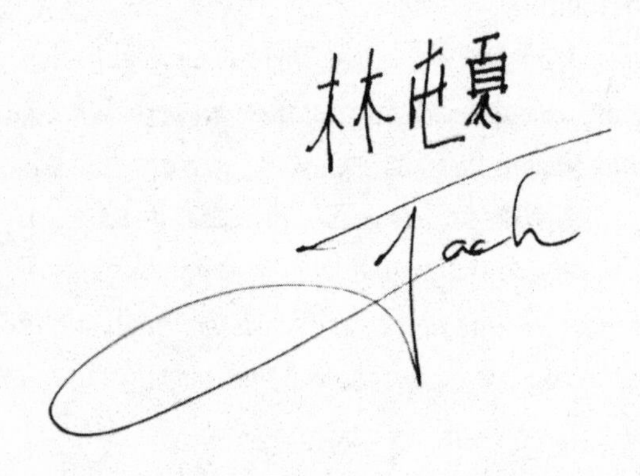

CHAPTER 7

The House on Huron

We have had some wonderful parties on Huron Street, parties that would spill up the stairs and out into the backyard, and on several occasions a guest landed in the fishpond.

Jack and I were two political peas in a pod, but by no means identical. We were different in a way that provided balance in our lives. He was sentimental; me, not so much. He was never impatient; I wish I were more patient. He could be loud and rambunctious; while I can work a room with the best of them, at heart I am quiet and deliberate. He was socially exuberant; I am far more careful.

In my university days, I was a huge fan of Ingmar Bergman. In one of his films, a character observes that a man and a woman in a long-term relationship sometimes become more, not less, like each other. That happened to a certain extent with Jack and me. Under my influence, I think Jack learned to listen more and become more strategic. Under his influence, I became more optimistic and bolder.

All the more so as we lived under the same roof.

To be political peas in a pod, you need the right kind of pod, and Jack and I found the perfect one when we bought our house on Huron Street in 1993. It was our home for the rest of Jack's lifetime, and my mother and I live there still.

In the heart of Toronto, the house became the centre of our personal and political universe. Its location couldn't have been more perfect. A couple of blocks to the south is the heart of Chinatown, where my mother shops at the Lucky Moose emporium and where we go to the Dim Sum King. A couple of blocks to the west is Kensington Market, where Sarah and Mike liked to hang out and shop and where I have my constituency office as the MP for Trinity-Spadina. A block to the north is the University of Toronto, where the kids went (and I before them) and where I go swimming when I have the time. A few blocks to the east is Toronto City Hall, where Jack and I both served on council. And even closer to the east, the hospitals that were to figure large in our lives.

In 2005, I was diagnosed with thyroid cancer and had to spend two days in isolation at Mount Sinai Hospital after taking a pill to radiate the cancer cells. Like a kid full of excitement, Jack e-mailed me: "My love, I can see your room on the top floor of Mount Sinai Hospital. Look out your window, and you can see our bedroom on Huron Street." Sure enough, he was right.

Jack's message continued, "Since I can't be there with you, look again, I am sending you a message." There in the distance I could see a flashing bright light. Ever the romantic, Jack was turning our bedroom light on and off to send out his personal SOS: I love you, I miss you, please come home safely.

The CBC biopic of Jack took artistic licence and added another scene much like that one. This time he was the one in the hospital bed—in the living room of our house on Huron, where he spent his final days. And I was the one flashing that light in the darkness. During all the time he was sick, in everything I did, I was constantly beaming loving and healing lights to him. And he had his shelter in the house he loved, looking out at the flowers I had planted by the window.

In *Toronto Life* in 2004, Trevor Cole, the much-lauded Canadian novelist and magazine writer, wrote a profile about Jack as leader of the NDP called "The Player." And while it focused on Jack, the article also considered—insightfully, I thought—the nature of our political partnership. As he researched the piece, I had told Trevor how even our wedding in 1988 (the choice of Ward's Island as a venue, the poem read to confirm our commitment to the city and to the environment) was designed by committee. "All these choices," wrote Cole, "were born of a belief that politics was less a job than a lifestyle." Later on, Cole referred to our "real and fairly daunting political partnership . . . There can be no doubting their effectiveness on council, where they acted as a kind of policy tag team, dividing up responsibilities in order to maximize their effort."

Trevor Cole spent several days just hanging around us at the house while he was working on the article, and I thought he captured my calming influence on Jack rather well. He wrote: "When Layton gets 'a little too energetic' in the words of environmental lobbyist Gord Perks, Olivia's the one person in the world who can say to him 'Jack? Earth to Jack. Put your feet back on the ground.'"

Cole described our house on Huron as "a political action centre," where Svend Robinson had launched his bid in 1995 to lead the NDP (and where Jack had launched his own successful bid, in 2002), where activists met and campaign workers set up banks of phone lines and where political thinkers gathered at our dining-room table to eat and strategize.

Our house on Huron is bright green—pea-green, really, most appropriate for a pod—although the south side has faded in the sunshine to more of an aquamarine. It's one of many large Victorian semi-detached houses on the street, and a Canadian flag hangs proudly from its west-facing front. More than 120 years old, the house has had many incarnations—once a synagogue, a general store, a bed and breakfast, and a vintage clothing store called, fittingly, Courage My Love. Of course it was decidedly not energy-efficient when we bought it in 1993. We would discover that horsehair had been used as insulation. Over time, we made it green—and not just the colour.

Today it's almost (though not quite) off-grid. We added a geothermal system to heat our home in winter and cool it in summer; we wrapped the entire house in a ten-inch blanket of insulation; we added solar panels and a solar system to heat and store hot water; we installed a sun tunnel on the roof to light a dark hallway by day; we installed triple-pane windows to help keep in heat during winter and keep out heat during summer; and we use energy-efficient light bulbs, low-flow toilets, the best energy-efficient appliances we could find and, outside, rain barrels for watering the garden, to reduce our use of water in the summer.

We also had fun doing what we could to spread the good news of going green (good for the pocketbook, good for the environment). In 2010, Rick Mercer of CBC-TV dropped by to film a segment for his program and he had a ready supply of jokes as he toured the house with Jack. Jack told him that on a sunny day in summer we produce more energy than we use, allowing us to sell the surplus to Toronto Hydro—and causing the electricity meter outside our home to run backwards. "That's what the odometer on my car did before I sold it," Mercer quipped. I also made a YouTube video of the same sort of tour of the house in which I pointed out that while a solar-heated water system may cost several thousand dollars, it pays for itself in about four years.

The appliances and green-energy devices in the building may be new, but little else is. I suppose that speaks to our priorities. Furniture was clearly not one of them—everything in the house is a hand-me-down, and nothing matches. Sarah picked out the brown couch in the living room, and it's a nice couch that matches another brown couch that came from Jack's parents, but both couches clash with the various rugs. The TV was given to us by Jack's brother David. At one end of the living room, Jack's guitars are set on stands, and there are two objects from Jack's grandfather—a nineteenth-century organ and a wall clock. One of my sculptures, a bronzed bas-relief, occupies a spot on the wall opposite. The other art and posters on the walls mostly came from auctions.

In one way, Jack and I were quite different. He liked to shop, whereas I loathe shopping and live by a less-is-more philosophy. Many items in the house followed Jack home after charity auctions; if an item couldn't find a buyer, he'd bid on it.

The centre of our lives together at Huron Street was always the kitchen-dining room. One of the few items that Jack and I bought together was a custom-built fourteen-person dining table with matching chairs.

At one end of the kitchen was a beer fridge, and nearby was an old wood-and-glass cabinet that housed several dozen plain wine glasses. (The cabinet remains, not so the beer fridge.) There would often be two or three different meetings happening at the same time in our house. Guests would spill out into the backyard as Jack and I would plan how to move an issue forward—such as building affordable housing or creating high-quality childcare.

And there was always great food. My mother cooked for everyone, and the best meetings took place in the kitchen-dining room area so people could eat wonderful Chinese food while the conversations flowed. Our house on Huron really reflected the new political style we were trying to build, where people of all ages and backgrounds come together for a common cause while having fun and breaking bread—or sharing rice—with each other. A standard greeting in Cantonese is *nay ho*—hello. But a warmer greeting is *Lay sic jaw faan may*—Have you eaten rice yet today? Invariably, when you left our house, you had.

My mother has always had her domain by the kitchen; Sarah and Mike had theirs in the basement. For Jack and me, it was our top-floor master bedroom. It has a deck—often invaded by raccoons—from which we can see through treetops to the CN Tower. Then there's the king-sized waterbed we bought when we first got together, and, in an alcove, there's a desk and computer, where we worked.

Being a visual person, I always wanted to make sure that Jack looked his best in the public eye. So Sarah and I would go shopping for his ties, and I always went with him when he needed to purchase a suit. During national election campaigns when he was NDP leader, Jack always had a personal handler; one year it was Mike, another year it was his nephew Alan, and for his last two campaigns, his sister Nancy travelled with him. To ensure that Jack's tie always matched his shirt and suit, I had developed for all of them what I called "tie principles":

1. Dark blue shirt with light yellow (or light green) ties. Use light-coloured ties with dark shirt.
2. Pick ties that can echo eye colour or colour in suit.
3. All dark orange, brown and burgundy ties go with white shirts only.
4. Grey suit with white shirt and burgundy ties. Light suits don't work in winter.

5. Light blue shirts can handle two kinds of ties: the two very dark blue-striped ties and the two yellow ties.
6. White shirts can go with anything.
7. Brown is a semi-boring colour; try not to use it in urban centres. Brown, though, is also a cool colour—and goes well with orange. Use in rural areas and small towns.
8. Leave the very bold ties (purple and dark pink, for example) for urban centres.
9. Patterns cannot be too dense or else the tie vibrates on TV and will distract.
10. Two suits have blue stripes in them. Try using ties with blue in them.

One of our friends referred to our house as a "total community centre." With all the political gatherings and meetings and dinners and parties, you never knew who was going to be there and you were never alone. Imagine the scene: people coming and going at all times of the day—politicians, artists, journalists, activists, students, friends of the kids, my mother's mah-jong ladies, new arrivals from all over the world, tenants, neighbours. The house on Huron has always drawn an extraordinary, diverse community that reflects our extraordinary, diverse city.

Mike Layton still laughs when he tells his favourite story about unexpected visitors at Huron Street. It happened while he was still at university and working part-time as the manager of a restaurant and bar. His job required him to work well past closing time, and that meant that he often slept in. One day, when he was just getting up and still in his bathrobe, the doorbell rang. The guy at the door said, "I'm here for a photo shoot."

Still bleary-eyed, Mike said, "Yeah, could you just wait one moment?" And he shut the door. You should know that we have an intercom system on our phone. Ours is the only house you are ever likely to see with an intercom system. Mike, who is now a city councillor, says it's more complicated than the phone system at city hall. In any case, he buzzed us on the top floor.

"Hey, Dad," he said, "some guy is here for a photo shoot."

And Jack replied, "Mike, that would be Steven Page of the Barenaked Ladies."

"Oh shit!" said Mike, and ran to open the door to one of his idols.

A word of explanation about the idiosyncratic telephone system at Huron Street. The phone lines—and there were four—were always ringing, as was the doorbell. With Jack and me on the third floor, my mom's bedroom on the second floor, the kitchen and living room on the main floor, and Sarah's and Mike's rooms in the basement, we figured that the best way to communicate was to install an intercom phone system instead of having to yell up and down the stairs. With the touch of a button, Mom could call everyone when dinner was ready. Or Sarah could tell her father that someone was on the line for him without having to run up three flights of stairs.

After the phone system was installed, of course, it had to be married with an Internet system. Before the age of Wi-Fi, we had wires dangling here and there and running throughout the entire house. In total, there were eight telephones and eight Internet drops.

Overkill, you may say. But it certainly came in handy when, for example, we needed to move our offices to the house while city hall was virtually shut down during a strike. It was handy for the university students who lived with us a long time ago. And even now, when the kids are grown and moved out, my mother, who is increasingly disabled with rheumatoid arthritis, can easily summon me from my top-floor aerie.

~

There is plenty of student housing in our neighbourhood, being so close to U of T, but none of the student houses could be more of a party house than ours became. We worked hard and we partied hard. We loved parties—and so did the kids—and we had them for every imaginable occasion. And we didn't even need a special occasion. Often our meetings in the house evolved into parties, as most of the people we worked with and met with were also our friends, and as so many dropped in. As well as being action central, we were party central—and not just party in the political sense.

Jack and I kept a database of people who were single and perhaps looking for a partner, and we would arrange for them to connect at our place. Hallowe'en parties were especially useful for such pairings. At one such party, we invited our then single friend Marilyn Churley, who had been a city councillor and later an MPP and Ontario cabinet minister. We introduced Marilyn to Richard Barry, a smart housing policy person and a good musician; not long after, they were inseparable. Betty Chee (a Toronto architect) married Michael Kaufman (an educator, writer and co-founder with Jack of the White Ribbon Campaign to end violence against women) after Jack and I introduced them. So the matchmaking sometimes worked—and sometimes without our even knowing because there were so many parties and meetings at the house.

We have had some wonderful parties on Huron Street, parties that would spill up the stairs and out into the backyard, and more than once a guest landed in the fishpond. One was a musician (who shall remain nameless) and another was an Iraq war resister (who had just moved to Canada from the United States). For big parties, Sarah and Mike would invite their classmates and camp friends (they went to summer camp every year, as campers and then camp counsellors), and invariably some of them slept over. It would be hard to calculate how many people used our house as a crash pad over the years.

Countless keys to the place are floating around out there; for many of our friends and friends of friends, our house was their community gathering space.

One party we called "Martini Madness," and it featured Mike Layton—a trained bartender—mixing cocktails while I was instructing guests on how to make sushi, so its preparation was part of the entertainment. Of course one can get thirsty with wasabi, and the martinis went down fast and smooth. It didn't take long for the party to hop. Sometimes these parties were dinner parties, meant as a thank you for individuals who had worked particularly hard for us. Sometimes the dinner party was a prize item at a charity auction ("Jack and Olivia will make you sushi in their home")—we raised a lot of funds for charities that way, and always had a great time with the winning bidders. But no matter the occasion, the parties always filled the house with laughter—and usually with song. Our sing-alongs almost always featured live music. If Jack wasn't playing his guitar and handing out song sheets, other musicians stepped up. One of Jack's treasures was a songbook called *Rise Up Singing*, a collection of some twelve hundred folk and popular songs.

My mother loved these wildly boisterous parties as much as anyone, and she would usually lead the cleanup afterwards. Whenever you invite that many people into your home, there is inevitably a certain amount of mess and chaos; Jack and I possessed a high tolerance for both. Mike would often join my mother, and they would talk, laugh and tease each other till early dawn. She was key to the smooth running of the place, and I owe her a huge debt of gratitude. Given the demands of our political careers, Jack and I were both lucky to live with my mother, who took care of day-to-day housekeeping, shopping, cleaning, laundry and, blissfully, cooking.

~

For all that we loved the house, there were times when we had to escape the political world, the parties, the city, the BlackBerrys, and get away from it all. When I was crushed by my loss in the 2004 federal election, for instance, Jack and I took a trip to the northern tip of Vancouver Island. We had to heal our wounds, recharge our batteries and put everything into perspective. We had to leave the work and the politics behind and enter a wilderness zone.

I had known about the healing effect of time in nature since I was sixteen years old, an immigrant not yet three years in Canada, and thankfully, Jack felt the same way.

Through the years, I would seek out the wilderness for a stretch of time to help put my life in focus. This love affair has sustained me. Jack and I were blessed to be able to paddle down wild rivers such as the Nahanni—feeling in sync as we went through wild rapids and sharing the exhilaration. We paddled past icebergs on the Alsek River, found eagle feathers while hiking in the Rockies and Haida Gwaii. We'd go on long-distance cycling and camping trips, taking Mike and Sarah with us when they were young—to Manitoulin Island northwest of Toronto, to Prince Edward Island, to Îles-de-la-Madeleine in the St. Lawrence River, to Prince Edward County in southeastern Ontario and the P'tit Train du Nord trail in Quebec. We snorkelled in remote atolls in Belize and Dominica, staying in straw huts with solar panels and using water from rain barrels.

On our post-election trip in 2004, we kayaked in the Pacific Ocean, at the northern tip of Vancouver Island. Jack and I were in a tandem kayak, part of a group led by guides through channels where we paddled alongside orcas and caught sight of humpback whales. At one point, en route across Goletas Channel to the aptly named God's Pocket at the entrance to Queen Charlotte Strait, we encountered three-foot-high waves. Tandem kayaks are difficult to flip, but there was still that risk and the fatigue factor was enormous. I think we sang "Row, Row, Row Your Boat" about two hundred times in an effort to safely make the crossing.

The height of that trip was hiking in the old-growth forest at Cape Scott Provincial Park, an area known for its rugged terrain, its sandy beaches and its violent weather.

If you were to ask me, what's your idea of bliss? I would say, swimming in a gently flowing river with mountains all around me.

As politicians who worked so much indoors, we felt bound by one rule when we were on vacation—we had to be in the great outdoors. And when we had our fill, we were ready, once again, for the beat of Toronto and our house on Huron.

CHAPTER 8

Food for Thought

Children living in poverty find it hard to thrive and to learn. A body not fed does not grow. Hungry children are inattentive, unfocused in the classroom, and they tire easily. Proper nutrition and brain stimulation during those first six years of life are absolutely critical, and damage done then is difficult to reverse.

I believe a child represents the soul of a city. It is our first duty to provide the best services to children. Whether as a family or a nation, our success is judged by how well we treat our children. I am constantly amazed by the creativity, the resilience and the hopeful nature of children. I was obsessed with playing when I was a kid, and now, as an adult, I want every child to have a chance to play joyously.

As a school trustee from 1985 until 1991, I fought hard for after-school programs, childcare and a good education. Later, as a Metropolitan Toronto councillor between 1991 and 1998, I was part of a team that pulled together a comprehensive report on how to put children at the centre of our city services. So when Mayor Mel Lastman appointed me in 1998 as Toronto's first Advocate for Children and Youth, I was thrilled. I had a rare opportunity to channel my passion in a way that could get things done for all the children and youth in the newly amalgamated city.

Based on my philosophy of putting children at the centre of all services, my first task was to ask the city's children: If you were mayor for a day, what would you do? They were able to respond by writing, drawing or painting, and many drew pictures of the CN Tower and parks and trees, while others printed notes about improving playgrounds.

One entry stood out in stark contrast to the others. A five-year-old girl named Sylvia had drawn a stick-figure child holding an oversized shopping bag. The accompanying note read: "I would ask God for money to buy groceries." I knew all too well that this little girl in the richest city in the country was not alone in her plight, and I could imagine Sylvia's mother struggling to make her money stretch till the end of the month and cover the rent with a few dollars left for groceries. Sylvia's plea has haunted me ever since.

Even then, the consequences of neglecting substantial numbers of the city's children were clear. The UN World Summit for Children in 1990 made the following commitment to children of the world: "The growing minds and bodies of children should have first call on society's capacities and . . . children should be able to depend upon that commitment *in good times and in bad*." Children living in poverty find it hard to thrive and to learn. A body not fed does not grow. Hungry children are inattentive, unfocused in the classroom, and they tire easily. They are also more likely to drop out of school, clash with police and have difficulty staying employed. Proper nutrition and brain stimulation during the first six years of life are absolutely critical, and damage done then is difficult to reverse.

The connection between poverty and reduced life chances is well documented. Children in low-income families tend to be less healthy than other children, and sometimes their health is compromised for life. They are more likely to be hyperactive and to be behind on vocabulary and math.

On the other hand, research shows that early intervention works. Intervention in this case means primarily a good diet and stimulation from caregivers. It means access to good public services. Above all, it means treating children as full participants in the life of the community.

In 1989, nine years before my appointment as Children and Youth Advocate, every member of Parliament had supported a motion made by Ed Broadbent, then leader of the NDP, to end child poverty by the year 2000. In 1998, with the deadline just two years away, the goal looked as elusive as ever. Toronto had the highest poverty rate in Ontario, with one in three children living below the poverty line. I felt that it was my mission to enrich the lives of those children, and I knew that I had to enlist all parents to join in the effort.

I knew another political truth. Programs that focus only on the poor will always be vulnerable to the axe. But programs that serve the majority—including the middle class, or better still a universal program that serves everyone—will withstand future political turmoil and elimination. Witness the semi-universal Old Age Security income program for seniors.

When Jack and I became a couple (in both the personal and political sense), the very first program we designed was a student nutrition program, in 1989. We noticed that the nutritious sandwiches we packed for our children would sometimes come home untouched. Taste was not the issue; Mike and Sarah and their friends were simply availing themselves of the opportunity to buy junk food from nearby corner stores at lunchtime. When I went to school in Hong Kong, all the kids ate lunch together, and I didn't quite understand why that didn't happen here in Toronto. Jack and I were more than willing to pay for nutritious meals or snacks in schools, but they were just not available. At the time, Jack was on the City of Toronto Board of Health and I was a school trustee. With the help of people such as trustees Pam McConnell and Tony Silipo, and the fundraising efforts of the Toronto Educational Opportunity Fund, we launched a nutrition program that became very successful and popular even though it wasn't universally available. In 1991, parent advocates and community groups such as FoodShare Toronto's Coalition for Student Nutrition convinced the City of Toronto to invest $180,000 each year to help fund a cost-shared model.

Many of these programs were limited to the old city of Toronto and had not been extended to outlying regions such as Etobicoke and Scarborough. When the city of Toronto amalgamated and these boroughs became part of a single municipal entity, I saw an opportunity to expand the nutrition program. Working with the executive director of FoodShare, Debbie Field (who was briefly my executive assistant when I was a Metro councillor), and Fiona Nelson (a long-time trustee and advocate for the rights of children), we submitted a proposal to expand the program across the newly formed city region. On that initiative, I was ably supported by the deputy medical officer of health, Dr. Jack Lee.

By this time it was accepted that all children, rich or poor, needed nutritious food at school. With millions spent on ads that pitch junk food to children, a universal student nutrition program is an issue not just for low-income parents but for all parents. A child who eats an apple a day at mid-morning snack will save our health care system millions. We also need to teach kids how to cook and how to grow food so they can become healthy adults capable of feeding themselves.

By 2013, this little program had grown tremendously. Now, every week, 144,000 Toronto students enjoy healthy breakfasts, snacks and lunches. Toronto's involvement brought in the province, and the Ontario government expanded the food program province-wide to 690,000 students, including those in First Nations communities.

But in 1998, while I was expanding children's food programs into the inner suburbs of Toronto such as Scarborough and Etobicoke, it occurred to me: Why stop at nutritious breakfasts or snacks for children? If their teeth are rotten, how can they eat? If they're in pain from a toothache, how can they learn? I had bad teeth when I was a child because of all the chocolates I ate, but thankfully my parents had money for good dental care when we were in Hong Kong. I know that any child who can't smile because of rotten teeth will quickly lose her confidence. Dental care is expensive, ranking third in health expenditures in Canada, after heart disease and mental health. How is a struggling parent supposed to pay the rent, buy groceries and still have money left over to take the kids to the dentist? Yet the consequences of not going to the dentist are serious. More than half the children in this country have had a cavity by age thirteen, and early childhood tooth decay affects almost 9 per cent of children, some as young as twelve months.

In the old regions of Toronto and North York, a program provided free dental care for children if their parents earned less than $30,000 a year. Why, I asked, should a kid with a toothache in Scarborough not get the same treatment?

Mayor Mel Lastman liked to play with children, and I surrounded him with happy kids so he understood and felt the emotional impact of his policy of putting children first. He came to feel the pain of kids who had dental problems, and he came to see how unfair it was that

Toronto and North York kids enjoyed free dental care while those from Scarborough and Etobicoke did not. And he saw how happy kids were when they had a nutritious breakfast in schools. So Mel Lastman supported my initiatives. When I was able to get the Royal Bank of Canada involved, his enthusiasm for our projects increased.

During my time working with Mel Lastman, I used a favourite strategy that Jack and I both learned from our dear friend Dan Leckie. I was "propositional" as well as "oppositional." This approach worked well, and confirmed to me that you can reach across political divides from the left to the right and bring people together to achieve important goals; the key is to appeal to our common humanity and connect.

Mayor Lastman and I worked successfully together on a range of initiatives for the benefit of children. And the ideas emerged from questioning the status quo. What about pregnant moms in the city, I asked. At the time, some two thousand babies a year in the city were born underweight, and almost 7 per cent were born prematurely. Malnutrition, addictions, homelessness and even a mother's poor teeth all affected the fetus.

Why not, I argued, give newborn babies a decent chance in life by helping them to be born full weight? Why not support high-risk pregnant mothers? And after the baby is born, wouldn't it be a good idea to ensure there are places where mothers could get answers about parenting, share the joys and frustrations of raising their babies, break the feeling of isolation and share some toys too? At the same time, they could learn how to prepare their own baby food (cheaper than buying it) and nutritious meals for themselves and their other children. Finally, at such places their children could play with each other and learn at the same time.

And what about children who were growing up in homes where there weren't any books around? What kind of library programs could we establish so these children could learn the joy of reading, just as

I had been able to do when I was a kid? Being stuck at home watching TV may be easy as a form of babysitting, but it can drive a child stir-crazy and be very isolating. How many children are latchkey kids, their parents both working? What about good recreation programs at nearby rec centres or local parks so these children could play with their friends, learn, exercise and grow up healthy?

And what about mothers without homes? Their kids were sometimes taken away from them—not because they were bad mothers but simply because they had no permanent roof over their heads. Shouldn't housing for them be a top priority?

There was absolutely no way I could tackle all these issues by myself. So at my dining-room table on Huron Street, I brought together experts and activists committed to creating a city that put children first. With the city's amalgamation, all of us saw a perfect opportunity to take the best practices of each region and share them across the new city so that all children and their parents could have equal access to these services.

As the first advocate, I had a lot of latitude to define the scope of my work. So I pulled in staff and resources from different departments: Health, Parks and Recreation, along with the Children's Services Division. I formed a formal Children and Youth Action Committee, or CYAC, at city hall with these city staff and added to it a "children first" citizens' group. I also invited like-minded city councillors to join the team. Later we managed to get librarian and author Ken Setterington appointed as the first Children and Youth Advocate for Library Services for the Toronto Public Library. I recently asked Ken what it was like to join the CYAC—since it all meant more work for him and other city staff.

"It was a period of excitement for city staff," he told me. "For the first time in our careers, those of us involved in services to children had a politician working with us championing the programs and services we deeply believed in. Besides, going to meetings with you was fun. Your sense of humour could be counted on to provide laughter at every get-together."

Fun and laughter have always been part of my political life, and fortunately, Mayor Lastman loved to have fun, especially with children. So my "kitchen cabinet" provided many opportunities for children and their service providers to interact with both city councillors and the mayor. We put together a "welcome baby package"—Fiona Nelson's idea—so that every new parent would receive from the City of Toronto a beautifully designed kit with information about neighbourhood services available to them and their newborns (the location of the closest libraries and public health clinics, for example, and available drop-in programs) and including a copy of the Toronto children's charter of rights. Included as well was a multicultural children's calendar, a cute "Read to Your Bunny" book to encourage reading, a growth chart and a fridge magnet picture frame provided by the Public Health Department. (Unfortunately, the program was later discontinued.)

Throughout the eight years I was the Children and Youth Advocate, from 1998 to 2005, I organized awards breakfasts so we could celebrate unsung heroes such as childcare workers (for they were unfairly paid low wages) and public health nurses who provided such important services to our children. At these events they had their photos taken with the mayor—there were literally hundreds and hundreds of Kodak moments at city hall.

We needed to send out a strong message that Toronto is a child-friendly city and we needed to engage the public so they could imagine a city that put children first, so my children's committee sponsored a design-a-flag contest. The contest was promoted in schools, childcare programs, recreation centres and libraries throughout the city, and we received more than two thousand entries. The winning design, "Small But Mighty," was by five-year-old Nathaniel Roda. The flag-raising ceremony at city hall was an example of how the CYAC gave a direct voice to children in the city.

Each year, we wanted to honour programs that demonstrated innovation and leadership in serving children. To that end, we established two Children's Advocate Awards, of $5,000 each, to highlight and encourage best practices from children's and youth organizations citywide.

In my new position, I knew it was important to capture detailed and factual portraits of the city's children. Especially important was to identify those children falling through the cracks. So with my staff, I initiated annual Children and Youth Action Committee report cards and action plans, so that year-to-year change in children's circumstances—for better or for worse—could be tracked and measured and we could see whether set goals had been attained. I put young Sylvia's drawing and her haunting quote about praying to God for grocery money on the cover of the inaugural annual report—a powerful message and motivation.

In that first report, in 1998, I wrote a letter that read, in part: "The present lives of our children will determine the future life of our city . . . Let us make a covenant with our children—to put them and their needs at the heart of our city."

The report card was compiled by city staff, using data from Statistics Canada and various children's services providers, and documented the needs of children in the city. Based on that information, I then issued an action plan that outlined the goals for that year—such as setting a target to reduce by half the number of homeless children living in shelters, the number of children waiting for childcare, the number of low birth weight babies or the number of latchkey children. By the end of each year, we had in hand a summary of what had been done, what still needed to be done, the barriers, the effectiveness of the services and the number of children and families served.

And, to provide a reminder of what these activities were really about, the CYAC wrote a Children's Charter (which the City of Toronto adopted), incorporating the spirit and substance of the United Nations Convention on the Rights of the Child. A copy of the city's Children's Charter was provided to all service providers so an overall framework could guide their day-to-day activities.

During the eight years that I was Toronto's children's advocate, we were able to expand the student nutrition program from 34,000 to 120,000 children and provide free dental care to all children whose parents earned less than $30,000. We set up many family resource centres for mothers and other caregivers to drop in to with their children, and we dramatically increased the number of children using libraries.

We also started a newsletter that provided updates every two weeks, and I enlisted Annie Kidder and her team at People for Education, a community-based parents' organization, to help write it. Through this newsletter, parents, librarians, recreation staff, public health nurses, hostel providers, cooks at children's breakfast programs, principals and city councillors—all got the same message of putting children first.

As for ending child poverty, though, there was only so much that the city of Toronto, alone, could do, without supporting programs from the provincial and federal governments. We hired a polling firm and undertook a five-year tracking program to see what strategies worked to break the cycle of poverty for single mothers. We discovered that one-third of single mothers on social assistance had a post-secondary education. Many were depressed, and their energy was sapped by welfare red tape. They couldn't break out of the cycle of poverty because they couldn't afford childcare, clothes or subway tokens in order to go back to school or work. We hired mothers on welfare to interview other mothers on social assistance to find out what could be done. What we discovered was that while childcare and tokens were fundamental requirements, these mothers also needed group support and encouragement to sustain hope.

Through the years, I met with groups of mothers who managed to break out of the cycle of poverty. Their stories were truly inspiring. Despite all odds, some worked three jobs in order to save enough to get into college; others talked about how difficult it was to stretch a tiny budget so there would be a bit left for their kids' pizza days at school. Others had heartbreaking stories. One mother was put in jail because she was caught stealing diapers; another was forced to endure violence from her spouse because she didn't have enough to pay rent and buy food at the same time, and in the end she was evicted.

I believe that the child-centred efforts we made in Toronto later became the basis of provincial policy. The practice of public health nurses visiting at-risk mothers at home started in Toronto and then expanded throughout Ontario, as did all-day kindergarten. So wherever you are—village, town, city—take the lead. Make a covenant with our children. Your determination and your accomplishments will influence levels of government to fulfill that all-important first duty.

My friend Laurel Rothman is national coordinator of a group called Campaign 2000, which has been striving since 1991 to focus a spotlight on child poverty in this country—in no small part by reminding all Canadians and all parliamentarians of that solemn promise made in the House of Commons in 1989 to end child poverty by 2000.

Laurel remembers how angry and frustrated she and her colleagues were in 1999—ten years after the promise and nothing had been done. "We said, 'This is crazy,' so we held silent vigils in one hundred communities across the country. They were called 'Silence at Six,' for they were all held at the dinner hour. And some were not silent: in some communities people banged pots and pans. In Nathan Phillips Square in Toronto, we put up a big countdown clock to show how much time was left before we reached the year 2000. A high school kid wrote a song called 'The Promise,' which we all sang."

But the shaming, the singing, the vigils, the clock: all had limited effect. The National Child Benefit Supplement was somewhat increased during this period, but overall, support for poor parents remained limited.

Canada is one of the few Western industrialized nations that do not have a national policy or program for student nutrition. The United States and the United Kingdom have nationally funded programs, but not Canada. So in 2006, as the NDP caucus member in charge of children's affairs, I pulled together a team with Debbie Field from FoodShare and Brian Cook from the Toronto Board of Health. That year, Jack and I spent our Christmas holidays finalizing a proposal for a national children's nutrition program.

The plan was to start small and build the program in partnership with existing community-based breakfast clubs. Our goals were to create jobs, support local farmers through bulk purchasing and ensure that Canadian children ate well, thereby reducing their obesity rates and enhancing their academic performance. Alas, the Conservative government of the day didn't see the merits of such a proposal. The plan remained in the NDP's 2008 and 2011 election platforms. One day . . .

Toronto's system of public services for children is more than a century old. In the early 1900s, there were childcare centres in Toronto's schools and public health nurses. There was also dawning recognition that our city was only as strong as its weakest member. A growing city needed skilled workers, educated children and resourceful families. Public services made for a safe, healthy, productive city.

What has happened? How is it that in this rich country of ours we have children growing up hungry? How could it be with so many political promises of ending child poverty, we still have children who can't focus in school because they didn't have breakfast? One child in seven is poor. One in five will have some experience of poverty.

The numbers were stark when I was Toronto's children's advocate; they have grown starker since, with almost half a million *more* children living in poverty. Use of food banks has increased by 90 per cent, and 40 per cent of food bank users are children. There is something wrong in this country. If we do not feed all of our children, how can we grow a healthy next generation?

I came to realize that cities couldn't do this alone. Canada's federal government was not providing the supports other countries' national governments were. Since the seventies, we have fallen behind on so many issues—childcare, housing, home care, transit, the environment. It's up to the federal government to take a leadership role on issues that matter most to Canadians, setting guidelines and national standards. What makes Canadians proud? Our national health care plan.

To make progress in Toronto and our other cities, the federal government would need to provide leadership on these vital urban issues. And that thought became more central to me in the years to come.

CHAPTER 9

Children First

Quebec has seven-dollar-a-day daycare. Theirs is the best childcare program in the country, and the results have been spectacular. A decade ago, Quebec women fared last when participation in the labour force was measured by province; today they're in first place. Child poverty rates have been cut in half.

In all the years and decades I have been pushing for universal, all-day public childcare, I have had all the excuses, all the clichés, tossed at me. *Taxes are already too high. If you want socialism, move to Russia. We can't afford it. A woman's place is in the home.* And my favourite, one I heard often when I was a city councillor and a regular guest on talk-radio shows: *If you can't afford to have a kid, don't have one.*

And when I was given the chance and the time, I would offer the following analysis in response. Few dispute the need for tax dollars to be spent on police protection, fire protection or military protection; anything that *protects* us is seen as a state priority. Such services are mostly provided by men, and our society deems it natural that these services should be a state responsibility. But when it comes to services typically performed by women—whether it's providing early childhood education and care or nursing care for the elderly—the thinking changes. These services are deemed to be a private responsibility or best done by volunteers. The state, it is thought, should neither shoulder some of these costs nor provide the service. This gender-biased analysis of public versus private responsibility has resulted in a poor and fragmented approach to home care for seniors and childcare for our young. Surely the state has a role to play in both domains.

Here's the problem. We remain stuck in a kind of time warp that continues to insist that early childhood education and care are the sole responsibility of women—as it was viewed in the fifties, when many families lived comfortably on just the father's income. Those days are gone. Ordinary workers' salaries have not kept up with inflation, and often both parents must work. Meanwhile, successive governments seemed to see nothing wrong with insisting, in effect, that women make a choice: Are you a mother, or are you a worker? You have to choose one or the other—but if you want to be both, don't expect help from the state. This blind ideology ignores two facts: more than two-thirds of women are employed, and the high cost of childcare is limiting the number of babies born in Canada. Families are, in fact, saying: we can't afford a child, so we won't have one. For a country with a declining birth rate, not having a universal and high-quality childcare program is short-sighted and counterproductive.

My experience as a city councillor from 1991 to 2005 was that although it took a lot of work to make the municipal government understand the importance of services for children, they did come around—in large part because those of us advocating for children made sure there was face-to-face contact between parents and children on the one hand and elected officials on the other. The mothers and fathers were able to talk from their own experience about the importance of high-quality early learning while three-year-old charmers were running around council chambers. Who can resist a three-year-old?

Encounters like this also happen at the committee level in the House of Commons, but there it's far more formal and more intimidating. When I was pushing my national childcare bill (more on this later), we did have parents speaking to the committee, but a committee consists of only fifteen or sixteen MPs, so the influence on the House of Commons is negligible.

And it's hard to reach the federal Conservatives at all. Their party line is that anything to do with health care, childcare or home care is a provincial responsibility. And that's a mistake, because just as with health care, the federal government—which collects the greatest share of the taxes we pay—should take a leadership role and partner with other levels of government.

Just a few blocks from my house in Toronto and near my office in Kensington Market, there is a wonderful childcare centre called Kensington Kids. My granddaughters, Beatrice and Solace, are lucky enough to go there, and their parents are both able to go to work knowing that their kids are in good hands. Sarah put Beatrice on the waiting list when she was four months pregnant just so she could get a spot.

But daily, across Toronto and across Canada, thousands and thousands of other parents are still waiting for spaces. And thousands of parents, in order to hold down a job, must pay far more for childcare than they can afford or must settle for programs where they cannot be sure of the quality of care their children receive.

Affordable, accessible, good-quality childcare is critical to breaking the cycle of poverty and it is critical to the participation of women at every level of education, in the workforce and in their community.

The lack of such daycare is a national problem with far-reaching implications: it hurts families, inhibits the progress of women, reduces the productivity of the workforce, increases the gender income gap, deprives children of vital learning and play experiences, and is a drag on the economy. This is a national problem that requires a national solution.

As a Toronto school trustee in the eighties, I became an advocate for childcare, and I carried that through to city hall. During my years on city council, and as Toronto's Children and Youth Advocate, I forged alliances with an extraordinary network of childcare providers, advocates and activists, who in turn forged alliances across the country. This was an incredible act of empowerment—and necessary, because childcare has been dismissed by male-dominated governments over the years as a "women's issue."

It was time childcare was on the table, and in the late nineties, I began gathering some of these advocates and activists at my own table. My oversized kitchen table, to be precise. We became a kitchen cabinet of determined supporters of early childhood education. My old friend and childcare ally Martha Friendly recently reminisced with me about our early efforts to generate a national program. "Olivia," she said, "the drive for a national movement really came out of the dinner meetings we had at your house. I'll never forget those evenings at your kitchen table. We bonded, relaxed, laughed, brainstormed, planned strategies and got energized, every time. I can't think of any other politician I ever worked with who went about things the way you did."

"Yeah, always lots of good food, and plenty of wine," I said. "Maybe that helped us think outside the box."

While we did make some progress in boosting the number of childcare spaces in Toronto, clearly we needed to increase the focus on the *national* stage. We held children's forums, at which parents could voice their concerns and make suggestions about how the city and other levels of government could move forward to better support their children. We put on summits and invited prominent speakers such as political scientist Jane Jenson of the Université de Montréal and the Canadian Policy Research Networks, as well as politicos from different parties and levels of government.

We knew the City of Toronto couldn't do this alone. I found support through the Association of Municipalities of Ontario. At one annual general meeting, Toronto hosted a successful children's breakfast with eighty-five of our colleagues from across the province. At the Federation of Canadian Municipalities, where more than two thousand municipalities are represented, we pulled in councillors from other regions to join with us to push other levels of government to put children first.

Jean Chrétien was still prime minister—years after he had promised, in his famous Red Book of 1993, to establish national childcare in Canada. He made the same promise in every election, and with three majority Liberal governments he had had plenty of opportunity. But the promises went nowhere.

Finally, thanks to the efforts of both the aforementioned advocates and some staunch Liberal champions of childcare—notably John Godfrey and Carolyn Bennett—we got word that there would be an announcement in the federal budget of 2000. So I booked a committee room at city hall and invited some of our kitchen cabinet—Martha Friendly and Kerry McCuaig—and other key stakeholders, including parents with children.

We sat and watched Finance Minister Paul Martin read the budget speech. As we listened, it sounded like good news. He announced that $1 billion would be transferred to the provinces for childcare programs. There were cheers and tears in the committee room as we celebrated this step forward.

But we soon discovered there was a catch to the Early Childhood Development Initiative. There was no national legislative framework, just a straightforward transfer of funds to the provinces. And the money was not earmarked for childcare programs. Only a few provinces, such as Quebec and Manitoba, actually applied the funds to childcare. But we in Ontario were not so lucky.

Mike Harris's ideology-driven Conservative government had been teaching us the ABCs—Anything *But* Childcare! They designated some of the federal money to children's health and some to family resource centres—drop-in centres where mothers who were at home could take their children to play with others but couldn't leave them unsupervised. These were all valuable initiatives—but they weren't early learning centres and they certainly weren't childcare. Yet childcare was the most pressing need.

Our kitchen cabinet pulled together. And we started gathering some good ammunition on the need for childcare. I set up the blue-ribbon Commission on Early Learning and Child Care—and on my recommendation, the city appointed as co-chairs Charles Coffey (vice-president of RBC, one of Canada's largest banks) and Margaret McCain (the former lieutenant-governor of New Brunswick), two well-known humanitarians and champions of children. The commission's report, submitted in 2002, was perhaps the most authoritative argument yet for childcare as a key to Toronto's and Canada's success and economic growth. At the same time, the City of Toronto sent letters to twelve thousand parents whose kids were on childcare waiting lists; the letter asked them to call their elected representatives and urge more investment in childcare.

Back on the national stage, Chrétien's Liberals gave evidence that they were paying attention. Martha Friendly and other leaders of the childcare movement met with Human Resources Development Minister Jane Stewart, stressing the need for a legislative framework at the national level to ensure that funds designated for childcare would actually create childcare spaces. Stewart made a step in the right direction, with a "multilateral framework agreement"—an agreement with the provinces to provide tax dollars specifically for childcare, with federal funding of $1 billion over five years.

But this was still not a national program, protected by legislation. Paul Martin then succeeded Chrétien as Liberal leader, and in the 2004 election campaign, he pledged he would go one better—with more money, and funding based on the provinces' meeting standards for quality, universality, accessibility and developmental programming—or QUAD for short. But once again, this program was based only on agreements, not secured through any legislative framework through an act of Parliament. Then, when Minister of Social Development Ken Dryden couldn't get all the provinces to agree as a group, he made individual agreements with each one. They all signed on and received a combined total of $250 million for the first year of the QUAD childcare agreement.

Unfortunately, when Martin's Liberal minority government fell in 2006, with the stroke of a pen and no debate in Parliament, Stephen Harper tore up those agreements. While $1.25 billion continued to be transferred to the provinces and territories for children's services, children in Canada still had no national childcare program on which they could rely. After the election of 2006, I did not wait for the parliamentary session to begin. As a brand-new MP and the NDP's childcare critic, I gathered together the old kitchen cabinet and our network of allies, and we set to work framing legislation for a national childcare program.

One of my proudest moments came when I stood up in the House of Commons to introduce the Early Learning and Child Care Act. In my speech in the House, I said that this act would enable us to entrench "the principles of quality, universality, accessibility, accountability and educational development." I noted that the OECD had confirmed that Canada was "at the bottom of the heap of industrialized nations" when it came to its spending on childcare. This was our "dirty little secret," I said.

"Too much of Canadian childcare is unregulated babysitting with no quality educational components. That is another failing grade," I said. The Early Learning and Child Care Act that I proposed was modelled after the Canada Health Act. In order to receive federal funding, provincial and territorial governments would have to provide high-quality and universally available and affordable early learning and care.

In the meantime, I worked closely with our childcare allies to build public support and I kept a spotlight on the issue. I tabled countless petitions, gave numerous press conferences, met with activists and parents, raised questions in the House—we were determined to leave no stone unturned.

Some of this advocacy was fun—and very creative. Children from childcare centres made oversized cards to present to the prime minister, begging him to save childcare. And on May 25 of 2006, we held a mothers' rally and press conference on Parliament Hill—a rally featuring thousands of dolls. Most significantly, the rally included the Liberals and the Bloc Québécois.

As a result of constant negotiation, careful wording, reaching out to childcare advocates and building consensus, on November 21, 2006, my Early Learning and Child Care bill passed second reading, by a vote of 144 to 116.

This was a major achievement: all opposition parties—including the Bloc—united and voted yes to a national childcare program. The Bloc's participation was the real breakthrough.

The Bloc Québécois, which ordinarily wouldn't support anything that would permit federal involvement in Quebec's affairs, voted for the bill because I had inserted an exemption clause. Quebec as a nation in Canada should have the right to receive federal funding without specific conditions, I argued. This condition formed the basis of what came to be called "asymmetrical federalism," and it's how the federal government would be able to introduce national programs while keeping Quebec on side. That policy showed that the NDP could connect with Quebec, which already had a universal childcare system—created by Pauline Marois, today the premier.

With that vote, we demonstrated that Canada could indeed achieve national childcare legislation—that we could unite to deliver on our commitments to our country's children in every part of the nation.

Since the bill dealt with financial matters, Prime Minister Stephen Harper had to give consent if it was to proceed to third and final reading. But even though the majority of parliamentarians supported the bill, and even though the Standing Committee on Human Resources, Social Development and the Status of Persons with Disabilities had approved it and sent it for a final vote in Parliament, Stephen Harper would not give consent and make it the law of the land. He and the Conservative Party would not take a leadership role in establishing a national early learning childcare program, as they fundamentally disagreed with such services.

I had to reintroduce the bill after the election of 2008, and once again in 2010. But the Conservatives maintained their wrong-headed ideology and refused to honour the views of the majority of members of Parliament and the parents of Canada they represented. And children of this country are still waiting.

When the Harper Conservatives won a majority in 2011, we realized that our push for national childcare had hit a brick wall. On the federal level, we must wait until an NDP government is formed.

For all our disappointment and for all our failure to achieve national childcare, we did make breakthroughs that cast things in a different light. We established that we could, indeed, build a national childcare program and win support for it. The national childcare movement, involving parents, providers and activists, gained force and shifted its focus to the provinces. Many provinces, aware of the benefit and value of good childcare to the economy, have increased their investments in early learning and care. Major business groups such as the Conference Board of Canada and the Canadian Chamber of Commerce support more government funding of childcare.

Moreover, we proved that, as a country, we could work together. In the federal election of 2011, that became the NDP's message in Quebec—"*Travaillons ensemble.*" That's what we did with childcare, and one day, universal daycare will come to pass in this country.

Our first duty as a society should be to our children. If we were to manage our cities, provinces and indeed the whole country with children in mind, everything would be so much better. I am proud of several accomplishments in my political life, and one of them is what we came to call Toronto First Duty.

My kitchen cabinet team came together to develop the Toronto First Duty pilot project. It featured a new model for delivering services, one was that child-centred and involved multiple sectors. This meant a seamless transition as the child moved through the day—from breakfast time to playtime to study time and finally to after-school activities. For the child, it meant an end to being lugged from place to place and from program to program; for the parents, it allowed them to continue working or studying while enjoying a deep involvement with what their young children were doing all day. Involving parents was a key element of Toronto First Duty, because once involved, those parents continued to be keenly interested in the education of their children.

Toronto First Duty took form in 1999, when the Atkinson Charitable Foundation convened a roundtable.

A few months before that meeting, I had put forward the argument at Toronto's Budget Committee that if mothers on welfare could get affordable childcare, they could work—and that it would be cheaper for the city to provide childcare than to trap mothers in the welfare/poverty cycle. Here was the math I put forward: a single mother on welfare was costing the city $12,000 to $14,000 a year; a childcare space was in the $9,000-a-year range. If we offered mothers childcare, they could come off the welfare rolls. As more mothers returned to work, we would save on welfare spending. As there was a declining number of people on welfare, I started a reserve fund to collect the savings and then transferred $3 million into the First Duty pilot project. I was able to lever another million from the Atkinson Foundation. The city agreed to put to the test both the economic and educational arguments in favour of early childhood education.

Charles Pascal was then the executive director of the Atkinson Foundation, and he recalls it this way. "Yours was the largest input, Olivia. You were the children's advocate then and you somehow managed to sequester $3 million from the city during a fiscally difficult time." In fact, I managed to procure $3.8 million in funding, but $3 million was the amount actually spent on Toronto First Duty.

Kerry McCuaig is now the Atkinson Charitable Foundation's Fellow in Early Childhood Policy, but when Toronto First Duty was yet to be imagined into being, she was one I called upon. "In 1999," she says, "we had this progressive report, the Mustard report, and its main recommendation was that every child should have the same good early experience. So when the thinkers gathered at Atkinson, the response was 'Build it, and they will come.'"

Still, there was a tall order in front of us. First we had to create a working model, then we had to prove its efficacy and then, once that was done, we had to communicate that message to the world. And there were many players to work with: city council, the school board, early educators, parents, community agencies.

Says Kerry, "We spent many evenings around this table"—and she pounded it for effect—"brainstorming and plotting strategies."

"There was a lot of plotting," Charles adds. "Childcare was always last on the list of government priorities."

"What was different about Toronto First Duty," Kerry continues, "was that it had legs. I learned this from working with Jack Layton: you create the political space. We had a number of things going for us. Olivia and her progressive colleagues had good relations with the city and the school board. We had a progressive funder outside and progressive people inside, and each leveraged the other."

Research at the five First Duty demonstration projects, which blended childcare, family support and kindergarten into one seamless program, showed tangible benefits for the children involved. Vocabulary, numeracy and reading levels all improved. Parents were less stressed, and an economic analysis showed that by combining several programs into one, more children could be served for the same cost.

Kerry McCuaig contributed to the final report on Toronto First Duty, published in 2012. She called First Duty "the little program that could." In her foreword, she went right to the heart of what was accomplished and the lessons learned: "how scientific evidence was turned into community action and ultimately public policy. It began with a simple but compelling assumption: it is only through public policy that permanent and sustainable change takes place."

Dozens of disparate programs merged into one that was anchored to the neighbourhood school. Players left their egos behind to create a single entry for children and families into a world of support and nurturing, beginning with pre- and postnatal care, right through to primary school.

Toronto First Duty's learn-through-play curriculum came to be adopted in most early childhood settings. The First Duty team was able to draw up a template for what to do and what not to do as schools are recast as child and family centres rather than remaining "no parents allowed" zones.

I had hoped that the exciting research generated by Toronto First Duty would move the entire country towards the Western European model of all-day preschool that is seen as part of the educational system there. That did not happen. Still, I count it as a great success that this pioneering blend of kindergarten, childcare and parental support was embraced first by Ontario and then by six other provinces. Policy-makers in the United Kingdom and Australia have changed their thinking on early childhood development, and when they wrote about those changes they referenced the Toronto First Duty model.

In the fall of 2013, September 3 to be exact, the benefits of Toronto First Duty came home to me—full circle. My granddaughter Beatrice had been attending Kensington Kids Early Learning Centre, at Kensington Community School. And that day, she started at an all-day kindergarten program—right across the hall from Kensington Kids. It was an easy, seamless move. Solace, her younger sister, meanwhile took her sister's place at Kensington Kids. The girls' parents didn't have to leave work early to shuttle either girl off to another program somewhere else in the city or secure a babysitter. They have Toronto First Duty to thank for that.

In 2007, Charles Pascal—the province's Special Advisor on Early Learning—was asked by then premier Dalton McGuinty to prepare a report on implementing all-day childcare in Ontario. Two years later, and after broad consultation, Charles submitted his report. Called *With Our Best Future in Mind: Implementing Early Learning in*

Ontario, the report noted that "the current fragmented patchwork of early childhood services too often fails the best interests of our children, frustrates families and educators, and wastes resources. The result? More than one in four children enter Grade 1 significantly behind their peers."

Key to the vision outlined in the report is that schools become community hubs offering opportunities for children's learning, care, health, culture, arts and recreation. Charles recommended that school boards be mandated to offer programs before and after traditional school hours for children aged four to twelve. Finally, the report recommended fee-based extended programming that would operate fifty weeks a year—including activities during school breaks and summer vacations.

In 2009, the provincial government announced that it was phasing in, over a five-year span, full-day learning for four- and five-year-olds, including the option of a fee-based extended-day program. This arrangement fell well short of what Charles had suggested, but still, it was a start.

I was not surprised to see a front-page story in *The Globe and Mail* on September 4, 2013, headlined in part: "Children Who Attend Full-Day Kindergarten Are Better at Speaking and Making Friends." The story arose from a landmark study of seven hundred children showing that children in full-day kindergarten "are better prepared for school, showing strong language development and better communication and social skills." *The Globe*'s education reporter, Caroline Alphonso, had interviewed Charles Pascal for the story, and even he was taken aback by this new study. "Even though we predicted high impact for kids and families," he said, "I never imagined the results would be so dramatic, so soon. The program even in its early years of early childhood development is showing that kids' lives are being shaped, and in many cases, saved."

Ontario need only look to Quebec to see a government taking early childcare seriously. In 1992, just around the time that I was wrestling with bringing various city childcare programs together, Camil Bouchard submitted his report to that province on the subject of childcare. The professor at the Université du Québec à Montréal had come up with a memorable title for his document: *Un Québec fou de ses enfants* (A Quebec Crazy for Its Children). In it he urged all Quebecers to treat the needs of children and youth with as much generosity, equity and compassion as they could muster.

And they did. Quebec has seven-dollar-a-day daycare. Theirs is the best childcare program in the country, and the results have been spectacular. Quebec's childcare system pays for itself. Montreal economist Pierre Fortin has shown that the entire cost of the program is paid for by mothers who are able to work—thanks to affordable childcare. A decade ago, Quebec women fared last when participation in the labour force was measured by province; today they're in first place. Child poverty rates have been cut in half in that province with a program that is self-sustaining . . .

Quebec has shown the way on this vital issue. When will the rest of Canada see the light?

CHAPTER 10

Giving Voice to the Voiceless

Key to my dealings with people, whether at the personal or the political level, is acceptance of another—regardless of race, religion, creed or sexual orientation. In my lexicon, there are two key words: contact *and* connection. *First you make one, then you make the other.*

On the warm afternoon of August 1, 2000, I strode across a stage at Nathan Phillips Square in front of Toronto City Hall, took a microphone in my hand and addressed a crowd of young people estimated at fifteen to twenty thousand. Organized by Will Chang, a young lawyer and a fan of electronic music, this rally was perhaps the largest the square has ever seen. People spilled out onto the nearby streets. They had come for one reason: to dance, to protest and to celebrate the music they loved. A banner above the stage proclaimed, "It's About Freedom to Dance."

"You need to be loud—loud enough that the mayor and city councillors over there," I said as I gestured towards the council chambers, "can hear you. Out of fear, they panicked and decided to ban raves on city property. Let me ask you the question: Who wants to ban raves in Toronto?"

"Noooooobody!" they shouted back, echoing a favourite saying of then mayor Mel Lastman.

"Instead of admitting defeat," I continued, "the rave community came together. You challenged this fear, you talked about the rave family. And volunteers spent *thousands* of hours educating the public about electronic music, about rave culture, about unity and respect."

Three months earlier, a majority of my fellow city councillors had banned all raves on city property and any rave, anywhere, after 3 a.m. This curfew would effectively kill the all-night parties—at least the open and sanctioned kind. I, along with many others, had spent months trying to debunk myths about raves: that they were havens for drug use, that raves were unsafe, that raves and death by drug overdose went hand in hand.

The party on the square continued for hours, and rather than spinning out of control into a clash with police, it was a peaceful and joyous event that ended with marshals and revellers alike cleaning up the space when the dancing was done. The next day, the *Toronto Star* described the rally as "a defiantly jubilant free party . . . an ebullient party/protest [that] put a professional face on a widely misunderstood cultural movement."

That movement had been imported from the UK and the US. Electronic music had become popular in Toronto in the late eighties, first with all-night parties in clubs and warehouses and then in government-owned buildings such as the Ontario Science Centre, Pearson Airport and even the SkyDome stadium. In general, the parties were defined by the music itself—often provided by DJs (also known as turntablists or spinners) playing highly danceable and multi-layered beat music, sometimes with laser shows. Peace, love, unity and respect were the buzzwords at these gatherings, which generated a true sense of belonging among the thousands of young people who flocked to them. Rave culture was decidedly different from the boozy hookup club culture that was another option for young people then—and still is today.

Yes, there was drug use, but as I often pointed out, drug use is a societal problem and not at all specific to raves. In fact, the decided advantage to having raves on city-owned property was that young people could be offered on-site information about drug use, harm reduction and safety. A major concern with the ban was that it would drive the movement underground, where security and safety would be at the whim of the organizer.

And make no mistake: electronic music was a movement. That summer of 2000, Detroit drew one and a half million people to an electronic music festival—without incident and with all proceeds going to support that city's parks and children's programs. Berlin was then drawing a million people to its annual Love Parade. Toronto was regularly hosting massive raves, attended by ten to fifteen thousand partiers, and was becoming known around the world as one of the best cities to experience drum and bass, breaks, house, trance and techno music, with many producers and DJs from Toronto becoming worldwide stars. The economic benefit of these events—for hotels, restaurants and the music, fashion and graphics industries—was enormous. One of the signs hoisted at that August 1 rally read, "Raves Make Jobs."

But when a twenty-year-old Ryerson University business student named Allen Ho died at a rave in a former shoe factory after taking a drug called ecstasy, what I called "moral panic" set in and Mayor Lastman and Toronto city council instituted their ban.

At this point, young people themselves still had little voice in this debate, but that was about to change. The apolitical ravers got political—in a hurry.

~

I first met Will Chang shortly after he had organized a gathering of Toronto's top rave promoters and nightclub owners to deal with the upcoming coroner's inquest into Allen Ho's death and the impending threat posed by politicians. It had become obvious, through press releases and comments they made to the media, that Mayor Lastman and Police Chief Julian Fantino had made it their mission to ban raves in Toronto. Chief Fantino had written a much-publicized letter to Prime Minister Jean Chrétien describing raves as "a health and safety emergency that could easily become an epidemic" and "threatening the very fabric of Canadian society." Mayor Lastman painted raves as havens for drug use, guns and criminal activity. The pair were hell-bent on killing off what was not only a fresh, youth-based entrepreneurial industry but also a movement whose main principles were peace, unity and acceptance.

On this night, the organizers who had built Toronto's rave scene—many of whom were fierce competitors—had come together to fight a common adversary. They formed the Toronto Dance Safety Committee (or TDSC for short) to speak on behalf of the city's rave scene when dealing with the media, the police and city hall. At my first meeting with the TDSC, it consisted of Will Chang and other leaders of the rave community. I recommended that bringing some diversity to the committee would give it clout, and so they added two members of the Public Health Board, an activist from the gay and lesbian community (which had faced similar profiling issues in the past) and a City of Toronto health worker. Will was chosen as the group's spokesperson, since we felt that his legal training would enable him to debate the issues well in the media, allowing us to put an educated and professional face at the forefront of the cause.

I was impressed with the TDSC. Here was a group of young people who were talented—as promoters, artists and entrepreneurs—and passionate about their industry. They had the kind of raw passion—a belief that their community was not just about making money but about promoting peace, love and unity—not often seen. And their industry was under attack—from the police, from politicians, from the media and, it seemed, from the court of public opinion.

When city council had, to my dismay, voted to ban raves from city property, I had been able to add an amendment to the resolution, requiring council to revisit its decision at its meeting on August 1—after receiving reports from the chief of police and Toronto Public Health.

I worked closely with Will and the TDSC in the months leading up to that vote. He was just starting his career as a corporate lawyer—he had not even been called to the Ontario bar yet—and here he was front and centre in a PR battle against the mayor and the chief of police, two adversaries who, by virtue of their positions, commanded a high level of public trust. I was happy to work with Will.

Will knew the arguments to make: that the best way to combat drug use among youth is to educate and inform rather than ban, which would succeed only in pushing raves underground, where they would be more dangerous; that ecstasy as a drug has caused fewer deaths than conventional activities such as snowmobiling (and you don't see politicians trying to ban snowmobiling); and that it is wrong to profile an entire community based on the actions of some members of that community.

Perhaps most important, it is wrong for elected officials to pass legislation that penalizes and harms thousands of patrons and hundreds of legitimate businesses that make up Toronto's rave scene (event promoters, venue owners, music stores, record labels, magazines, clothing stores and so on) in a knee-jerk reaction to a movement that they do not understand.

Will and the TDSC knew all the right arguments, but their plan was to deliver all of them at once, which in my view would have been a mistake. My advice to the committee was to develop a media and PR strategy, and to feed the arguments to the media bit by bit in order to gain support as the story and the public debate developed in the months before the August 1 vote.

Our PR strategy consisted of the following: one, deliver the arguments one by one over several weeks so that each time the press picked up the story they would recap all the arguments previously made. Two, create a series of "rules" by which the rave community would self-regulate (these came to be known as the Toronto rave protocol), thereby reducing the risk that legislators would impose their own rules. And three, host a large rally, to take place at the doorstep of city hall on the very day on which council would be voting on the rave issue. And thus the iDance Rally was scheduled for August 1, 2000, at Nathan Phillips Square.

Organization for the rally quickly got under way. I could help the TDSC shape their message, but it was up to them to get the numbers that they would need to sway city council's decision. The committee knew that a large rave could easily attract ten to fifteen thousand attendees, but could they attract such large numbers to a political rally at city hall on a Tuesday afternoon?

The answer was a combination of an intense marketing campaign within the rave community and the participation of top DJs, many of whom were international stars who flew to Toronto on their own dime to participate. The TDSC enlisted the aid of Toronto's top rave promoters and persuaded all participants—DJs, MCs, dancers, sound and light companies, security, professional PR advisors and others—to donate their time and services to the cause.

Countless volunteers showed up to act as marshals at the event, to hand out flyers, to make political signs such as "Ravers Are Voters" and "Understand Before You Legislate," to hand out free water and to clean up the square afterwards. Toronto's MC Flipside produced a brilliant fundraising CD called *It's About Freedom to Dance*, with seven original tracks showcasing different styles of electronic music by Toronto musicians and looping in Mayor Lastman's most outrageous and misinformed comments on the rave scene (obtained by my staff from city council recordings). I wonder if Mel Lastman in his wildest dreams expected his voice to be the vocals in hiphop and drum and bass songs on the radio.

The iDance Rally was promoted not just as a political event but as the party of the year, and boasted what is to this day one of the most impressive gatherings of DJ talent that Toronto has seen. They even managed to suspend what is perhaps the largest disco ball ever used in the city, high above Nathan Phillips Square—suspended from a construction crane. When the sun went down, the disco ball showered the downtown core with glittering light, while revellers danced and splashed around in the reflecting pool beneath the appropriately named Freedom Arches, making for a sight I will never forget.

We also gathered an impressive list of speakers at the rally, including former Toronto mayors Barbara Hall and John Sewell (the optics of two former mayors criticizing the current mayor were priceless) and prominent civil rights lawyer Alan Young. As the vote was happening inside city hall, we would project on a large screen the names of councillors who had previously voted against the ban, those who had voted for it and, most important, the ones who were changing their minds. We wanted those gathered in the square to apply pressure to the councillors who still supported a ban.

The success of the iDance Rally was immediate and unmistakable. Hailed by *The Globe and Mail* as "one of the most significant events in a long time in Canadian music," by *NOW* magazine as "one of the biggest events ever held at Nathan Phillips Square" and by the *Toronto Star* as "a seminal moment for the city," the iDance Rally received unprecedented praise from the community, media and city politicians. Two days later, Toronto city council lifted its ban on raves by an overwhelming vote of 50–4.

Will Chang was named Activist of the Year by *NOW* magazine, and the *Toronto Star* called him one of "the faces that shaped 2000." I later learned that Will's involvement with iDance caused Osgoode Hall Law School to offer him a teaching position, making him, at twenty-four, perhaps the youngest instructor in that school's history. (Will went on to work at two Bay Street law firms and is today general counsel at Granite Global Solutions.)

The following year, Will Chang, with help from my office, organized iDance 2001, again at Nathan Phillips Square but this time as a "show of strength" by the rave community. That event drew an estimated thirty thousand people and had corporate sponsors that included Microsoft and the *Toronto Star*. While some members of the rave community bemoaned the inclusion of corporate sponsors, our message was clear: the rave scene would not be an easy target for future persecution.

From my experience as a school trustee, I knew that young people constituted a largely untapped source of energy, passion, intelligence and insight. I had encouraged student council presidents to get involved in board of education decision making and I had always made a point of taking on very young volunteers and giving them positions of real responsibility. I was never disappointed.

So when I was elected to city council in 1991, I thought: let's do the same thing here. Along with a city planner, I produced a report on how to make the city more youth-friendly, and one of our recommendations was a youth council. That led at first to a Metro Youth Council and, in 1998, a Toronto Youth Cabinet.

In its first year, the cabinet comprised ten young men and women. There was no pushback from anyone on city council, because some councillors thought having a few kids around city hall was just the kind of window dressing they needed. It looked good on paper but posed no threat to the status quo. Maybe the young people would want to do some charitable work, or put on a dance?

Well, when these young people put on a dance, it was not just about some tunes, punch and potato chips. It was a rally, organized, enormous, and put on to make a political statement.

During the first iDance Rally at the square, an executive member of the Youth Cabinet, Ryan Teschner, was constantly moving back and forth from council chambers inside to the protest outside. He would ascend the stage and tell the crowd what was going on in council chambers, then hurry back to council, where he took particular councillors aside and passed on messages from their constituents—young voters (or their parents) who were outside, demanding that the ban be overturned.

Ryan had been a member of the Youth Cabinet for almost three years, and he had learned a lot from me and by simply hanging around city hall. He knew how the place worked, how to lobby politicians, the dynamics on council and how to conduct a press conference. And just as important, he had learned how to leave a lasting impression on the press.

Fast-forward a few years to May of 2002. Mayor Mel Lastman is holding a press conference to discuss an infusion of millions of dollars to fund a comprehensive strategy to make the city safer for youth (the previous summer had seen fifteen young Torontonians die violently). What was striking about both the strategy and the press conference was how the Youth Cabinet placed its stamp on both. *Toronto Star* columnist Royson James was there and he later wrote a piece in which he quoted Ryan, calling him "an eloquent representative who stole the show at the news conference in the mayor's office." Here's more from that column:

> *When challenged by a skeptical media as to why the youth-offered approach will work where others have failed, Ryan tackled every preconceived notion and shredded them.*
>
> *For one, he said, the strategies were suggested by the very youths themselves. Young people across the city told youth cabinet members what they wanted and now it's important that their views hold primacy, Teschner said with the facility of a seasoned politician.*
>
> *By the time he was finished, Mel was saying "Ryan for Mayor." And Chow, council's youth advocate, was beaming, as puffed up and proud as a mother hen.*

It's true. I was proud—and I still am. The amazing, talented and passionate young people who joined the Youth Cabinet were key to its success. People such as Ryan Teschner and Kehinde Bah.

My modus operandi with the Youth Cabinets, as with all groups, was simply to bring young people of different backgrounds and cultures together, helping them connect, understand each other and recognize their common goals. Ryan—who came from a somewhat privileged white Jewish family in North Toronto—found himself working closely with Kehinde Bah, a black youth leader who had grown up in a rough neighbourhood. They got along famously, so much so that Catherine Porter of the *Toronto Star* once called them "a dynamic duo." As Ryan remembers their partnership, "Kehinde taught me that what we did was relevant and to communicate that. I taught him, I hope, strategy. We played off each other."

Kehinde had direct experience of violence and had endured the violent deaths of friends. Through the local Boys and Girls Club in his neighbourhood, he understood the importance of after-school activities, and the importance of having role models and mentors to help dissuade young people from joining gangs. Ryan, who had only read about violent crime, had endless patience for policy-making and the political process; Kehinde was cynical about politics. But, working together, both young men came to understand that something as basic as a basketball court was important to a neighbourhood, and the absence of such play space could have dire consequences.

One way we had of bringing together Youth Cabinet members, especially as it grew (today the cabinet features several hundred members), was to hold retreats at a camp north of Toronto. The members were mostly apolitical kids, though some already leaned left or right (one year at the retreat, a basketball match pitted a right-winger against a left-winger in a winner-take-all game). These youth were all colours and races and religions, from the working class, middle class and privileged class. Some of them had joined up thinking that being in the cabinet would be a good way to fulfill the forty hours of volunteering required of every high school graduate in the province. But, through the Youth Cabinet's work and the empowerment that came with acting as a voice for Toronto's three hundred thousand youths, virtually every one became engaged in a cause to better the city. The Youth Cabinet, quite literally, changed people's lives.

Ryan now practises law at a prestigious Bay Street law firm (Heenan Blaikie), where he regularly applies his skills as an advocate to further the causes of his clients—much as he did as a member of the Youth Cabinet. Kehinde works for the Remix Project, which strives to offer work in the arts to disadvantaged youth. Both now say that their time as members of the Youth Cabinet helped build skill sets that will serve them for the rest of their lives. Not only did they learn the dynamics of municipal politics but they also learned how to set an agenda, how to develop a strategy and how to execute it.

Members of the Youth Cabinet came to feel that city hall was just as much their domain as it was the politicians'. These youths knew when each councillor was likely to be in his or her office and they were not shy about approaching them to talk up a proposal, to lobby or to educate. They looked at maps and voting results, liaised with residents and community groups, and learned how to use strategic levers to convince a particular councillor. They wrote motions and amendments. They learned about informed decision making, and they learned some hard political truths, including this one: everything comes at the expense of something else. Will buying new police helicopters lead to the closing of libraries on Sundays? This was the kind of political knowledge that transformed these "kids" into a sophisticated political presence.

"The idea," says Ryan, "was for us to integrate into the web of city council and not to act like we were an external body throwing stones. We became a shadow council. We had training in lobbying, in communications. We mapped out where we should partner with other youth organizations. We devised budget strategies. What was an idea to bring in youth became a sophisticated machine whose tentacles spread through the city."

There was no shortage of issues for the Youth Cabinet to tackle, and no shortage of victories either. At one point, they persuaded council not to cut $5 million from the budget—a cut that would have required young people to pay user fees to play in recreation centres and parks. They obtained additional funding to build basketball and skateboard parks and to hire youth outreach workers. The Youth Cabinet helped stop the closures of swimming pools across the city, successfully opened the lines of communication between Toronto's police and young people, developed initiatives to bring out the youth vote during elections and fought hard to secure millions upon millions of dollars for youth violence prevention strategies across Toronto.

As a baby in 1957, with my mother, Ho Sze Chow.

At age two, with a favourite toy.

My father, Wai Sun Chow, performing in the opera in the late 1950s.

At the age of three, in a rare photo with my half-brother Andre.

At fourteen, learning to paddle at the Toronto Chinese Baptist Church summer camp.

Standing outside my future workplace, Toronto City Hall.

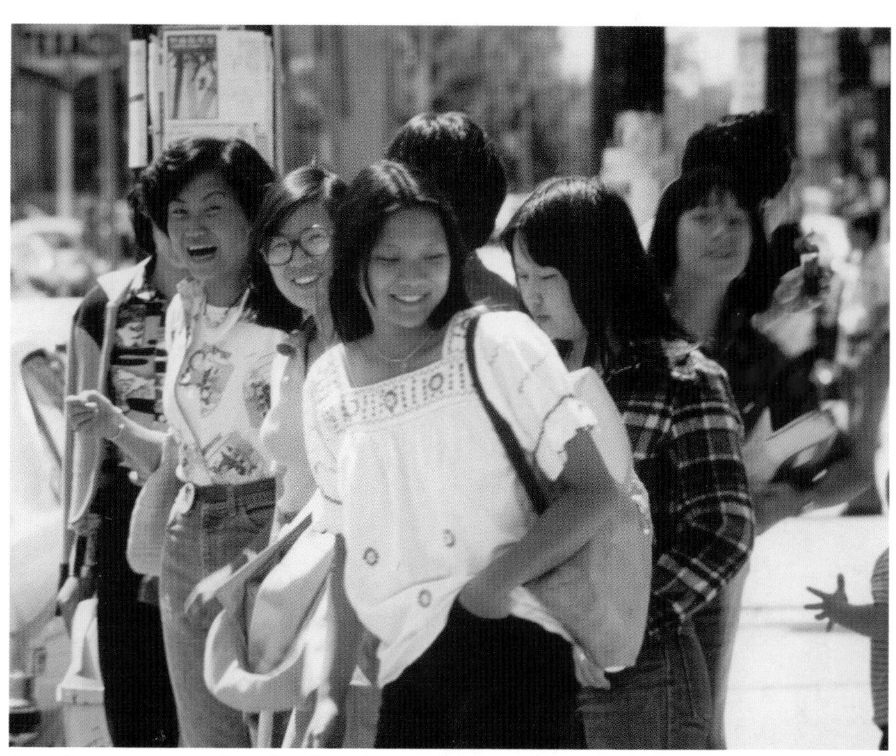

At eighteen, as a Sunday school teacher, with my students in Chinatown.

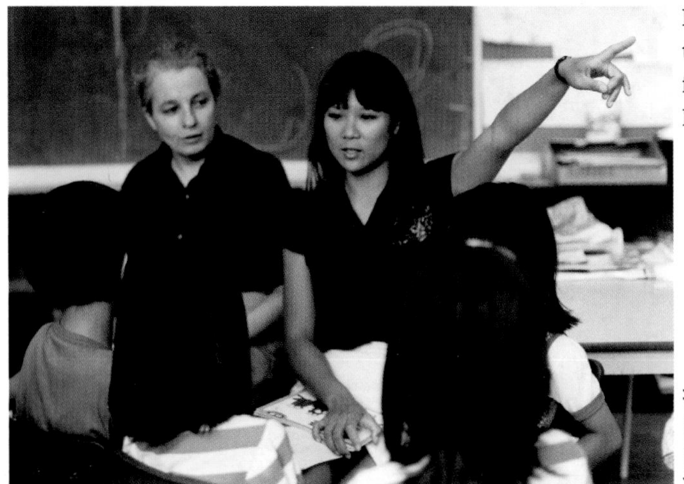

Alex MacDonald

Back to school as a trustee in 1985, with fellow trustee Joan Doiron.

David Smiley

With Dan Leckie, friend and political mentor.

David Smiley

With the other Dan—MP Dan Heap—and City Councillor Jack Layton in the 1980s.

David Smiley

Auctioneering with Jack in the late 1980s.

A photo-booth strip, taken not long after we met in 1985.

Alex MacDonald

Court and spark.

Dear Olivia,

So many images have captured my mind that I wish I were a poet. I would weave the music of our love through the images that have made it real. I would speak of the great loves of history – for we are one of those. The world will know this in years to come. I would set your beauty against the strength I feel when we love; and your strength against the challenges that we are joining hands to confront: our strength.

I have said that I was searching for the mysterious, the mystic and profound sensations which can develop between a man and a woman. I have said that I wouldn't rest until I found these elusive goals.

A declaration of love, 1985.

On our wedding day, on the Toronto Islands, July 9, 1988.

Sarah and Mike Layton in the mid-1980s.

Sally Roy

The extended Layton clan in the early 1990s.

With my mother, my brother Andre and my niece Althea.

Toronto Star/Tony Bock

Star Trek fans in our matching Trekkie outfits in the 1990s.

Brian Summers

Modelling in the Dare to Wear Love fashion show, for the Stephen Lewis Foundation.

Canadian Press/Robin Rowland

With Jack on the tandem bicycle at Toronto's Pride Parade.

Toronto Star/Andrew Stawicki

Jack wins the NDP leadership race in 2003.

Toronto Star/Ron Bull

As children and youth advocate at Kensington Kids childcare centre in 2004.

Rob Andreacchi

Promoting the Liberal-NDP coalition government in December 2008.

Susan Kwong

Presenting the "Lucky Moose Bill" to small-business owner David Chen in 2012.

Hugh Campbell

Our first grandchild, Beatrice, born in 2009.

Bruce Kirkby

With Jack in the Arctic, on the Alsek River, on his sixtieth birthday.

Canadian Press/Darren Calabrese

Celebrating my election on May 2, 2011, as Jack led the party to Official Opposition status.

Canadian Press/Sean Kilpatrick

At Stornoway, the official residence of the leader of the Opposition.

Canadian Press/Ryan Remiorz

Holding an eagle feather at the state funeral, held on August 27, 2011, as Jack's casket is borne away.

Canadian Press/Adrian Wyld

Responding to tributes to Jack in the House of Commons.

Susan Kwong

At Necropolis cemetery, by the bronze sculpture of Jack that I created for his gravesite.

Dean Goodwin

Adding my own chalk message at Nathan Phillips Square on the first anniversary of Jack's death.

David Pelletier

In the spring of 2013, working on the tandem sculpture "Jack's Got Your Back."

Hugh Campbell

The next generation—our grandchildren, Beatrice and Solace Layton Campbell.

Mitchel Raphael

Ready for the future, in the summer of 2013.

All this work by members of the Youth Cabinet changed the city, but it also changed them. Ryan learned how, as he says, "to put together a proposal to get something done. I learned that it was not about screaming but getting people together." He and his unpaid colleagues were absorbing valuable lessons about strategic thinking, how to rally around a cause and build consensus, and how to change the minds of policy-makers.

The key to their training, it struck me, was to give them independence. They would bounce ideas off me, and I certainly gave them my insight and whatever information might be useful. But I never told them how to proceed. I had brought them in from the *outside* and given them some space *inside* the political domain, but how best to represent their constituency, which issues to focus on and when—that was all for them to know and discover. After all, the city belongs to them also, and we are made richer by their involvement.

We are made richer through our diversity.

Consider the extraordinary strength that Toronto has gained while becoming the most multicultural city in the world. Immigration and its resulting diversity have been a secret weapon for Canada, but the benefits are not always appreciated, and immigrants, like youth, have been kept on the outside all too often, without a voice. Calls from desperate people facing deportation are a regular occurrence at my Toronto constituency office, and I have met too many people crying for help as they were about to be booted out of the country in a few days' time. Of the thousands of people I have assisted through the years, two stand out in my memory.

One is Matthew Nguyen. He was like thousands of Canadians who live in fear of deportation because they do not have regular immigration status. Often they are faceless and voiceless. They work, live and attend school quietly, but always living in fear of being discovered and deported.

Soon after I became a member of Parliament in 2006, a teacher at my old high school, Jarvis Collegiate, came to me with the story of Matthew. He and his two sisters had been brought from France to Canada at a young age on visitor visas after the death of their mother. For most of his teenage years, says Matthew, he was kept home as a domestic servant and not allowed to attend school. He was robbed of his childhood. Desperate to get an education, he ran away at sixteen, lived in youth shelters and went to vocational and high schools in Toronto.

With an expired visitor visa, Matthew was facing deportation. I wrote and called the minister of immigration, urging him to allow Matthew to stay. A team of teachers and fellow students organized a Help Matthew Stay campaign and garnered the attention of thousands of people within a short time.

While I was on holiday and on the road that year, I took a call from the minister's office—Matthew would be allowed to stay and continue his studies in Canada. Eight years later, he is now finishing his studies at York University, has his own apartment and is living proudly as a Canadian.

Two days before Christmas in 2010, I received another cry for help. A neighbour ran over to my house and said his friend's pregnant wife was to be deported a few days after Christmas. He urged me to speak to him. I found out that Jimmy Wu had come to Canada nine years before. He met his wife, Juan Yun Chen, at the Catholic church he attended in Chinatown, they fell in love and married, and now they had a ten-month-old son, with another child on the way.

Jimmy had applied to sponsor his wife close to a year before, as her visitor visa had expired. The problem was the huge backlog: reviewing a sponsorship application takes at least a year. The Immigration

Department had a Kafkaesque policy of deporting spousal applicants while they were awaiting approval. Once Juan Yun was deported to her home country, in this case China, Jimmy would have to start all over again and submit a *new* application to sponsor her and wait for a year or two before she could come back to Canada.

If Jimmy's wife were deported, who would take care of their son? Was she to give birth to her baby alone, without her husband's support? Deporting her because of sheer government incompetency was absurd, inhumane and a giant waste of taxpayers' money. And to do it at Christmastime to a devout Catholic family just added insult to injury.

I took the story of Jimmy and Juan Yun Chen to the media and wrote an e-mail to the minister of immigration. Just three days before Juan Yun Chen and her young son were scheduled to leave, she received a Temporary Resident Permit, a direct intervention from the minister allowing her to remain in Canada while her husband's sponsorship was being processed. Soon Juan Yun secured her residency status in Canada and gave birth to a healthy son in Toronto. A new Torontonian. Well, two new Torontonians, actually.

The politics I practise is the politics of inclusion, and that's also how I live my life. Key to my dealings with people, whether at the personal or the political level, is acceptance of another—regardless of race, religion, creed or sexual orientation. Jack Layton was the same way. This was just one more point of contact and connection between us.

In my lexicon, those are two key words: *contact* and *connection*. First you make one, then you make the other. Whether I was trying to bring a potential ally to my side or attempting to understand the thinking of someone who opposed me, it seemed to me critical that I sat down with these people, over tea or a meal. Face-to-face encounters always worked better than a phone call or an e-mail. For me, it was a question of respect.

Bob Gallagher, more than most, knows that to be so. Bob is a close family friend who was my executive assistant when I was a city councillor, and he was later Jack's chief of staff in Ottawa. In his spare time, Bob's a horseman who competes as an eventer, that most demanding of equestrian sports that combines cross-country, dressage and show jumping. He formerly taught political science at Trent University in Peterborough, Ontario, but he gave up academia for the push and pull of front-line politics, and it was easy for him to slide into working for us. "My hobby," he likes to say of that decision, "became my vocation."

For decades, Bob has been an activist for gay rights and is now director of communications with the United Steelworkers. So when Jack and I got married and planned a wedding ceremony that gave prominent roles to gay friends, musicians and the Chinese community, Bob was not surprised. As he told *Maclean's* magazine more recently, "They were truly urban modern people who believed you don't just tolerate difference, you celebrate it."

Bob has had many years to observe closely how Jack and I operated as a political couple. One thing he understood was how we made the most of community banquets and other public functions—we never sat together and actually preferred to attend different functions if, as often happened, two events coincided.

"They worked in tandem," Bob once told a reporter. "I'd ask Olivia if she was going to go to something. And she'd say, 'If Jack's going, I don't need to. He's got it covered.'" In fact, at one point a rumour was circulating in the Chinese community media that Jack and I had split up. When a reporter called our house, any number of people might pick up the phone—a male volunteer, friend or relative—but never Jack. The fact that I seldom showed up with Jack at Chinese banquets

(I would often go alone or with staff or a volunteer) led some imaginative journalists to speculate on the state of our relationship.

I was unaware of such gossip until one day, a cheeky journalist, thinking Bob was my partner, asked him outright, "Are Jack and Olivia separated?" Bob burst out laughing and could barely repeat the story with a straight face.

Bob strives for efficiency, and used to complain good-naturedly—especially when I was still in Toronto on council and Jack was a rookie MP in Ottawa—that our chats on the phone several times a day slowed things. "Working with Olivia," Bob says, "meant being interrupted by Jack calling at any moment of the day. Then I moved to Ottawa to work for Jack, and I can't tell you how many times Olivia would be brought in on speakerphone to be part of the decision. And it wasn't just rubber-stamping, it was truly input."

Bob remembers the exact moment he met Jack: February 6, 1981, the day after police raided the four largest gay bathhouses in Toronto and arrested more than three hundred men. Bob helped organize a demonstration to protest what was clearly an assault on the civil liberties of these men. This rally and others like it played a role in the early years of Pride Week, which has grown to become one of the largest gay pride festivals in the world. Today, when anyone talks about "the LGBT community," it's widely understood that the initials stand for lesbian, gay, bisexual and transgender. But three decades ago, it was a different story.

Bob remembers that "in those days, the gay community got very little support. Politicians avoided the issue and the community like the plague. Jack was an exception. He made contact with Bob within hours of the raid." Jack was not a typical politician, Bob says. "He had an amazing comfort level with gay men and lesbians. In 1981, few people in authority felt comfortable around me as a gay man. Jack did. He had met gay people in a variety of settings, and never felt uncomfortable joining us for a beer at a gay bar. It takes that contact to enable a comfort level." First face-to-face contact, and then communication.

Bob believes (as Jack did) that you need opposition, and sometimes confrontation, to move the yardsticks, and we agree on this ironic point: there would be no gay marriage in Canada today had the police not conducted those bathhouse raids. The politically sophisticated community and institutions that resulted were essential to the battle against AIDS and the fight for marriage equality.

So the yardsticks did move. On the issues of gay rights and the freedom of people of the same sex to marry, Canadians did change in their thinking. And yet, of course, there persist barriers that force gays and lesbians to remain outside and less included than heterosexuals. It's why I stood up in the House of Commons in the spring of 2010 to comment on the newly revised citizenship guide. Tens of thousands of copies had been printed, but to my dismay there was not a single reference to gay rights, gay history or the LGBT community as part of Canada's diversity.

I think it is vitally important for newcomers to this country to understand the history and cultural evolution of Canada as a stronghold for human rights. We receive immigrants from around the world, including countries where gays, lesbians and bisexuals face prison, torture and death.

Canada's new citizenship guide, I argued in the House, should have spelled out that Canadians are protected against discrimination based on sexual orientation. The section in the citizenship guide entitled "Towards a Modern Canada" should have noted that homosexuality was decriminalized here in 1969 and that civil marriage for same-sex couples was legalized nationwide in 2005.

It is important that this history and the rights of the gay and lesbian community be recognized, celebrated and documented in our citizenship guide, I argued then. For us not to do so, especially for our new immigrants, I said, is unfair, unjust and a missed opportunity.

A year later, the citizenship guide was reprinted and gay rights in Canada were given a place. It is part of who we are.

When I was elected to Metro Toronto council in 1991, discriminatory treatment towards the gay and lesbian community came to my attention—and from a very close source.

In January of that year, I hired Bob Gallagher as my executive assistant. He had left his teaching job at Trent and returned to Toronto to look after his partner, who was gravely ill with AIDS. Bob told me that the financial costs involved in caring for his partner were not insignificant; neither would he be eligible for bereavement leave. The frustrating part was that Toronto city council had offered *all* its staff—heterosexual and homosexual—benefits since 1990; Metro council did not. This had to change.

Looking back on the campaign we launched, I can see my familiar pattern: assess and research the problem, then forge alliances—in this case with Kyle Rae, an openly gay Toronto city councillor, and with a legion of community volunteers.

Our volunteers drew up a petition calling for same-sex benefits and canvassed some of the streets in Toronto. On Summerhill Avenue, for example, every house but one signed up. We then took that sampling to the Metro councillor representing that area. We got her vote. We also countered the argument that extending benefits would incur extra costs; the experience of Toronto city council debunked that myth.

Then came the strategic part. By speaking with some Metro councillors, we discovered that religion was a huge stumbling block. For example, Councillor Raymond Cho, my longtime colleague and good friend, a member of the Korean United Church, was convinced that voting yes to same-sex benefits was an affront to his religion. We urged the head of his church—a very progressive man—to call him. The burden of that call: in voting yes, no church doctrine would be broken.

With Metro Councillor Mario Gentile, a devout Roman Catholic who thought homosexuality was a sin, we persuaded his niece—his lesbian niece—to talk to him. And she convinced him that even if she was a "sinner," sinners and their partners still needed health care.

When it came time for the vote, I arranged for Mario to speak first. And he simply said that while his religion compelled him in one direction, compassion moved him in another. His was a very simple yet powerful statement—and the vote was won.

A related issue in those days was the creation of a hotline for young people struggling with their sexual identity. There were plenty of generic hotlines around town, but they were typically staffed by adults who would suggest counselling options. Which was fine, to a point. But in 1993, two young gay people walked into my office and met with Bob Gallagher. What they said was this: "Kids in crisis should be able to talk to a young person our age who has been through this."

I knew from my experience working in the crisis intervention unit in a Toronto hospital how important these hotlines were, but Bob and I also knew that setting up the infrastructure would be a major challenge. We needed reliable funding, around-the-clock staffing and of course a physical location. And again, through further investigation, we discovered that the need was province-wide: a troubled gay teen living with ultra-conservative parents in downtown Toronto was just as isolated and vulnerable as her counterpart in a Northern Ontario outpost.

Throwing down the gauntlet, Bob told the two visitors in my office: "Find fifty young people who can work on this for a year." Two weeks later they came back—with fifty dynamic, energetic youths. We launched into fundraising, we started training staff, we procured funding from the NDP provincial government of Bob Rae, and the hotline—the Lesbian Gay Bi Youth Line as it was then called—started rolling.

But in 1995, when the Mike Harris Conservative government came in, one of the first things they did was to end funding of the hotline—and 90 per cent of its budget was suddenly gone. We swung into action again. And when those same youths began fundraising in the community, one of the really helpful people on the board we created was Kathleen Wynne, then an openly gay school trustee and now the premier of the province. The hotline survived and endures to this day (with some funding from the province).

So when a young man or woman facing bullying at school or eviction from home needs to talk to someone, they can call the city's hotline (now called the Lesbian Gay Bi Trans Youth Line) and speak with a peer, one who has been there and knows the territory. It's contact and connection that makes the difference.

CHAPTER 11

Bully in Black

I'm a committed progressive and social democrat. But just because I'm progressive doesn't mean I have to roll over in the face of bullies.

I don't like bullies. I never have. For all of my adult life, I have worked hard to stop schoolyard bullies, political bullies, corporate bullies or anyone who uses power or wealth to lord over people who possess neither.

In one case, the bully I was up against was dressed in a black suit during all public appearances. I'm speaking about the head of the association that represented the Toronto police force in 2000. I want to make it clear: I do support the Toronto police force. The men and women who protect our neighbourhoods do so proudly, and they perform an important service. But in the year 2000 I found myself up against their de facto union, the Toronto Police Association, where all of the union's executives were dressed in black.

That year, the association launched a telemarketing campaign to solicit funds from Toronto's citizens, with the money raised going to the police association itself. And how would the money be used? To support politicians who in turn supported the police, and to challenge politicians who dared hold the police accountable to the Toronto Police Services Board (which handles civilian oversight of the police).

The scheme would have involved the sale of wallet cards or car decals, with gold, silver and bronze decals going for, respectively, $100, $75 and $25. The decals featured the words "Toronto Police Association," "Gold Booster" (if you opted for the gold), a red maple leaf, the scales of justice and an outline of the city that included the CN Tower. Those who purchased decals would be encouraged to stick them proudly on the bumper, dashboard or window of their car.

You can imagine the pitfalls of such a thing and how it might leave the wrong impression. Let's say you're a driver who has run a red light or been caught speeding. The officer who pulls you over notices as he or she approaches your vehicle that you have a gold sticker—or no sticker at all. Does the officer reduce the fine because of that decal, or issue the harshest fine possible because you are decal-less? I don't think police officers think that way, but the temptation to be swayed, at least, is there. As for citizens who donated to the campaign, they might be under the impression that these decals had special power to exempt them from obeying the law.

Operation True Blue pitted the Toronto Police Association, which then represented the seven thousand unionized members of the Toronto Police Service (including five thousand officers), against the chief of police and the police services board. The union wanted Operation True Blue to continue; as a city councillor interested in policing matters, I wanted it stopped in its tracks. I firmly believe that the cornerstone of a democracy is civilian control over policing. Elected officials should not be beholden to the police, the RCMP or the army.

After only a few weeks, the telemarketing firm hired by the police association had raised $300,000. At the annual conference of the Law

Union of Ontario, a body of progressive lawyers and legal workers, I urged them to take action.

That night during the conference's party at the University of Toronto's Faculty Club, lawyers Paul Copeland, Howard Morton and Bob Kellerman and I began to plan a course of action to stop the police union's fundraising campaign. Thirty-six hours later, on a Monday morning, we held a press conference denouncing Operation True Blue.

Howard told the press that day that we in Canada take our democracy for granted. "We lose our democracy piece by piece," he said, "and every time we lose a piece of it, we lose something that took centuries to obtain."

For Paul Copeland, the police campaign was the thin edge of the wedge. As he suggested during the press conference, "You don't want the police and the army backing political candidates. For one thing, police regulations—specifically the Police Services Act—forbid it. The police have power, and that fact and the fact that they are publicly funded should rule out things like Operation True Blue."

The head of the police union, Craig Bromell, of course couldn't see the problem. He's heard on CBC-TV's *The Fifth Estate* program, in a four-part series titled *Bully*, telling a scrum of reporters that money raised by Operation True Blue would be used not to investigate "enemies" of the police but simply to lobby politicians to advance the police union's law-and-order agenda.

I didn't buy it, and neither did the Toronto press, who were all over the story. In a column headlined "$25 Ticket to a Police State," *Globe and Mail* columnist John Barber slammed the campaign. "Are we there yet?" he wrote. "Have we driven our democratic, civil society to the point where it has come to resemble an old-fashioned Latin American thugocracy? The answer is no. Not yet. But police association chief Craig Bromell is speeding us along as fast as his considerable energy can manage."

Letters to the editor continued in that vein, as did radio hotline shows. The *Toronto Sun* ran a headline that riffed on the To Serve and Protect motto of the Toronto police: "To Serve and Protection Racket?"

If you search YouTube for Craig Bromell, up will come the *Fifth Estate* documentary. In it, host Victor Malarek interviewed then deputy chief of police Robert Kerr. The interview is breathtaking. Kerr is wearing his full uniform, but the epaulettes and medals seem to bestow little in the way of power or confidence. On the contrary, he appears edgy, emotional and, on one occasion, on the brink of tears. He tells Victor about a police officer apparently loyal to him bringing him snippets of an overheard conversation. Something to the effect that if Kerr does not retire from the force, damaging information about him will be made public.

When Victor asks about the source of the threat, Kerr replies: "My interpretation is that the police association executive has some dirt on me that they're going to use."

Victor then asks Kerr whether he is afraid of Craig Bromell. There is a pause. "Yes," comes the reply.

Victor follows up. "You're the deputy chief of the Toronto police, and you fear Constable Craig Bromell?" There is another pause as the deputy chief appears to wrestle to control his emotions. Same answer. "Yes."

"What does that say to the public?" Victor then asks.

"It's all very frightening," says the deputy chief. The thirty-five-year veteran of the force, a self-described hard-nosed and liberal cop who believed passionately in police accountability and civilian oversight of the police, retired several months later.

Never offered in the interview is evidence to support Kerr's claim that he might have been blackmailed or what information he feared might be used against him. Palpable, though, is his fear and the source of that fear: Craig Bromell.

Victor Malarek interviewed Craig Bromell for that same documentary. Like me, Victor can't stand bullies. He grew up in Montreal, "a ward of the state," as he often puts it—playing for laughs but making a point. "My dad," he says, "was in prison when I was growing up and when I asked him about bullies, he just said, 'Smack 'em back.'" And, in his own inestimable way, Victor Malarek has consistently done just that.

When he interviewed Craig Bromell for *The Fifth Estate*, Victor's first question was not a question at all but a statement: "You've been called dangerous, a thug, a bully."

Bromell responds: "You can call me a bully."

In those days, challenging police union power often meant provoking a response. I remember being interviewed in the company of a member of the police association. He was tall and lanky; I am . . . less so. He would just tower over me in what I felt was a clear attempt to intimidate me. Judy Sgro—now a Liberal MP but back then vice-chair of the Toronto Police Services Board—resigned from that position when police intimidation became too much for her. At one point, the police union threatened to sue her for defamation over comments she had made during a *Fifth Estate* interview. Sympathetic police officers told Sgro that she was under surveillance and, in one informal and almost two-hour-long meeting between the police services board and the police union executive, every member of the executive attacked her and insisted that she not speak to the press without their permission. Sgro told *The Fifth Estate* what her instruction was: "You call us, and we'll tell you what to say." She referred to the entire police union executive as bullies.

The police services board has seven members, and their job, no easy one, is civilian oversight of the men and women in uniform. Old police culture—the thin blue line, as it's called—insisted that anyone who is not with them was against them, and certainly anyone making comments critical of policing could expect to feel the heat. Jeff Lyons served on the board in those days and he actually had his office swept for listening devices because he feared the police union was keeping tabs on him. (The sweep turned up no bugs.)

By the end of January 2000, and after working together with like-minded allies, we had kicked up a firestorm over Operation True Blue. But Mayor Mel Lastman rarely spoke out against the police union, and his appointees on the police services board would not vote to stop the campaign. As a result, the decision to denounce the police union's campaign and seek an injunction to stop its activities would have to come from city council. I had already garnered enough votes, but I was worried about Mayor Lastman's defence of Bromell. It was widely anticipated that he would weigh in on the union side. But just before the vote, his chief of staff made him watch *Bully*. Then the winds shifted—in a hurry.

Mayor Lastman was angry as he blasted the union and urged rank-and-file officers to dump their executive. "There is no way this police union executive is going to hold our city hostage," he said. "I'm a strong supporter of the police. They do a tough job but the union has gone overboard. The bullying and the intimidation by the union have got to stop." With his biggest ally jumping ship, Craig Bromell called off Operation True Blue.

Of course the battle to maintain civilian control over policing didn't end there. The issue of the police cozying up to certain political candidates (while targeting others) and the broader issue of the police flexing political muscle continued to simmer for years. "Soft on crime" is the epithet usually applied by candidates on the right to anyone who dares to suggest a slightly different approach.

Advising the Toronto police union around this time was the Texas-based Police and Fire Labor Institute. I am a firm believer that just as church and state should be separated, so should police and politics. But that's not what that Texas body thinks, as contained in volume 1 of their book, *Police Labor-Management Relations*, published in 2006: "What separates the police union from the police executive in the world of politics is that the police union has the ability to endorse a candidate and work in the candidate's political campaign. Perhaps the union's greatest political advantage is its ability to contribute money to the candidate. In many parts of the United States, the police union's political action committee is the largest campaign contributor to a candidate. Despite protests from the editorial boards of newspapers about the perceived political power of many police unions, candidates for public office continue to seek the endorsement and resources of the police union."

The book describes how police unions can influence public opinion directly through press conferences, direct mail, billboards, radio and TV. "The union's ability to make a political end run frustrates law enforcement executives and government administrators." I'll bet.

The Toronto police also took advice from the Los Angeles Police Department union, and their suggestion (this came up in the *Fifth Estate* documentary) was to win instant respect by taking down a mayor or city councillor. Craig Bromell talks freely in *Bully* about using private investigators to gather "dirt" on those he perceived to be the rank-and-file police officers' political enemies ("scumbags," he called them).

I have a cameo in Victor Malarek's documentary. I'm seen entering a room and passing Gary Clewley, one of the police union's lawyers, and Craig Bromell. I cheerily ask Clewley if he's been enjoying his summer, and he assures me that he has. Then he says, rather playfully, "We're ready to rumble."

"Any time," I reply.

~

On September 27, 2003, less than a week before the provincial election, a full-page ad ran in *The Globe and Mail* under a heading that read: "The Toronto Police Association Board of Directors proudly endorses Ernie Eves and his fellow Progressive Conservative candidates." The ad depicted a photo of Eves, a police car and the police association's logo. Conservative candidates in the Toronto area were listed, and voters were offered this note in bold print at the bottom of the page: "Help Keep Ontario Safe. On October 2nd, vote for Ernie Eves and the P.C. Candidate in your riding."

A year later, the police services board sought a legal opinion on whether such ads were legal. The opinion came back: No, they were not. In 2005, the board adopted a policy that prohibited political activity by police officers and their association. At every election, the chief is asked to remind everyone about this policy and to enforce it.

Meanwhile, the Ottawa police union tried to endorse mayoralty candidates in the 2006 election. That plan was quickly stopped when the Toronto Police Services Board sent the legal opinion as well as its policy to its Ottawa counterpart, reminding them that all police unions in Ontario are bound by the Police Services Act—which prohibits police officers, in their official capacity, from either backing or opposing political candidates. In fact, the chief of police is supposed to discipline any officer who does so. (As private citizens, of course, these officers enjoy the same political rights and freedoms as anyone else.) Ottawa then created its own policy along the lines of Toronto's prohibition.

The act also prohibits officers from suggesting that their political positions are those of the police force or from participating in any partisan political activity when they are on duty or in uniform. This includes endorsing or soliciting funds for political parties or candidates. It's a different story in Texas, but that's the Canadian way.

I support working people, including public sector workers, such as nurses, teachers, daycare workers, firefighters—and police officers. I think they have a right to have a voice in public affairs. But an elected public official's first duty is to the public interest. And so, if a union leadership loses sight of its principles and turns to tactics like the ones I've been discussing in this chapter, that must be addressed. I'm a committed progressive and social democrat. But just because I'm progressive doesn't mean I have to roll over in the face of bullies.

On June 15, 2000—five months after the True Blue campaign—an anti-poverty demonstration saw about a thousand people gathered at Queen's Park, including many homeless people. They were demanding the right to address the legislature to voice their concerns about social housing and other matters. But a few troublemakers in the crowd started to become unruly and violent.

Jack Layton was there, as he had been pushing for the building of more affordable housing and was greatly affected by the homeless. He called me as police horses were charging, and I had the sense of general chaos. Worried about his safety, I ran to Queen's Park.

When I arrived on the scene, Adam Vaughan, now a Toronto city councillor but then a reporter with Citytv, asked me about these police horses charging at people. I answered that it would be better if the police de-escalated the violence. (I was then a member of the Toronto Police Services Board, having been appointed because of my leadership role during the True Blue campaign and my efforts to contain the police budget.) Craig Bromell immediately saw an opening. He went on the offensive, claiming that I had violated the Police Services Act by telling officers what to do via the media.

The police union then demanded my head on a platter. To back that demand, they began circulating a petition—in police stations right across the city—which called for my resignation from the police services board *and* my seat on city council. Here again, the police were meddling in politics. For an entire week, the public debate dragged on, which only served to distract from another, more serious discussion: Did charging demonstrators with horses and escalating the violence constitute adequate and effective policing? What protocols should be in place on how to handle mass demonstrations?

Police board chair Norm Gardner and Police Chief Julian Fantino were of the same political stripe, and I knew which way the political winds were blowing. Though I was confident that there had been no breach on my part of the Police Services Act, I knew I lacked the support of a majority of police services board members, including those appointed by Mike Harris's Conservative government. Before any vote could be taken on the matter, I resigned from the board.

The Law Union of Ontario had reacted immediately when Operation True Blue was unveiled. And they likewise responded quickly when I was hounded off the police services board by the self-styled bully Craig Bromell. Bob Kellerman of the Law Union told reporters that the board had broken the law by forcing my resignation and that by refusing to rein in the police union they had actually emboldened it, so much so that the union didn't hesitate to go after politicians.

"People elect politicians," Kellerman said. "They don't elect the police. But if politicians are afraid to stand up to the police, and if the police are giving orders as they tried to do with Judy Sgro, you have a police state. You have essentially unelected officials running the show."

With my resignation, the principle of civilian oversight had been trampled. That principle remains front and centre when police activities are questioned by the public. After witnessing the brutality and the violence seen during the G20 demonstrations in Toronto in 2010, the Toronto Police Services Board commissioned the Independent

Civilian Review into Matters Relating to the G20 Summit. The resulting report, authored by former Ontario associate chief justice John W. Morden, focuses on the long-standing misinterpretation of the board's statutory mandate and makes recommendations with a view to correcting this misinterpretation so that the principle of civilian oversight is given the life it was intended. Among other things, these recommendations do away with the problematic "policy vs. operations" divide that has often been used to keep the board out of matters that are properly its business.

The report places emphasis on the concept of civilian oversight in policing, and makes clear that Ontario legislation gives police board members the statutory duty to ensure "adequate and effective policing." Board members are not prevented from seeking operational information and details before a significant event, discussing these matters with the chief, making recommendations to the chief or obtaining a full debriefing after an event.

As the report states: "Civilian oversight of our police is essential. It acts as a check and balance against the legal powers society has given the police to enforce the law. Effective oversight of the police is the way that the public and police remain partners in the preservation of public safety. For the police to be effective in our communities, the public must have respect for those that perform the policing function. The governance and accountability that civilian oversight creates work in tandem."

I couldn't agree more. Civilian oversight of our police is an integral component of a Canadian society premised on the rule of law.

In a book that strives to paint a picture of a political life that has spanned decades and continues to unfold, I can't tell every story, but some absolutely must be told. And one of them is the story of Jane

Doe. What I remember most about this time was the courage of many women, not least Jane Doe herself.

One night in August of 1986, a Toronto woman (her identity was never revealed, and she continues to be known as Jane Doe) was raped at knifepoint by a man dubbed the "balcony rapist" for his pattern of entering apartments through balcony doors. Police knew that a serial rapist was on the loose in the Church and Wellesley Street neighbourhood (Jane Doe was the fifth victim) but failed to warn women what was happening and to take precautions. Women, in effect, were being used as bait.

The Jane Doe case established many precedents. In a legal battle that would go on for eleven years, she became the first woman to secure her own legal representation in the criminal prosecution of her rapist. She also sued the Toronto police for violating her constitutional right to equality and for breaching the duties they owed her as an identifiable target of a serial rapist. In 1998 she was awarded a verdict against the police. She then worked with me for another ten years on a document that became known as the *Jane Doe Social Audit*—an attempt to ensure that police implemented changes to their policies and practices around the investigation of rape. This, too, was unprecedented.

In her memoir, *The Story of Jane Doe*, she writes: "In Ontario, only four per cent of all reported rapes that reach trial result in guilty convictions . . . At four per cent, we have disaster, farce, permission to rape."

But another remarkable thing happened. Under the leadership of Councillor Pam McConnell, a female caucus had formed at city hall around this case, and we were not going to allow this rape to be ignored—never mind the opportunity the case offered to rethink the entire approach of the Toronto police to rape. A number of female councillors spoke passionately about this case at a meeting of city council on July 10, 1998. I led this charge, and it resulted in a motion being passed urging that both city council and the police services board issue an apology to Jane Doe and the women of Toronto and that "city staff expeditiously settle all of the monetary issues arising from the Jane Doe decision."

Just seven days before that council meeting, Madam Justice Jean MacFarland had ruled in favour of Jane Doe on all three counts on which she had launched her suit against the Toronto police: negligence, a violation of her Charter equality rights, and an infringement of her Charter right to security of the person. The judge held that the police owed a duty of care to the women in Jane Doe's neighbourhood and that they had "utterly" failed in that duty. The judge called the police investigation "irresponsible and grossly negligent." The judge also accepted Jane Doe's argument that the reason for the shoddy investigation was that the police did not take the crime of sexual assault seriously. Jane Doe was awarded $220,000 in damages, which, eleven years after the legal battle began, amounted with interest to almost $500,000.

Now the question before city council was this: Do we appeal the decision? Several male councillors expressed misgivings about the legal and financial obligations for the city of paying the compensation. I urged council to think about the emotional cost to this woman—who had already suffered for many years—of dragging this case on. I was furious that the whole thing had persisted so long, and the thought of a costly appeal by the city made me doubly angry. As more and more female councillors spoke, the tide turned. Finally, council voted 51–1 to issue an apology and to forgo an appeal.

Why was I already angry? You should know that there was not just one Jane Doe case around this time—there were three. I remember a Toronto Police Services Board meeting when Maureen Prinsloo was still the chair. I told her that I was going to say something out of turn—something that was not on the agenda before the meeting got under way. I had given Maureen a heads-up—something to the effect that we won't make a huge fuss if you don't. What I wanted to talk about was the case of another woman, who had been staying at Nellie's, a downtown women's shelter. She said she was raped by two police officers in the underground garage of a Toronto mall one night. She brought a complaint, but the case dragged on for five years and she finally killed herself. Two months later, the officers she accused were found guilty of discreditable conduct and were dismissed from the force.

In another case, a Toronto police sergeant had been accused of extorting sexual services from a sex worker by threatening her with arrest. The woman hired a lawyer and made a complaint, and although there was a disciplinary hearing (the presiding officer called the sergeant's conduct "a totally despicable abuse of police power and authority"), in the end no criminal charge was laid. He kept his job as a police officer, although he was demoted to first class constable. This third Jane Doe, like the second one, took her own life.

My friend Anna Willats—then the coordinator of the Toronto Rape Crisis Centre—and I came together with friends of these Jane Does. We wanted things to change. We wanted an acknowledgement from the police of the wrong that had been done, and we wanted an apology.

We had gone to the police services board several times urging the police to revamp their way of investigating sexual assaults, to survey victims to ensure they received necessary support and that the case had been adequately investigated, and to provide more intensive training to front-line and investigative teams.

On paper, the police supported all these recommendations, but reports from the front line pointed to little progress. So I proposed an audit of police practices on sexual assault investigations. The author of the audit was Jeffrey Griffiths, the city's own financial auditor, who had consulted with almost two dozen groups—including the Toronto Rape Crisis Centre—that work with women who have been sexually assaulted. What an extraordinary document it was.

In great detail, it showed that former chief Julian Fantino had not implemented all the improvements to how sexual assaults were to be investigated—even though he had repeatedly told the civilian board that he had. This audit and the report that followed it became a template for real change in the handling of sexual assault cases in Toronto. The board set up a steering committee, with Councillor Pam McConnell; the new chair of the board, Alok Mukherjee; the new chief of police, Bill Blair; Deputy Chief Jane Dick; as well as Jane Doe and several other women activists. As a result of this committee's work, the entire approach has changed, including a longer training as recommended by Jane Doe and others, faster referral from the divisions to the Sex Crimes Unit, and precise, sensitive and balanced notifications and warnings. As well, a community advisory committee now works with the Sex Crimes Unit so there have been continuous improvements.

More recently, in order to reflect the multicultural community it serves, the Toronto Police Services Board has been bringing in officers with a wider range of cultural backgrounds and who speak a wider range of languages. Board chair Alok Mukherjee, who was the director of race relations at the Toronto Board of Education when I was a trustee, provided a tremendous amount of leadership in this area. By 2006, the year after I left my city councillor position to become an MP, more than half the 144 graduates from the police college were women or visible minorities. The board also ordered systemic reviews to remove barriers that had prevented the proper promotion of diverse officers. To ensure continued successes, all new chiefs of police will be held accountable to ensure the force reflects the citizens it serves. These officers are able to build trust from diverse cultural communities that, in turn, are able to support police initiatives.

One example of such a partnership in my own neighbourhood was the Croft Street Revitalization Project. Working with neighbourhood residents, students and artists, local officers transformed Croft Street: graffiti gave way to aesthetically pleasing murals. Officers were part of a program that brought in young people who had experienced minor conflicts with the law and had them trained by professional artists. Croft Street, and my neighbours, were the clear beneficiaries.

But while I see many advances in the area of community-based policing as more officers are redeployed from support functions to front-line staff, the entire community-based policing concept cannot be made to work perfectly unless shift work—or the "compressed work week"—is changed. Officers work through rotating shifts—day shifts, evening shifts, night shifts—and move from one neighbourhood to another within their division.

This system has drawbacks. Let's say your house or store is robbed. The officer who begins the investigation may find her shift ending, and continuing to work on the investigation involves expensive overtime. If the officer waits to continue the investigation next time she is in the area, precious time is lost. But if she hands off the paperwork to another officer, precious time is also lost—you have to go over old ground with a new officer unfamiliar with the case. No relationship is built up between you and one or two or more officers, and that can lead to frustration—as David Chen will attest.

Mr. Chen owns Lucky Moose Food Mart—a great Canadian name for a Chinese neighbourhood grocery not far from my house in Chinatown. Many independent neighbourhood stores are owned and operated by hard-working immigrant families. Lucky Moose, for example, is open seven days a week, from nine in the morning until ten at night. The tireless owner, David Chen, gets up at five to go to the Ontario Food Terminal, spends all day running his store and catches up with paperwork late into the night. He works long hours in a low-margin business.

My mother shops at Lucky Moose all the time, checking out the mangoes from the Philippines, the hoisin sauces from Hong Kong, the fish and lobster swimming in tanks. And the beautiful flowers and plants, including one known as the money tree plant. (One story has it that a truck driver in Taiwan was briefly out of work after a typhoon and turned to braiding women's hair in his wife's salon, where it occurred to him that braiding the bark of bonsai trees might make him some money—as indeed it did.) Unfortunately, money doesn't grow on trees, but the plants are very popular, and, at about sixty dollars each, they are a big-ticket item for a small enterprise. Losing even one plant could mean losing a chunk of the day's profit.

On May 23, 2009, Lucky Moose got unlucky when a shoplifter stole twelve money tree plants and took off on his bike. David and two co-workers chased the man, bound him with twine and tossed him into a delivery van until police arrived. The case garnered national headlines when it was Chen and his co-workers who were arrested, strip-searched and charged with assault and forcible confinement. (I heard about it when my mother called me that day in a state—"Ollie, Ollie, something has happened. Somebody stole from Lucky Moose, but David Chen got arrested!") The thief, a career shoplifter with forty-three previous convictions, was lightly punished with a thirty-day detention.

In theory, citizen's arrests are allowed in Canada, but at the time, the law allowed only for such arrests during the actual commission of a crime. But shoplifting is a different kind of crime—it doesn't become a crime until the shoplifter *leaves* the premises without paying for the goods. The plight facing small entrepreneurs like David Chen is twofold. Unlike the chains and bigger stores, they can't afford security staff.

And while the police view shoplifting as a petty crime, shop owners see it as a crippling blow to their slim profit margins. Often it takes hours for officers to arrive on the scene, and some of them may not be familiar with the history of crimes in the community.

The arrest of David Chen struck a nerve with small storeowners everywhere in Canada. Clearly, they were not getting adequate protection from police or the law. One part of the solution was to revise the Criminal Code—and that is what I started to demand. As a member of Parliament, my position was clear: hard-working store owners should not be punished when protecting their property. And I repeated that again and again—in the House of Commons, in committee, in the gym—everywhere.

I started talking to small business owners in my riding and across Toronto. When I was in Vancouver, I went door-to-door to small businesses and shops in Chinese and ethnic communities, gathering signatures on a petition. From this one little neighbourhood grocery, we built a nationwide movement—and the rallying cry was "Lucky Moose." After we had gathered ten thousand names on our petition, my old friend Chi Kun Shi, a lawyer who had been defending David Chen from the start, drafted a private member's bill that I called the Lucky Moose Bill.

On November 2, I made a motion for the bill to be expedited through second reading by unanimous consent. I knew that all parties agreed in principle, but the Conservative government was dragging its heels and not taking any action. Loath to support another party's legislation, they voted no. However, four hours later, during Question Period, Stephen Harper announced that the government would present its own bill, using the same language as my Lucky Moose private member's bill.

The Citizen's Arrest and Self-Defence Act was passed by unanimous consent and became law in 2013. The change means that someone in David Chen's position may now rightfully make a citizen's arrest—assuming the police are not immediately available and assuming that no more than reasonable force is used. The act does not allow store owners to harm or assault anyone, nor does it give these owners any more power. The only difference is in the timing of the citizen's arrest.

Citizen's arrest shouldn't be necessary in the first place—people and their property should be protected by the police. By generating greater awareness of the plight of small business owners and neighbourhood stores, the Lucky Moose story has helped generate demand for community policing.

The kind of community policing I have in mind is the kind of policing you see in old black-and-white movies—where the beat cop knows not just the couple who own the grocery store but their children, too. That's why I want cops on the street, not in the sky.

Between 2000 and 2005, Police Chief Julian Fantino lobbied long and hard for helicopters. We need them, he pleaded, what with gangs and post-9/11 security fears. When nearby Durham Region got choppers, helicopter envy set in and the campaign ramped up.

It really irked the chief when I did some research and found that although helicopters were indeed sexy in a kind of *LAPD* way, setting down metal spike strips was an effective and far less costly way to end a car chase. A suspect fleeing police in a vehicle poses a real danger to both pedestrians and other drivers. It struck me that although a helicopter allowed police to keep a suspect in view, it didn't end the chase (witness the O. J. Simpson pursuit). Spike strips, on the other hand, fit in the trunk of a police car and can be set down on the roadway in the path of a fleeing car. Also called stingers and stop sticks, they pierce the car's tires. There is also a device that blends spikes with netting, gumming up the tires should the driver try to continue driving on flat tires. The point is this: the Toronto police could do the job without helicopters.

"We want cops on the street, not in the air" was my line at the time.

Fantino did manage to get council to fund a six-month trial. But that was all, whereupon the chief started courting private donors and senior levels of government. Then people started to wonder what the police wanted in return. Fantino accused the quibblers of being paranoid and took them to task for questioning the integrity of the police (his usual response to questions he considered impertinent).

The Tory provincial government promised him $1 million in temporary funding, but when the Conservatives lost the 2003 election, the Liberals cancelled it. That was the last gasp for the helicopters, and with none of the dire consequences Fantino had predicted. We're getting along just fine without them. The Toronto police already have a plane and can do any kind of aerial surveillance required.

Fantino then entered federal politics, but he never lost his desire for metal toys. Briefly associate minister of national defence (in 2011–12), he was part of the campaign to acquire those famously overpriced F-35 fighter jets. "This is the aircraft that is absolutely essential to what we need to do in this country to maintain our sovereignty," Fantino told the CBC in 2011—even though the F-35 has trouble flying in extreme cold weather, something we have a lot of in the Canadian Arctic.

As I write this in the summer of 2013, the campaign to acquire those billion-dollar jets is on hold.

CHAPTER 12

In Search of Safe Shelter

The City of Toronto did a follow-up report two years after the Tent City eviction to check on the well-being of these folks. Almost all of them still lived in their housing and were doing well. So many people who had been seen as beyond rescue had been rescued. The turning point was a decent roof over their heads.

At the mouth of the Don River, where it flows into Lake Ontario, stand linked and gently curving concrete silos—once part of a sugar refinery called the Canada Malting Company. Near the end of 1997, several dozen homeless youths began using the thirty-seven-metre-tall silos as a refuge. Built in 1928 and abandoned in the 1980s, the silos were a dangerous place to seek sanctuary because old equipment there had rusted and leaked PCBs into the soil. I do remember the smell of the place: a fetid brew of rancid oil, raccoon feces and rotten grain. Outside, some bold artist had scaled one elevator and painted a nine-metre-tall rooster. Thus the name, Rooster Squat.

Jack and I wanted to know more about these young people. Why were they homeless? What did they need in order to leave this terrible place and come into a shelter? So we went and visited the Rooster Squat and listened to their stories.

The majority of these young people had run away from physical, verbal or, in some cases, sexual abuse at home. Others had mental health or substance use issues. Jack and I were very alarmed by a young woman who was coughing violently, and we tried to persuade her to see a doctor. Most of these people were lost and frightened, yet defiant. They didn't want to leave because here, at least, they finally had some friends and a sense of community—even though the conditions were deplorable.

That winter was bitterly cold, and Christmas was only two days away. We wanted to help these young people celebrate the holiday season as best we could and be sheltered from the bitter cold.

Jack called a childhood friend in Hudson, Quebec, a guy named Philip Habib, who owned a tent company called E-Z Up Canada. "Can you deliver some tents?" Jack asked him.

"But this is the morning before Christmas, Jack," came the reply.

"All the more reason these homeless young people should have a roof over their heads," said Jack.

"Okay, let me see what I can do," said Philip.

So Philip rounded up some friends and loaded some tents onto a bus. On the night before Christmas, the tents arrived in Toronto. They were beer tents, constructed of plastic and designed to protect against summer rain, not winter cold. Still, they gave comfort to those who felt they were being discarded by society, and the tents became a symbol that someone was willing to do something about their plight.

Something else had brought us to Rooster Squat in 1997. Almost a year earlier, on the night of January 4, 1996, I was walking home with Jack after a typical late night at city hall. A blizzard was raging, and as we neared home, around midnight, we passed a couple of homeless men in sleeping bags tucked inside doorways—at least protected from the swirling snow if not from the bitter cold.

That night a man named Eugene Upper died in a Spadina Avenue bus shelter—not a block from our home on Huron Street. Jack later wrote a book about homelessness and he dedicated the book to this man.

In *Homelessness: The Making and Unmaking of a Crisis*, Jack described waking up the following morning, hearing the news of Eugene Upper's death and realizing that we had perhaps passed him the night before. "A shiver ran down my spine. Is there anything more awful for a Canadian to imagine than freezing to death? How could this have happened in Toronto? Were there no shelters? Were there no emergency services for the homeless? Wasn't this the richest city in the country? What the hell was going on?"

The death of Eugene Upper was a catalyst for both Jack and me. We were mobilized.

In 1998, about eighteen young people from Rooster Squat moved over to another piece of vacant land on the waterfront. They were soon joined by others, and what became known as Tent City emerged. Jack and others arranged to have trailers brought in, and once they were renovated, those shelters offered much better protection against the cold than tents. Over the course of four years, Tent City grew to include about 130 homeless individuals living in shacks and lean-tos. The Toronto Disaster Relief Committee brought in portable homes and toilets, while social service agencies offered health care and food. Then came logistical help—generators, wood stoves, toilets, blankets, candles, propane and first aid supplies—as if disaster had struck. As it indeed had for those seeking shelter.

Jack was always going to bat for these folks, insisting that they get housing. He was at the very least trying to save or relocate Tent City, and we offered support in whatever way we could. But as Tent City grew, tensions rose—especially when Home Depot, the owners of the property, put up a high razor-wire fence all around the land and eviction loomed. The presence of Tent City also brought Canada-wide and even worldwide attention to the plight of the homeless in the city of Toronto. When *The New York Times* ran a piece describing the conditions at Tent City, Toronto's reputation as a model city was tarnished.

On September 24, 2002, security guards hired by Home Depot forced the squatters to vacate the site. They were not allowed to retrieve their clothes and personal belongings. These residents, some of whom had been living there for four years, would not leave the site. They were dazed, sad, angry and frightened. Some wept, others paced and still others cursed. They were all given pink notices informing them they had been charged with trespassing and would face fines of up to $2,000. Most didn't have $200 to their names, never mind $2,000.

Meanwhile, citizens of Toronto who were upset at the eviction rushed down to Tent City to show their support; others were calling on Mayor Lastman to find homes for these hundred or so homeless people. Tensions grew as the standoff continued between the Tent City residents who wanted to retrieve their belongings and the security guards hired to keep them out.

I was chair of Toronto's Community Services Committee at the time, and worked closely with the mayor's point person on housing, Sean Goetz-Gadon, to find a solution to the crisis. By nightfall, we managed to broker a deal with the Conservative provincial government of Mike Harris. The residents of Tent City would be moved into apartments, with support and counselling from a community centre. Over a hundred people had found shelter. It was a start.

~~~
~~~

Many Canadians would be shocked to learn that the homeless are not just those one sees walking the streets with small backpacks or lining up at shelters at the end of the day. The visible homeless are the tip of the iceberg, as a far greater number are couch-surfing or living in rundown motels. (The Kingston Road motel strip in east Toronto is a well-known state-run depository for homeless families and for mothers and children fleeing abusive partners.) Some 20 to 30 per cent of the homeless in this country are children, and I knew from my time serving on the board of the Children's Aid Society the incalculable consequences of homelessness for these children.

Every few months, they and their families are uprooted as the search for decent housing drags on. These young boys and girls have no opportunity to attend school regularly, develop relationships or maintain friendships, and that's a recipe for anger and frustration. I would often point out that being stingy with childcare and affordable housing was penny-wise and pound foolish: some of these children would follow a course that ended in jail, which is many times more expensive than subsidized housing and childcare. Jail is the worst kind of shelter. Love and optimism can flourish in a home, but jails are hotbeds of hate and despair.

All too often, parents roaming in search of housing suffer unbearable strains and lose their children, who become Crown wards and land in foster homes. But there aren't enough foster homes, either, and certainly culturally appropriate ones are in short supply. It's even worse for older people who lose their housing—there are no foster homes at all for adults and seniors. Sometimes I think of my unstable father and how easily he could have landed on the streets or in jail. Seniors in Toronto in need of affordable housing are told the wait is ten years long. It's ironic that in our society, parents need to put their babies on waiting lists for childcare before those babies are even born, while seniors need to go on a waiting list that may be longer than the years they have left. On a waiting list before birth, and still on a waiting list at the end of life.

As for the young people of Rooster Squat, I knew that many of them had been abused—verbally, physically, sexually. And some suffered from mental health problems or drug dependency. But I also knew that their lives could be turned around through decent, affordable, dependable housing coupled with the right counselling and support. I had seen it.

After years of intensely focused activism, a tiny amount of funding is available to build supportive housing, and more shelters with supportive services have been constructed. But still, Canada does not have a national affordable housing program.

One lesson of Tent City is the importance of housing in helping homeless people with substance use or mental health issues. The key is not to plunk individuals into apartments, walk away and hope for the best. They need evaluating, they need support—and the leader in providing that support is WoodGreen Community Services. I have been connected to WoodGreen for decades, having taught English as a second language to immigrants there in the early eighties, and I know what they have to offer to those who would otherwise have no hope.

One of the largest social service agencies in Toronto, WoodGreen has been in operation for more than seventy-five years. It serves thirty-seven thousand people each year and in a wide variety of ways—by finding safe and affordable housing for homeless or marginalized people, by helping seniors to live independently, by helping parents who are searching for childcare or by assisting newcomers needing to get a start.

For many of the former denizens of Rooster Squat and Tent City, WoodGreen provided a lifeline of support and counselling.

The City of Toronto did a follow-up report (*From Tent City to Housing: An Evaluation of the City of Toronto Emergency Homelessness Pilot Project*) two years after the Tent City eviction to check on the well-being of these folks. Almost all of them still lived in their housing and were doing well. Tent City presented a dramatic illustration of the plight of the homeless (one that continues today and is actually worse), but for those particular people, at least, help was forthcoming. So many people who had been seen as beyond rescue had been rescued and their quality of life improved. The turning point was a decent roof over their heads.

How fitting that on June 9 of 2013, a building at 1070 Queen Street East in downtown Toronto was renamed Jack Layton Seniors Housing. The affordable housing facility had opened twenty years earlier under the auspices of WoodGreen Community Services, but had never been given a name. Now it had the best possible one. The building houses seniors who had been living in difficult or inadequate circumstances, and WoodGreen offers them twenty-four-hour support along with classes in tai chi, art and music—and a chance to live independently. I was there for the unveiling, along with Sarah Layton and many others.

We listened as a tenants' choir sang a musical rendition of Jack's letter to Canadians. "Canada is a great country," they sang, "one of the hopes of the world. We can be a better one—a country of greater equality, justice and opportunity."

For me, the link between mental health and homelessness is very personal and powerful. The numbers on homelessness in this country are still staggering: the most recent data suggest that two hundred thousand Canadians experience homelessness in any given year, with some thirty thousand without a home to go to on any given night and another fifty thousand couch-surfing with friends and relations in the absence of any other option.

"First you have to have a roof over your head, and then your life can really come together," I told the gathered that day in both English and Cantonese. "This building, this housing, this is where love grows. This is where friendships are created and where we come together to celebrate each other and support each other."

Brian Smith was president and CEO of WoodGreen when I first went there decades ago and he's still in that job. In 2013, he received the Canadian Urban Institute's City Champion award for transforming WoodGreen into one of Toronto's leading social services organizations. We need more visionary leaders like Brian—and more WoodGreens.

When I was young, each of my embattled parents would ask me an impossible question: If they separated, which one would I choose to live with? Almost fifty years later, I am again facing a similar question: Which of them do I care for most?

Today, my father has dementia and would get lost if allowed out of the apartment alone. My mother's mind remains razor sharp, but she is increasingly prone to falls—she has cracked ribs on three occasions and broken her arm. She receives an injection every six weeks to control her old nemesis, rheumatoid arthritis. Still, she is indefatigable and cheerfully grumpy. Her domains are the kitchen in our house on Huron Street, a little sunroom off the kitchen where she watches her Chinese soap operas and both the front and back gardens.

I know that despite the battles between them, and despite my father's demons, my mother and father love each other. My mother still goes to his apartment in St. James Town, cooks his favourite foods and tends to him whenever she can. At our dim sum on Father's Day in 2013, she made sure he had everything he wanted and was the centre of attention. She laughed with delight when I took him home in style, cruising through Chinatown in a friend's convertible. We are and always will be a family, but my parents simply cannot coexist under one roof.

She's an intriguing mix, my mother: generous, jealous, territorial, tough, resilient, hot-tempered, quirky, amusing, impatient, stubborn. She has a great sense of humour, but doesn't suffer fools. I like to think that I have my mother's common sense and my father's artistic bent. Unlike my mother, I have no temper. And like my father, I am not judgmental. My mother is *very* judgmental.

A total of six caregivers—working in shifts from morning to evening—now tend to my father. They help him with shopping, cooking and personal care, or take him to Toronto Chinese Baptist Church, which he still attends regularly. As well, a nurse gives him his insulin shots, a home care doctor sees him every six weeks, and cleaners come by to keep the place tidy.

My father understands who I am, but he cannot care for himself. I dreaded those calls from the police when my dad was found lost or injured or both. One time, for example, he fell into a car, banged his head and suffered a minor concussion, but he wouldn't go to the hospital. I was in Ottawa and couldn't go to assist him. A wonderfully patient police officer walked him home, and friends of mine went over to make sure he was okay. After a similar incident when he landed at the emergency department with severe bruising and gashes in his head, doctors were insistent that my dad no longer leave the house without someone by his side.

But finding round-the-clock home care for him has been nightmarishly difficult. The health care system offered ten hours of care per week, but since he couldn't even remember to take his medications, let alone look after himself, ten hours were not enough. After a few more accidents, his hours were finally increased to twenty-one.

Public services provided to patients with advanced Alzheimer's are woefully inadequate and fragmented. In order for my father to stay in his own home, I spend many hours making sure all services are coordinated, medications ordered and picked up, supplies and food purchased.

Since I live with my mother when I am in Toronto, managing her care is a bit easier. Although her needs are not as extensive as my father's, she also requires two public caregivers (ten hours a week total) and one private. I have wall charts to manage the medical, caregiving, financial, food, drug and toiletry needs for both of my parents, along with the close to twenty people I am coordinating.

In the summer of 2013, I finally gave in and agreed to have my dad go to a nursing home (well, at least put him on a waiting list for a nursing home). I calculated that placing him in a nursing home would be more manageable for the family, but more expensive for the government—much more so if my dad was to be subsidized (no need because of my income). Failing to subsidize home care is false economy.

If Canada had a comprehensive home care system, our seniors would be better served by being helped to live longer at home, and at far less cost to the public purse. I can't imagine how a senior with children living far away, or with no spouse, could manage. And what if the senior can't speak English and is not familiar with social services? How would that person or that person's family navigate the maze that is our fragmented home care system?

I understand the senior care system inside and out, having been chair of the City of Toronto's Community Services Committee. Today my office regularly answers questions from constituents regarding pensions, seniors' services, tax laws and benefits, and we are on top of the issue. When I think of how difficult and time-consuming it has been for me to look for care solutions for my father, I can't imagine what other families who don't know the ropes must go through.

Getting into a nursing home is like winning a lottery because the waiting lists for high-quality homes are so long. The wait is even longer if government subsidies are required. Some Canadians are so desperate that they take early retirement or remortgage their homes in order to care for their parents. With an aging population, this home care crisis desperately needs leadership from the federal government. In the federal transfer of health dollars to the provinces and territories, there should be a partnership and conditions established to make possible a coordinated, high-quality and comprehensive national home care program.

Such was the recommendation of Roy Romanow's Royal Commission on the Future of Health Care in Canada, whose report was delivered in 2002. Yet successive governments have been unwilling to tackle this crisis. Throwing more health dollars at the system will not solve the problem, but leadership and partnership will. When Tommy Douglas created a universal health care program, ensuring access to doctors and hospitals was just the first phase. The second phase envisions home care and affordable medications and dental care. Without these components, many Canadians will fall through the cracks and find themselves unable to live in dignity in what should be their golden years.

Just as the first years after the birth of a baby should be a joyous, precious and memorable time, so too should the last years of a parent's life. Electing a government with the vision and political will to establish national programs for childcare and home care services could make those precious times a reality for all Canadians.

Finding a safe haven can be a challenge for anyone, not just the homeless, and the safest haven is a safe community. When I lived in St. James Town in the seventies, the community was not all that dangerous, but it was *perceived* to be dangerous. And, truth be told, I was on a few occasions followed home from the subway stop, flashed on the subway stairway and, one time, chased. I was vulnerable because I was a teenager walking home late (from my shift at the Shoppers Drug Mart that ended at 2 a.m. or perhaps the graveyard shift when I volunteered at the Toronto East General Hospital's crisis hotline).

I would get off at the Sherbourne subway stop and then walk up the stairs to Howard Street. On my left was a tunnel that led to Rosedale, that other (affluent, mostly white) world. To my right lay St. James Town, my (multicoloured, mostly immigrant) world. At that time of night, I would walk on whichever sidewalk was most illuminated, with a key between my knuckles, prepared to roll under a car should someone threatening approach.

Some things have not changed in that block since I lived there. The elevators in some buildings are slow and prone to malfunction, leading to long lineups. On the other hand, some things have changed and much for the better. There is a library now, and support programs, and a few years ago the new Wellesley Community Centre opened up. Led by local councillor Pam McConnell, we banded together and fought for that on city council. Offered at this beautiful building at the corner of Wellesley and Sherbourne are preschool programs, day camps and sports programs for children and fitness and yoga programs for adults. The beauty of this community centre is that it reflects the diversity of the community and kids of all races and colours go there. It's aesthetically pleasing, and for the condos built in the area, it's a draw, so that means privileged kids mingle with kids from lower-income families. Bringing together kids from different backgrounds is key to their working with each other as adults.

I also love the co-ops that have grown up in this area—many with gorgeous rooftop gardens where people come together. In these co-ops, many of the units are subsidized for qualified tenants while others are rented at full market value to those who can afford it. Tenants live side by side, regardless of the rate they pay, and no one need judge the other.

When Jack and I lived with Mike and Sarah and my mom in a co-operative at Dundas and Jarvis Streets—hookers' row, as some still call it today—Sarah, then a gorgeous fifteen-year-old, was sometimes approached. But we armed her with knowledge and confidence. We could have moved back to the much safer Annex neighbourhood where the kids had grown up, but we loved the downtown and we thought it was important to practise what we were preaching. Some of their friends' parents wouldn't let their sons and daughters come to our place for visits. Too dangerous, they said.

We didn't think so. In fact, what we felt at our co-op was a sense of community. The co-op was called Hazelburn, named after a nineteenth-century farm on the site that had tried to make a go of it raising hazelnut trees. Jack and I were among the first tenants. (We had each applied to the co-op—me with my mother and Jack with his children—shortly before we met, and not long after we met, he moved into an apartment on the tenth floor, and my mother and I moved into ours on the fifth.)

What distinguishes co-op housing is that it does away with the traditional landlord and lease arrangement. Hazelburn is a non-profit corporation, and anyone planning to live there must sign an occupancy agreement that outlines one's rights and responsibilities. A board of governors elected by the membership oversees administration, and a host of volunteer committees look after everything from maintaining the rooftop gardens to custodial arrangements and planning social events.

I remember cleaning the foyer of our building with Mike and Sarah along with children from other units. I saw it as a good experience for our kids. Certainly compared to some children in that co-op, they had come from a position of privilege. Why shouldn't they work with and play with children who came from other socio-economic backgrounds?

Both Jack and I paid full market rent for our apartments, while the rents of about half the other tenants were subsidized. When Jack and I married in 1988, I moved into his tenth-floor two-bedroom, for which we paid $1,200 in monthly market rent. My mom stayed on in our one-bedroom and I also paid market rent for her, around $750.

As a family, we paid close to $2,000 in combined rental fees in the late eighties. For that sum at the time, we could have rented a nice house with a backyard in a more child-friendly neighbourhood with an added bonus—my mother, our children, Jack and I all living under one roof. But we chose to stay and pay the price because Hazelburn was a model of co-operative living, and we loved it. The idea is to blend two populations: those able to pay a full rent share, and those who need help paying. No one in Hazelburn knew who paid full rent and who did not; it's when you isolate the fortunate and the less fortunate into separate housing that badges are pinned on people, the one saying "Look, I'm well to do" and the other saying "Look, I need a handout."

Unfortunately, our wonderful experience at Hazelburn was used against us when political opponents saw an opportunity to distort the facts and smear us with slanderous attacks. False accusations of our living in "subsidized social/government housing" were circulated—without mentioning that by paying full market rent in that co-op, we were actually subsidizing others. Our political opponents even organized hostile demonstrations in front of our building at the end of a school day, and harassed Sarah and Mike when they returned home from school. The self-appointed lynch mob sought to destroy the safe haven that Jack and I sought not just for our family but for the community. To this day, the slander is repeated by people who mistakenly believed it at the time—as well as by opponents who know better. But Jack and I were never deterred by lies and slander. We always lived our principles and were proud to do so.

I have called this chapter "In Search of Safe Shelter," and although I have always felt safe in my house on Huron Street, I can recall many times when home sweet home was less than sweet.

In our Hazelburn days, we had lived near a well-known strip club. A few years after we moved to Huron Street, we came to the aid of these women and others working in similar clubs. A small and courageous group of them complained that they were being forced to offer lap dances in backrooms where the word no was not always respected. These women came to us and said that they were dancers and strippers—not prostitutes—and that they, not the customers, should have control over their own bodies. So Jack and I launched a campaign to ban lap dances, which enraged some bar owners. After some intense campaigning, we were able to outlaw lap dancing in private rooms and the unwanted touching of dancers.

At the height of intense political debates, be they about housing, lap dancing or smoking in public places, we have always received hate mail—nasty, threatening letters. We have had demonstrations outside our home. We have even had rocks thrown through our windows—twice.

One Sunday morning we woke up to discover that we could not open our front and side doors no matter how hard we tried. After the initial shock subsided, we were able to leave the house by the back door leading out to our backyard. The front and side doors had been duct-taped shut and rigged with a cut garden hose so they would not open from the inside. A few days later, someone set our wood fence on fire—a fence that is right next to our *wood* house. Thankfully, a neighbour across the street, Mrs. Lee, spotted the smoke and urgently banged on our door. It so happened that Sarah was at home that afternoon, and together they doused the flames. No doubt someone was trying to send our family a message. But apart from reporting these incidents to the police, Jack and I never gave in to intimidation. We always felt that the best way to feel safe ourselves was to forge ahead and work to build safe communities offering safe shelter to all.

CHAPTER 13

Win Some, Lose Some

No political loss ever hit me as hard as that one did. I felt I had let Jack down, let our team down and let down the people of Trinity-Spadina. And Jack felt equally devastated.

During all the years I have been in elected office, some local residents have felt reluctant to ask me for assistance. I have always reminded them that they are my employers and that every few years, I would reapply for my job and they would have a chance to re-evaluate my performance. I have held elected office since 1985, and in all my municipal election campaigns, I received anywhere from 60 to 70 per cent of the vote.

In 1991, Metro Councillor Dale Martin stepped down in the same ward I represented as a school trustee, and I decided to run for his seat on the regional Metropolitan Toronto council (that was in Toronto's pre-amalgamation days). At the same time, Jack launched a campaign for mayor of Toronto, and we had high hopes of advancing progressive policies we had worked on for years. After a fierce and long nomination battle, and an election campaign, I became the first

Asian woman to achieve city-wide office when I won my election. But that victory was bittersweet, because while I won handily, Jack lost in his bid for mayor. That was my first real taste of defeat, and I felt it as keenly as if it had been my own.

When Liberal prime minister Paul Martin called an election in 2004, Jack had been leader of the NDP for close to two years, but had not yet had an opportunity to win a seat in Parliament. As he prepared for his first national campaign as leader, I saw an opportunity to make progress on the national stage on my career-long effort to better the lot of children, especially those living in poverty. I wanted to establish a national legislative framework and funding for a high-quality early learning and childcare program. So I tossed my hat into the ring and ran for the NDP in the riding of Trinity-Spadina. (Jack, meanwhile, ran in the riding of Toronto-Danforth, which he had represented on city council.)

Jack and I had high hopes for that election. We wanted to work together in Ottawa, as we had effectively for so many years in Toronto.

The Liberals, at this point, were in terrible shape and mired in scandal. Earlier in 2004, Auditor General Sheila Fraser had exposed corruption in a federal Liberal sponsorship program in Quebec, with abuse of public funds in federal government advertising. Paul Martin had established the Gomery Commission to look into the scandal, and it was very much in the headlines.

Closer to home, many of us felt that the Liberals, who held most of the seats in Toronto, had taken the city for granted. The city's waterfront was still looking stale, boring and shabby—despite many political photo opportunities and election promises of federal support. Thousands of desperate families were waiting for childcare or affordable housing, there was no employment strategy, and the federal government had done nothing to promote Toronto.

Trinity-Spadina was then held by Tony Ianno, the Liberal incumbent of eleven years and a man who hardly spoke in the House of Commons. (During the entire 393 sitting days of the 37th Parliament, he spoke only four times. He also owned a terrible attendance record, missing more than 70 per cent of his committee meetings.) So I thought we had a great opportunity, and over the years I had developed close working relationships with many neighbourhood and community groups in Trinity-Spadina. But the population base in the riding is constantly changing, as one-third of the residents move in and out each year. Connecting with newcomers, especially in the newly built condominium towers, was a challenge. And while many citizens knew of me as a progressive person, they didn't necessarily see me—or themselves—as a New Democrat. So I knew that winning the election would not be easy. But I was determined.

My campaign, managed by Bob Gallagher, moved into high gear. I love campaigns—I love canvassing, meeting people, strategy and passionate debate on issues that matter. I love the teamwork. I love the energy and the commitment of volunteers.

Our campaign team managed to attract supporters from across party lines, notably with a strong group of former Progressive Conservatives who had seen their party lose its progressive credentials (and name) when it merged with the Reform Conservative Alliance Party in 2003. One of these "Red Tories" was Kiloran German, a like-minded and passionate advocate for equal participation of women in politics. We had become allies and close friends on the original steering committee of Equal Voice, the multi-partisan organization dedicated to the advancement of women in elected office. Ironically, Kiloran had helped manage a campaign for a female Progressive Conservative candidate in Trinity-Spadina a decade earlier—losing to Tony Ianno—and she was determined to help me win.

So we seemed to have a groundswell of support, and I was buoyed by polls that put me well ahead of my political opponent. Indeed, I was faring better in the polls in my riding than Jack was in his, and there was some speculation that he might not win his seat. The odds were looking better for me.

But the local campaign was hard-fought, particularly on the ground. At the door, Ianno's team argued that if you liked having Olivia as your local councillor, you could keep her at city hall by voting for him as your MP.

Election day was exciting. On a beautiful morning in early summer, Jack and my mom and I voted at the polling station around the corner from our house. As the day wound down, I felt good, and I went to Jack's hotel to take him some fresh ties and catch up with him before the election-night events. The hotel visit was necessary: as party leader, Jack was assigned RCMP escorts during election campaigns, and he wasn't actually allowed to stay in our house until the election was over. And, as the spouse of the leader, I, too, had to be protected when I was with him.

Our election-night party was slated to take place at the convention centre, by the waterfront. I made a few more visits in the riding, did some media interviews and then went down to the Westin Harbour Castle hotel, where Jack's team had taken a suite to watch the election returns. I could see by the early returns that Jack's chances were looking good, which was a huge relief. The party had made some gains, and it looked like the Liberals would be held to a minority, which would give the NDP opportunities to influence legislation. But when the results from the condos in Trinity-Spadina started coming in, I could also see that I was in trouble. It became clear that these newcomers to the riding, who hadn't had a chance to get to know me or my work as a city councillor, were voting Liberal in order to stop the Conservatives from forming a government. I was winning in the other neighbourhoods in the riding, but my total number of votes and Ianno's were seesawing all night.

After an agonizingly long wait, and with my heart sinking and beating so fast that I could barely breathe, Bob Gallagher sent me the news through my BlackBerry: "It's over," he wrote. "Not this time." I had lost by less than 1.5 per cent—eight hundred votes. I had faced defeat before—against the same Tony Ianno, in 1997. And I know that losses go with the territory. But no political loss ever hit me as hard as that one did. I felt I had let Jack down, let our team down and let down the people of Trinity-Spadina. And Jack, who was taking calls from people across the country while finishing preparations for his speech, felt equally devastated. And he would soon have to make his way down to the convention centre, where the victory party was under way and the cameras were waiting.

I went on stage and lived Jack's moment with him while he gave a stirring speech. But he, too, was holding back tears as he left the stage. And later, after the cameras were gone and the crowds had thinned, I went out and spoke to my own team, thanking them for their wonderful work and encouraging them not to lose hope.

Jack had to be in Ottawa the next day, and I went home by myself to mope and cry. Bob and I went out for dinner at my favourite sushi restaurant, and it was the first time in my life I could not finish a dinner. I was in a state of shock and feeling a sense of loss on a scale I had not felt before. I was feeling guilty, I was second-guessing myself and I was feeling rejected. Bob and I watched some escapist movies to try to put this defeat out of our minds. Now I understood better how Jack had felt when he lost his mayoralty bid. In 1991, he lost and I won. Thirteen years later, our fortunes were reversed.

For a few days, I didn't want to venture out and face the public. But when I did, I found something astonishing. In the Annex, where I had earned the greatest support, I had people coming up to me and saying: "Olivia, so glad you are still here as our councillor!"

A number of my loyal supporters through the years had not voted for me—because they wanted me to stay put as their local councillor. I remember one constituent and supporter telling me that he'd prefer to see me getting the neighbourhood a beautiful park rather than have me tackle some abstract "make child poverty history" concept far away in Ottawa. I could understand that kind of thinking.

Another lesson from my defeat: even though it is difficult to connect with people who live in high-rises, I must try harder, must work smarter.

After the election, Jack and I spent some time sea kayaking out in British Columbia, near Port Hardy. One night we slept on the sidewalk outside the Nanaimo bus station because the bus was late and I was too cheap to rent a car or stay in a hotel for just a few hours. Those were beautiful and memorable moments spent together as we contemplated living a life miles apart and Jack travelling his political journey without me by his side.

Then I did what I have always done after a setback. I snapped out of my funk and went back to work as city councillor.

With Jack in the House of Commons in Ottawa and me at city hall in Toronto, we felt the separation keenly. He packed many of my photos into his small room in Ottawa, and I continued to live in our house on Huron Street. Well, at least our kids, my mom and the cat, Mauie, were with me in Toronto. In Ottawa, Jack chose to stay with his cousin Diane McIntyre, just as his dad had done when he was an MP. Even though we lived in two different cities, we were able to stay in touch by BlackBerry, discussing everything and anything, and he came home most weekends. And I focused on my work at city hall.

Just before the 2004 election was called, the Art Gallery of Ontario had announced an ambitious expansion plan. With the generous support of

Ken Thomson and his family, the AGO commissioned world-renowned architect Frank Gehry to design the expansion. Though based in Los Angeles, Gehry was born in the Grange neighbourhood where the AGO is situated. This was a coming-home project for him, and the expansion generated much excitement and anticipation—though not among the AGO's own neighbours.

In the early eighties, during a previous round of expansion, the gallery had promised the city that it would not expand any further. This new venture was seen as a betrayal. Neighbours argued that the proposed four-storey south wing was too massive for the area and that it would overshadow the park beside it. The disagreement between the AGO and its neighbours was acerbic and deeply felt, and the gap between the two sides was wide.

As the local councillor, I held a series of meetings at city hall so each side could hear the other out. When that didn't solve the disagreement, I asked the city to strike a committee that would have both sides work out solutions together. I chaired weekly meetings of this working group for several months (right through the 2004 election) and I did what I love best: brought opposite sides together and pushed them to listen to each other and find common ground and solutions. There followed intense negotiations, creative dialogue and a great deal of listening. Gehry's team was video-conferenced into one meeting, and neighbourhood residents passionately debated built form with one of the best architects in the world.

In the end, to minimize the perceived weight of that southern portion of the expansion, a blue tinted material was used so the building blended into the sky, giving it a much lighter feeling. Curved staircases, a Gehry signature, were added to provide a pleasing visual effect. Through the long and involved process, I felt, a better building was created.

The Art Gallery of Ontario also built tremendous goodwill with the neighbours by opening up the gallery to them and by participating in the beautification of Grange Park, which is right behind the gallery.

My campaign team was not happy with me for chairing these meetings during the election campaign, when I was supposed to be canvassing. But for me, finishing this project was important. I doubted it would have made any difference to the election results.

One of the highlights of 2005 for me was a very different kind of political campaign—my role on CBC Radio's fantastic *Canada Reads* series, an annual competition in which panellists promote and defend a favourite book as the must-read for Canadians. The only political figure, I was up against artists and writers—Donna Morrissey, Molly Johnson (subbing in for Rufus Wainwright), Roch Carrier and Sherraine MacKay.

My choice was Margaret Atwood's *Oryx and Crake*, a bleak view of a future dominated by pharmaceutical companies and genetic engineering, with manufactured viruses more or less wiping out the human race. Not particularly cheerful.

"Why?" That was the question my friends asked.

I had two reasons. First, Margaret Atwood is a great artist—one of the most important contemporary writers in the world, with extraordinary prescience and insight into the human condition. She also happens to be a fellow Torontonian, a constituent in Trinity-Spadina, someone who has helped put Toronto at the forefront as a centre for the arts and culture, and someone who has been a valiant champion of our libraries as a central feature of community life. I've been reading her books since my high school days. My second reason was that I saw *Oryx and Crake* in fact as a hopeful book.

"Why hopeful?" my friends asked. "It's hopeless! The end of the human race!"

"It's hopeful," I replied, "because it's showing us where we could go if we don't change. So it gives us an opportunity to wake up and change course." That, to me, is why art and artists matter to society, to culture, to political life. They help us see things differently. They inspire.

I love research and I always like to be prepared, so I approached the *Canada Reads* experience as I might prepare for a campaign debate—with briefing notes, role-playing, rehearsals and a dry run. I contacted friends (including Kiloran German and Jane Koster) who are voracious and critical readers and asked them each to play the part of one of my opponents. Then I staged a *Canada Reads* session up the street from my house at the Lillian H. Smith Library—part of our vital Toronto Public Library system and a wonderful community gathering place, with a great children's section.

To make it fun, I hosted a feast back at the house after the practice session, with food from each of the contending novels—fried chicken for *No Crystal Stair*, smoked fish for *Rockbound*, Montreal smoked meat for *Beautiful Losers*, chop suey for *Volkswagen Blues* and Thai green curry in honour of Oryx.

We had a great time—and I was pumped up for the series itself. I made it to the final round—where Donna Morrissey, a fabulous author from Newfoundland, prevailed with the obscure book *Rockbound*. Even though I didn't win, I loved every minute of the experience—particularly the opportunity of being able to talk about art and creativity as a political act.

After my defeat in the federal election, I returned to city council and there embarked on another one of my favourite initiatives—improving services for children. After years of focusing on early childhood education and care, I was mindful of launching programs that would help parents figure out what to do with their children after school.

There weren't enough after-school activities for six- to twelve-year-old children. Nor was there enough childcare support.

When I was a school trustee, I had created many after-school activities, but school boards are not supposed to deal with children after school. Activities after school are run by the City of Toronto. So in 2005, I persuaded the city to initiate a pilot project called the After-School Recreation Care—or ARC—program. Expert staff would hire young people with a skill to teach, then train them to become good leaders and teachers for young children. While providing safe, affordable sports, arts and other learning opportunities for children aged six to twelve, ARC would also train young people to nurture these children—especially young men, so they in turn would know how to nurture and teach children. Just as important, these young teachers would become role models and mentors to children—a counter to the gangs that were recruiting in some at-risk neighbourhoods. Not only would these young instructors (140 were hired) earn a decent hourly wage, they would also receive a credit from Seneca College towards their diploma. (The college continues to provide training, apprenticeship and education opportunities to workers in the program.)

The pilot projects were so successful that the City of Toronto has continued to run this service in many high-needs neighbourhoods. In 2008, the ARC programs received the Public Sector Quality Fair Gold Level Award. Today, close to one thousand children benefit from these services.

ARC was really the continuation of my First Duty project. Just as First Duty led to all-day kindergarten across Ontario, ARC was supposed to lead to after-school activities for all Ontario children from six to twelve. Charles Pascal, the Premier's Early Learning Advisor, had recommended that school boards be mandated to offer out-of-school-time programs for children aged four to twelve. Unfortunately, the

Ontario government's early learning initiative only covered children four and five years old, leaving out the rest.

Being in Toronto full-time had a side benefit: I finally had time to deal with some personal matters. A few years earlier, Jack had noticed a lump on my throat. I had some ultrasound tests and biopsies, and everything came back negative. But my doctor suggested that I should have a thyroidectomy to excise the lump. I did a lot of reading about thyroid cancer and I became convinced that since the lump was apparently benign, the excision was for cosmetic purposes only. So I put it off.

The lump became noticeable to others. A CTV cameraman noticed it on his viewfinder and warned me about it. Doctors likewise spotted the lesion on TV and called into my office, urging me to have the lump checked out. So finally, in the fall of 2004, I had the thyroidectomy—a relatively straightforward procedure. I had the surgery at Mount Sinai Hospital on a Thursday and was back to work at city hall on Monday. But then I got the news from my surgeon. I had cancer.

While Jack and I were shocked by the news, we were also very calm, since the growth had already been removed. We also knew that most thyroid cancers are very slow growing and are more treatable than most other kinds of cancer. So the next step involved taking a radioactive iodine pill—which meant being kept in an isolation unit at Mount Sinai for the weekend, since the treatment would actually make me radioactive. I passed the time by reading books. My main physical activity was skipping so I could sweat out the radioactive iodine.

After a few months, when it was clear that I remained cancer free and remission was well established, I learned a lot from my doctors and also the Thry'vors, or thyroid cancer survivors: that thyroid cancer is more common in women than in men, that many women don't get checkups for the disease and may not be aware of treatments and, finally, that there were few visible role models. Doctors suggested that an announcement from me could raise awareness of thyroid diseases, lower the fear of thyroid cancer and promote thyroid cancer research. I decided to go public with my story.

I was very touched by the response, particularly from the medical community and from cancer patients, who did indeed feel encouraged. They felt hope. I discovered new friends. Thyroid Cancer Canada gave out critically important information and support both to newly diagnosed patients and to those living with thyroid cancer. I greatly admire these volunteers' dedication and advocacy efforts. A common drug used in treatment, I would discover, is not covered by the government. Since then, I have occasionally joined the group's meetings and helped out with their fundraising activities.

Cancer is the great equalizer. It attacks indiscriminately, randomly and unexpectedly—often striking otherwise healthy individuals. No one is immune.

When the federal government fell to a motion of no confidence in November of 2005, I immediately resigned from city hall so I could focus on the task at hand—the election.

This time, I redoubled my efforts to ensure I wouldn't lose. I accompanied Jack for the launch of the election and for the leaders' debate, but I never strayed from Toronto. And a good thing, too, for the Liberals had targeted my riding. Astonishingly, Paul Martin took the time to campaign in Trinity-Spadina, not once but three times. Aggressive and negative tactics piled up. A political operative from another riding wrote a blog post in which he compared me to a chow chow dog. Apparently this dog and I were "separated at birth." Using one's ethnicity as the butt of a joke was not even remotely funny. It was offensive and reinforced negative stereotypes about Asians working like dogs.

But I stuck to the issues that mattered to the people of Trinity-Spadina—childcare, transit, housing, good jobs, our waterfront and support for the arts—all areas where we wanted to see leadership in Ottawa. And our organization on the ground was superb. Our team was leaving nothing to chance. Meanwhile, Jack ran a great national campaign.

On election day, January 23, 2006, we stayed focused. Again, Jack and my mother and I went to the polls, and then we went our separate ways. Oddly enough, I can't remember if I had dinner that night.

This time, the story unfolded more to our liking. Jack was re-elected by a wide margin, and the NDP gained ten new seats, including Trinity-Spadina. We had doubled our votes across Canada.

The streak of electoral good fortune has continued since then. Like his father, Mike Layton is a master of grassroots politics. He cares deeply about environmental and social issues; he likes people, and he has a knack for bringing people of different views together. So when, in December of 2009, it became apparent that there would be a city council vacancy in Mike's municipal ward in Trinity-Spadina, I was not surprised that he told Jack and me that he was interested in running.

Jack was thrilled, as was I. Mike had all the right skills and instincts. The challenge would be building and mounting a successful campaign in a very competitive downtown ward. It was here that Mike's long-time friend Joe Cressy arrived.

Jack and I had known Joe almost his entire life. Joe's parents, Gordon Cressy and Joanne Campbell, were well known community leaders in Toronto. Both had been elected to Metro and city councils and both had played active leadership roles in various organizations such as the United Way, the Urban Alliance on Race Relations and the Centre for Addiction and Mental Health. In fact, our connection with them extended back even further, as both Joanne and Jack had grown up in Hudson, Quebec.

But Joe Cressy is one of those people not known for living in the shadow of others, let alone his parents. Joe had been one of the youth leaders of the peace movement in the lead-up to the war in Iraq, and both Jack and I had taken notice of this young leader who we knew would go far. Over the years our paths continued to cross as Joe took on challenges near and far. Sometimes this work was in the NDP, but usually it was outside, in the world of non-governmental organizations. We took note as Joe did HIV and AIDS work in Ghana, anti-poverty work in South Africa, literacy work in Northern Ontario aboriginal communities and environmental organizing throughout Canada.

In December 2009, Mike showed up at our house with Joe, who had recently returned to Toronto to become a director with the Stephen Lewis Foundation. This was our first formal meeting to talk about Mike running for city council. Over the next ten months, Mike and Joe were joined at the hip. "They're kindred spirits," Jack used to say. With Mike out in the community earning every vote, Joe was in the background serving as his campaign chair and building a young and talented campaign team.

One of my favourite memories of that campaign goes back to the campaign kickoff event, where more than three hundred people packed Mike's campaign office. A few nights before, Mike, Joe, Bob Gallagher, Jack and I had been on a conference call talking about the need for a clever photo-op for the event.

"How about I give Mike my pair of canvassing boots?" suggested Jack. That was it! Jack would pass on to Mike his signature Blundstone boots—to send a signal that Mike was going to walk in his father's footsteps into Toronto city council and to convey the importance of earning every vote on the doorstep. It made for a great photo-op. Mike still wears Jack's canvassing boots, which apparently work quite well.

Mike won an overwhelming victory, with nearly 50 per cent of the vote. Jack and I couldn't have been more proud. Mike had arrived and won by doing what he does best—by bringing people together, focusing on the issues and working hard every single day.

As for Joe Cressy, since that election he has played an increasing leadership role in my own political career. He was my campaign chair for the 2011 federal election. He has also taken on a more active role in the NDP, serving on our elected federal council and acting as one of the party's most effective television pundits.

Joe is the kind of young leader we need in Canada. He's a strategic thinker and an extremely effective communicator, but above all else, he cares deeply about the issues. He is someone to watch.

CHAPTER 14

The Politics of Engagement

The press was in the council chambers, cameras running. The mayor was furious, especially because the huge screen on which the Simpsons *excerpt was played overlooked his chair. We lost that vote, but eventually the Adams Mine proposal died. Homer Simpson, as it were, to the rescue.*

I learned early on in politics that you have to find creative ways to tell your story and to gain media attention.

One of my favourite examples of creative political expression dates from 2000, when Jack and I and many others were trying to stop a plan to ship the city's garbage to the abandoned Adams Mine, south of Timmins in Northern Ontario. The abandoned open-pit iron mine stretched over sixteen square kilometres, and the plan was to transport garbage by train to the mine site and dump it there—for the next twenty years. The security of the local water supply was just the first of many concerns. The whole saga is brilliantly told by Charlie Angus—the musician and current federal NDP MP for Timmins–James Bay. In his book *Unlikely Radicals*, he describes how First Nations people, farmers, environmentalists, miners, retirees and volunteers formed an alliance to stop the dubious plan.

Toronto city council was mostly supportive of the plan, so our camp faced an uphill battle. But shortly before a crucial vote, the Layton family came up with the perfect way to capture the public's imagination and turn the tide against the mine. Mike was a devoted fan of *The Simpsons*, and every Sunday night all of us—Mike, Sarah, Jack and I—would sit down to enjoy the antics of Homer Simpson.

One night, as we sat around the dinner table talking about the upcoming Adams mine vote at city hall, there was a wait-a-minute moment.

Jack turned to Mike and asked, "Wasn't there a *Simpsons* episode about something like this?"

"There was," replied Mike. "Homer was put in charge of garbage and he put it in some sort of mine."

Thus ensued this scene on the day of the vote. For a full meeting of council, a few hundred people from Northern Ontario had jammed the chambers to witness the vote. Some of them had camped in Jack's office or at our house on Huron Street. The night before the vote, I quietly huddled with the audiovisual technician at city hall. I wanted no glitches. Like every other councillor, I had been given ten minutes to speak on the garbage issue, and my plan was to devote seven minutes of that time to a key part of *Simpsons* episode number 200—"Trash of the Titans" (which won an Emmy Award for Outstanding Animated Program).

In it, our bumbling hero Homer Simpson, after complaining about trash collection, manages to get himself named sanitation engineer for the community of Springfield, and he decides to bulldoze his trash into an abandoned mine—to disastrous effect. Garbage starts popping up out of holes in the ground, especially after other cities are invited to send their garbage as a way of bringing new income to counter Homer's overspending. He gets fired, and the town becomes an environmental disaster and has to be moved . . . It was perfect.

The press was in the council chambers, cameras running. The mayor was furious, especially because the huge screen on which the excerpt was played overlooked his chair. We lost that vote, but the other side eventually succumbed to our poison pills (a long list of amendments that made the plan unworkable for its proponents). Eventually the Adams Mine proposal died.

Homer Simpson, as it were, to the rescue.

You may think that the House of Commons is all about table thumping and "Hear! Hear!"-ing. There is a lot of that, but sometimes there is also intrigue, and that was certainly the case in May 2005, when the minority Liberal government under Paul Martin required NDP support if it had any chance of staying in power. A deal was struck between the Liberals and the NDP, and the result was a budget that had NDP (and Jack Layton) written all over it.

The drama had started in the spring, when there was talk of an early election being forced in the wake of testimony at the Gomery Commission, which focused on the Liberal government's misuse of taxpayers' dollars. The scandalous sponsorship program, you may remember, was an ad campaign meant to highlight the contributions of the government of Canada to the Quebec economy—a counter-narrative to the one being offered in that province by the Parti Québécois, which sought an independent Quebec. But spending irregularities were uncovered, and it looked like this could bring down the government. There was a growing sense that the Liberals had lost the moral authority to govern.

In a bold move, Jack Layton went on live television to say he was open to supporting the Liberals' budget, thereby keeping the government alive, if the budget could be made acceptable. His was an offer the prime minister found intriguing—and impossible to resist.

The Liberals were scrambling to stay in power. They held fewer than half the seats in the House, and their first budget that year was at first supported by the Conservatives and then rejected by them—as it already had been by the Bloc Québécois and the NDP. The Liberals desperately needed the NDP's support to stay in power.

Those four days in May resulted in what many later called "the first NDP budget" at the federal level—or "the Layton budget."

Jack called me one day, excitement in his voice. "We might get a budget deal with the Liberals," he told me. "I've put $4.6 billion of corporate tax cuts in play. Instead of giving that away to big corporations that don't need any help from the government, help me figure out how to invest it where it should go." Both Jack and I deplored these gifts to corporations, for they came at the expense of less fortunate Canadians and their children. We had both spoken out many times against such tax cuts. Here was our chance to spend the funds differently.

From the financial documents of our previous election platform, I pulled together a list of priorities. The wish list totalled $4.6 billion and was broken down like this: $1.6 billion for affordable housing construction (including aboriginal housing), a $1.5-billion increase in transfers to the provinces to reduce tuition, $900 million for the environment (with one more cent of the federal gas tax going to public transit), $500 million for foreign aid (to bring us in line with promises that Canada had already made) and $100 million for a pension protection fund that would offer compensation to workers should a company go bankrupt.

I look back on that time and I see it as a perfect example of Jack and me working together to get something accomplished. He sought my advice and I gave it. With Jack coming up with the ideas and me working on numbers, and with NDP negotiators wrestling with their Liberal counterparts over the course of four long days, we amended the federal budget—one that meant a $4.6-billion boost to the people who needed it most.

That was the deal we were proposing; now the deal had to be sealed. It was agreed that the venue for negotiations would be a suite at the Royal York Hotel in downtown Toronto.

On a Thursday, Jack gathered his negotiating team: the NDP's House leader, Libby Davies, and Bob Gallagher, his chief of staff. Those three were to meet with Prime Minister Paul Martin; his party's chief of staff, Tim Murphy; and his party's House leader, Tony Valeri. But before that meeting, Jack et al. met to pore over the spreadsheets and to confirm the numbers by double-checking them against our previous election platform costing sheets.

Meanwhile, word had leaked to the media that the two sides were meeting at the Royal York, and reporters had staked out positions at all the main entrances. But neither Jack nor Paul Martin wanted to walk that gauntlet. For his part, Jack didn't want the distraction. Martin, meanwhile, recognizing that a deal was more likely if his finance minister was *not* there to throw wrenches into the works, had not invited the minister. But the prime minister did not want that exclusion broadcast—for this, too, would distract the negotiators.

Martin's team was staying at the hotel, so they were safe. But how to get Jack's team into the Royal York Hotel without being spotted? Jack knew a way. He had attended many fundraising functions in that hotel, and invariably he would wander into the kitchen after the dinner to thank the staff. That was his style. He always thanked the kitchen and serving staff, not from a stage or from behind a lectern but face to face in the place where the workers worked with their sleeves rolled up and their aprons on. Not only did my husband as a cyclist know just about every back laneway in the city, he knew the back ways into many hotels through the employees' entrance. So Jack led Libby and Bob into the hotel's kitchen and up a back elevator into what Libby Davies remembers as "Martin's fancy suite," where the prime minister and his cohorts sat down to negotiate.

"They looked tense and nervous," Libby remembers. "Our job was to make this all feel normal and doable. Keep it cool." Paul Martin had dreamed of being the prime minister for a long time, and it looked like that ambition was in tatters—unless he could pull an iron out of the fire.

All details, of course, were hammered out at the eleventh hour. Negotiations started that Thursday, and the deal was announced the following Tuesday. What Libby Davies and Bob Gallagher remember is how the talks started with huge unease on the Liberal side, followed by a growing confidence that a deal could be struck—especially because our side had specific numbers and specific programs in mind, ones that were easy to sell to the public because they were so popular.

Layton and Martin established the framework at the first meeting. Jack was firm and specific: there were $4.6 billion in corporate tax giveaways, so all those would be turned into social and environmental investments that Canadians believed in and had been asking for. When Martin saw the specificity and insistence of Jack's position (knowing he had precious little time left for this government), he agreed, and Jack and he left the details to be worked out by the negotiators.

With the outline established, Valeri, Murphy, Davies and Gallagher had but a few days to come up with an agreement. Libby and Bob's tactic was to constantly remind their counterparts that virtually all their requests had been promised by the Liberals at one time or another.

Tension rose as the Tuesday deadline that Jack had set came closer. And as if there wasn't enough inherent drama that weekend, more came our way. That's because, true to form, the negotiation wasn't the only item on our plate.

With Peter Tabuns (then policy director in Jack's office and today an MPP) at the wheel, Jack and I set off for Cobourg, in southeastern Ontario. The occasion was a fundraiser for the Northumberland–Quinte West NDP riding, honouring the legendary author Farley Mowat. Jack and I were then going to attend a birthday party in Port Hope in honour of Dorothy Thomas, an old friend and a former Toronto councillor who was gravely ill. Many of Dorothy's old friends and neighbours were gathering at Bloomsbury, the grand Port Hope home of our mutual friends Kiloran German and Elizabeth Fowler, with Dorothy and her son participating by phone from a Toronto hospital.

En route we got a call from Kiloran with the news that a plastics factory in Cobourg had burst into flames and half the town had been evacuated. At that point, the fundraiser was relocated to Bloomsbury, and Jack and I arrived an hour or so early—with an entourage. We were being followed by a CBC van, a CTV van and a reporter from the *Toronto Star*—and all those journalists set up in the living room as Jack did interviews to offer updates on the budget negotiations. CBC and CTV then took off for Cobourg to film the fire (the blaze and the negotiations were the two top stories on the news that day), and Jack and I headed upstairs to the master bedroom, where Jack stayed in constant touch by phone with Bob and Libby. Meanwhile, the fundraiser continued in the Great Hall below. It was quite a party, by the way, with Farley Mowat in his kilt and in fine form.

Finally, on the following Tuesday, Jack called a press conference to announce the details while I was still hammering out precise wording for the pension protection fund. Jim Stanford, an economist with the Canadian Auto Workers union, was picking up his child at a Toronto daycare when I finally reached him on his cell phone. He pondered my questions and came up with wording for that final piece.

Once the deal was sealed with the negotiating team, Jack was going to announce it at the televised press conference in Ottawa. However, he could announce nothing without the agreement in writing. Confirmation in e-mail from Tony Valeri that the deal was good had yet to come.

Before we knew it, the press conference was about to begin. Bob Gallagher was in Toronto with Libby Davies, who in turn was on the phone with Valeri. "Get him to say yes!" Bob was shouting to Libby as Jack approached the podium. Bob, for his part, was on his cell phone with Karl Bélanger, Jack's senior press secretary, who was also at that press conference. We got Valeri's e-mail moments before Jack started speaking. Bob conveyed that news to Karl, who gave Jack a big thumbs-up, and Jack was all smiles as he got to the podium. Whereupon we all heaved a huge sigh of relief!

This is what was sweet about the deal reached that day. Yes, we were tolerating a scandal-ridden government (one that finally tumbled later that year), but at the same time we had enabled the largest single transfer of money back into social programs that the House of Commons had seen in twenty years.

The negotiations also showed that the NDP was quite capable of negotiating and that we could handle power and finances wisely and responsibly. We did not ask for the moon. We were practical and specific. A small political party had created an enormous social benefit while calling attention to Liberal corporate tax cuts that would have robbed the public purse.

Further, the transfer of funds for transit systems was based not on a per capita basis, as had been done in the past, but on the number of transit riders in a city. This was a special boost for Toronto, with its huge numbers of public transit users, and it allowed the city to buy desperately needed subway cars. (One upside of the crushing loss I had suffered while vying for a federal seat in 2004 was that I then became vice-chair of the Toronto Transit Commission and was part of procuring the contract for those new "built in Ontario" subway cars.)

Finally, the talks—as Libby Davies later put it—"showed Jack Layton as a real player."

"This was a time," Bob Gallagher says, "when Canadians were focused on federal politics. The weight of what we were doing was felt in that room at the Royal York. We realized that this was a key moment in history. We were negotiating for things that we would not normally get from a Liberal government. The Liberals had *talked* about doing these kinds of things in the past, but they hadn't done them. Now we were holding their feet to the fire."

Negotiating with the Liberals in this way was not without risk. Had they walked away from the table, we would have been seen as trying but failing.

Voting on the budget in the House of Commons ended in a tie, broken when Speaker of the House Peter Milliken voted in favour of it. And although the Liberals took a long time to implement the deal, and though the Conservatives tried to back out of certain parts of the package when they formed a minority government the following year, the deal was locked in. So the benefit was lasting. In my hometown Toronto, I came across people who were finally living in newly built affordable housing. As a country, we had not built any affordable units since the national housing program was eliminated in the mid-nineties, leading to massive homelessness and contributing to deep poverty.

~

In late 2008, Anne McGrath, a long-time party stalwart, was mulling over an offer to become chief of staff for Jack, who was leader of the federal New Democrats. She was, for the moment, his interim chief of staff, but would she take on the job full-time? Jack was waiting for her at La Strada, a fine Italian restaurant and long a favourite dining destination in Ottawa of those who fight under the orange banner.

Anne was not yet at the restaurant when she made up her mind. She would take the job. Indeed, she was perfect for the job. A former activist in the student movement, the labour movement and the women's movement, she had worked previously for the Canadian Union of Public Employees and Oxfam Canada and was at that time president of the federal New Democratic Party. Anne is extremely smart and supremely organized.

Jack and Anne talked briefly before Anne shook hands with her new boss. Anne didn't realize that Jack had a much bigger decision on their table at that Bank Street restaurant. That afternoon, the Harper government had presented an economic update that totally ignored the recession then facing Canada.

"What an opportunity" were the first words out of Jack's mouth. Then he said, "Let's think outside the box here." A coalition government—almost unprecedented in Canadian history—was what he had in mind.

This was Anne's welcome to her new job. The room began to spin just a little, but not from the wine. Anne would be Jack's chief of staff for almost three more years after this point, and she would learn to adopt what she calls "the rule of three." Jack had so many ideas, some sustainable and some not, but if he came back to an idea three times, she knew he was serious. This night he was serious from the get-go when he instructed her, "Call the Liberals." He meant, let's start negotiating with all the other opposition parties, because if all could agree on a power-sharing agreement, we could boot out Stephen Harper and the Tories.

The phones started ringing. I was called to join the dinner. Libby Davies, the NDP House leader, was called. Party strategist Brian Topp was called. That very night, Jack's office on the tenth floor of 131 Queen Street became HQ. On one wall hung an obituary of Jack's father, and in one corner sat a bust of Tommy Douglas—two reminders of Jack's roots.

What had triggered this sudden burst of adrenaline was a Tory "fiscal update" (or "the FU," as some later called it). Tabled the day before in the House of Commons, the document enraged opposition parties on several counts. First of all, the global economy was reeling from a recession, and many Western governments had already launched stimulation packages to get their economies back on track. But the fiscal update contained no stimulus spending. The Tories were as much as saying, "What recession?" The fiscal update also destroyed pay equity (which allowed female workers to earn the same as their male counterparts for doing jobs of similar value), banned civil service strikes and ended public financing for political parties according to how they performed in elections. Anne called the latter move "a poison pill," and it was one that the NDP, the Liberals, the Bloc Québécois and the Green Party would all oppose.

Politics is sometimes a game of brinksmanship, and the Tories had gambled that the Liberals posed no threat. The Liberals' leader, Stéphane Dion, was on the ropes, and the party was looking for another saviour. The last thing the Grits wanted was an election. What the Conservatives had not counted on, however, was Jack's bold move to oust them, not by going to the polls but by forming a coalition government. Too late, the Tories withdrew the most contentious clauses of the bill. And because the bill was a money bill—and therefore open to a confidence vote—opposition parties had a choice: accept the bill or bring down the government. Then what? That was the question.

We all started working the phones, and sleeping and eating took a back seat to collective action. Each side brought in the vets. The Liberals called in former prime minister Jean Chrétien and our side brought in Allan Blakeney (the former NDP premier of Saskatchewan) and Ed Broadbent (the former national NDP leader). Our lead negotiators were Dawn Black (a veteran and well-respected member of Parliament) and Brian Topp (a top-notch and experienced negotiator). We definitely had the A-team working for us.

This was a very exciting, very charged time. But, as often happens in these times, you find something to laugh at. Anne McGrath was with Ed Broadbent, who had been chatting with Jean Chrétien as the two parties haggled over some pretty important issues. Who would be the prime minister in this coalition? How many cabinet posts would go to the NDP? Ed had written Chrétien's telephone number on a newspaper, which he had left back at his apartment. Now a staffer was dispatched to collect it. Meanwhile, Ed's cell phone was ringing and he was frantically searching for it (it was buried in a briefcase). Was it Chrétien? Too late—the call was missed.

"Not to worry," Anne told Ed. "We can push the 'last caller' button and retrieve the number."

Ed looked at her in astonishment. "You can *do* that?" he asked. Ed was seventy-two years old at this point, and apparently some of the finer points of modern technology had passed him by.

In the end, Stéphane Dion and all Liberal MPs, and Gilles Duceppe and his Bloc Québécois, agreed to support the coalition on confidence motions for the next eighteen months. We agreed on cabinet posts and we agreed on a $30-billion stimulus package for the softwood lumber and auto industries, along with money for infrastructure, childcare and post-secondary education. This was an extraordinary and unprecedented moment in Canadian history.

For my part, I was ratcheting up support for the coalition. In an op-ed piece in Toronto's *NOW* magazine on December 2, 2008, I wrote: "Last week, Canadians looked to Ottawa for leadership. Canadians need hope and want cooperation between parties. Economists and business leaders advised bold action. But instead of an economic plan, or cooperation, Mr. Harper delivered an ideological plan to sell off public buildings, kill off opposition parties and roll back the rights of workers and women." I urged everyone to come to a rally at Nathan Phillips Square on December 6 or to attend one of eighteen town hall meetings like it being organized all across the country.

In my article, I pointed out that 62 per cent of Canadians had not voted for the Conservatives. "We are at a remarkable crossroads in our shared history as Canadians," I wrote. "You are the majority. Be part of the change."

On that bitterly cold Saturday, several thousand people came to the rally at city hall to hear Jack Layton and Stéphane Dion, along with comedian Mary Walsh and singer Feist.

After the three leaders signed the accord, Jack Layton urged Prime Minister Stephen Harper "to accept this gracefully." In the House of Commons, a furious Harper accused the Liberals of recklessness and of wanting to give veto power to "socialists and separatists." The Tories quite cleverly reframed the key question. For us in the NDP, the question was: Should the coalition replace a government that had lost the confidence of the House of Commons? The Tories turned the question on its head: Do you want the Bloc Québécois governing Canada?

On December 4, Harper advised Governor General Michaëlle Jean to prorogue, or suspend, Parliament. She had a choice: she could allow the coalition to proceed or she could do the unexpected—allow the prorogation. One of Harper's ministers had called the coalition "irresponsible and undemocratic." But what could be more undemocratic than padlocking Parliament?

All day long the TV cameras focused on the grand door of Rideau Hall. Jack and I were dumbfounded when Michaëlle Jean finally announced that Parliament was being prorogued.

Jack and I went on holiday at Christmas. By that time, Michael Ignatieff had replaced Stéphane Dion as the leader of the Liberal Party of Canada, and during that time we were clinging to the belief that Ignatieff would continue to support the coalition since, before it was announced, he, along with all Liberal MPs, had signed a letter agreeing to the coalition. When we returned to Ottawa, Jack spent all of January trying to reach Ignatieff and convince him of the merits of working together. But when Harper came back in January with a stimulus package, the Ignatieff-led Liberals supported it, and our Coalition for Change was officially toast.

What had Ignatieff been afraid of? Perhaps he feared the New Democrats more than the Conservatives. He could not imagine a better country run by the joint force of the Liberals and the New Democrats. While Jack was pouring all his energy into bringing about a progressive government, Ignatieff thought he could do it alone, without the support of other parties.

For many years, Brixton's, a British pub on Sparks Street in Ottawa, has been the NDP watering hole of choice—especially on Wednesday evenings, when Alexander Keith's India Pale Ale is the drink of choice. Late in December of 2008, we had retired to Brixton's to celebrate finishing the coalition document, the culmination of countless hours of work. Late in January of 2009, we went back to Brixton's, but this time to drown our sorrows.

I remember Jack coming to the caucus in the wake of that vote, putting on a brave face and saying something positive. In fact, he was furious—and hugely disappointed. He lamented what he called a victory for the triumph of fear and the politics of mean. Mean-spirited, that is.

I look back on the coalition that wasn't and I see another lost opportunity. On the other hand, I think that the forming of the coalition forced Harper to introduce an economic stimulus package that wouldn't otherwise have seen the light of day. The coalition also put the NDP at centre stage and in many ways prepared the way for the 2011 campaign in which we surpassed the Liberals in an unprecedented election.

Jack kept on saying as the coalition formed, "Let's work together to get something done." That thinking resonated with Canadians, especially in Quebec, where his "*Travaillons ensemble*" message found a ready audience.

CHAPTER 15

The Redress Express

As old friends got off the train—some from Vancouver, others from Toronto—we hugged and shed tears and held our heads high. I felt and shared a sense of wonder, pride and joy.

My first true encounter with the Chinese head tax—that distasteful episode in Canadian history—occurred when I got a summer job in 1977 working on a slide show that documented the history of the Chinese in this country. Later, while working in MP Dan Heap's office, I came face to face with some of the elderly Chinese workers who had come to Canada to build the Canadian Pacific Railway in the latter part of the nineteenth century.

Some fifteen thousand Chinese were brought to Canada as a source of cheap labour. The work was both backbreaking and dangerous, especially when mountain passes were dynamited to make way for the rail line. More than a thousand Chinese labourers died. Many workers who had gone back to China when the railway was finished then wanted to return; still others had stayed and wanted to bring their wives and children to Canada.

That hope was crushed as the federal government, responding to growing anti-Chinese sentiments, singled out Chinese immigrants and imposed a $50 immigration fee through the Chinese Immigration Act of 1885. This so-called head tax kept rising, and by 1903 it stood at $500 (equivalent to the price of a house at the time). That act was replaced in 1923—but not because the government had come to its senses and realized that the legislation was racist and exclusionary. On the contrary, the Chinese Immigration Act of 1923 was aimed at stopping Chinese immigration entirely, and in that it pretty well succeeded. By this time, some eighty-one thousand mostly male Chinese immigrants had paid the head tax, enriching federal government coffers by some $23 million, or $300 million in today's dollars.

In 1947, after Chinese Canadians had fought alongside other Canadians during the Second World War, that hideous act was at last repealed. In 1983, Dan Heap's NDP colleague MP Margaret Mitchell started pushing the federal government to formally apologize and provide redress to those who had paid the head tax. As Dan's constituency assistant, I met more than two hundred of them at his office as they showed me their "head tax certificates," and I was told many sorrowful stories about fathers who had been separated from their children and wives for decades and who had toiled long hours for years so they could save the $500 needed to bring their families to Canada.

There were other stories, too, of fathers having to make terrible decisions—which child to bring to Canada and which one to leave behind in China because the father could not afford more. And the stories of the wives who finally made it to Canada only to see their elderly husbands soon pass away. I remember the faces of these aged men and women who entrusted their stories to me in the hope that justice, finally, would be done. For decades, and to any who would listen, I had been recounting their stories of suffering. Families torn apart. Men separated from their loved ones for decades and forced to live a lonely life in Canada. Wives who endured tremendous hardship raising their children alone, and children deprived of their fathers. All because they were Chinese.

"But why not the Irish?" these seniors would ask me. "Why not the Italians or any other European immigrants?" These elderly Canadians of Chinese descent asked me this question because, to them, I represented "the government." I still remember the hope in their eyes as I talked about our campaign to seek redress, to have the government finally apologize for this historical wrong.

During more than two decades, successive Canadian governments had refused to apologize for this racist and discriminatory policy, or to offer redress to the remaining head tax payers. Brian Mulroney's Progressive Conservative government had offered a program commemorating the contribution of Chinese Canadians in building the CPR, but no apology or redress. Jean Chrétien's Liberal government ignored the issue. Paul Martin's Liberal government supported a commemorating program but also shied away from either a formal apology in the House of Commons or any offer of redress.

Nevertheless, the Chinese Canadian National Council never gave up, nor did the families of head tax payers, nor did New Democrats. In a way, we knew that achieving redress would affect very few people directly—many head tax payers had died waiting for justice. But in another way, those of us working on this campaign knew that the formal apology would and should affect all Canadians—not just Chinese Canadians—because it would be an affirmation of the right of all citizens to be treated equally under the law. Yes, we wanted to see redress for the remaining few. But even more, we wanted to see Canada acknowledge that barring immigrants to this country based on their race was wrong. A racist immigration policy should not be tolerated, and unless we learn from history, such policies could return in times of economic downturn or social unrest.

We were adamant: the pain and suffering of all these men, women and children must be acknowledged formally and publicly in the House of Commons. The Canadian Pacific Railway had united our country, and the contribution of Chinese migrant workers must be recognized. Canada must learn that institutionalized racism in the form of immigration policy must not be repeated in this magnificent country of ours.

As the leader of the New Democrats, Jack made it clear that the party would never give up the fight for redress. Gilles Duceppe of the Bloc Québécois also pledged support.

During the 2006 federal election campaign, an NDP TV ad, written in Chinese by the descendants of head tax payers, focused squarely on the tax and the importance of achieving both an apology and redress. Although the Liberals still didn't budge, Stephen Harper of the Conservatives seized the opportunity and promised his support for redress. With Harper's first minority government, we realized that we had a window of opportunity. And by now, I was a member of Parliament.

There was a clear signal in the Speech from the Throne that opened Parliament in 2006—a simple line, spoken in the Senate Chamber by Governor General Michaëlle Jean: "The Government will act in Parliament to offer an apology for the Chinese Head Tax."

While recognizing that this was an unprecedented commitment, none of us in the front lines of this fight wanted to risk delay. We wanted to see justice done at last. Only a handful of those who had paid the head tax were still alive, and we wanted them to live to see the day.

A few days later, and twenty-three years after I heard those stories in Dan Heap's office, I rose in the House of Commons to give my maiden speech—and I drove the point home. I spoke about the history of the Chinese in Canada and described the injustice they had endured. I repeated the demands with questions during Question Period, and I moved a motion in the House of Commons. And Jack brought it up with Stephen Harper during their occasional meetings.

I continued to work with the Chinese Canadian National Council to pressure the government to act, and to act properly and promptly. Together we mapped out how the apology and redress would be staged, while community leaders such as Dr. Joseph Wong worked behind the scenes. We wanted to ensure that this historic event had its moment—the sense of occasion and dignity that was so richly deserved.

There was no time to delay, and this wonderful network of people quickly organized the "Redress Express"—a train journey for some remaining head tax payers and their spouses, along with the leaders of this long, hard campaign through its many decades. Margaret Mitchell, the New Democrat MP who had been the first to stand up in the House on this issue twenty-one years beforehand, went with the few survivors to the train station in Vancouver. And then the Redress Express travelled east, over the railway built by thousands of Chinese workers in the nineteenth century.

Whenever I go to the Ottawa station to take a train back home to Toronto, I think of the incredible, long hoped-for moment when the Redress Express rolled into the station on the last leg of a decades-long journey. As old friends got off the train—some from Vancouver, others from Toronto—we hugged and shed tears and held our heads high. I felt and shared a sense of wonder, pride and joy.

And then, the next day, on June 22, 2006—just a few months after I took my seat as an MP, the prime minister of Canada stood in the House of Commons and said: "On behalf of all Canadians and the Government of Canada, we offer a full apology to Chinese Canadians for the head tax and express our deepest sorrow." Harper referred to "the shameful policies of our past" and vowed that his government would strive to ensure that similar unjust practices are never allowed to happen again.

I felt enormous pride, and for all kinds of reasons: I was part of the Chinese-Canadian community, I was a New Democrat and I was a member of Parliament. I felt enormous pride in Jack, for he had been relentless in his pursuit of justice through the years. And I felt enormous pride in being a Canadian.

There was a recognition that we, as a Parliament, had done something that we should do. What we were elected to do. We had bowed in recognition that there are no second-class citizens in Canada. And it was, therefore, a victory for anyone who had ever been subjected to discrimination in our country.

As I read Jack's words in Hansard today, I am still moved: "This is a momentous first step toward achieving full justice, reconciliation and closure to right the historical wrong of the head tax that has been a stain on our national conscience for a century . . . The next step should be the action that would give full meaning to these words: full justice, full reconciliation, and full closure to all of those who suffered from this racist and unjust policy. That step would entail redress that is more than symbolic, redress to the descendants of the head tax payers who died waiting for this day."

"Symbolic" payments of $20,000 were paid to surviving head tax payers or their widows and a community program was put in place to commemorate this terrible history so it would not be repeated. However, the descendants were unjustly excluded from the redress package, even though sons and daughters of these head tax payers were also severely affected by this exclusionary immigration act.

My riding of Trinity-Spadina is a very diverse one, in the most diverse city in Canada. At our constituency office in Kensington Market, our team spends a great deal of time helping people with immigration issues.

Among the most heartbreaking stories we hear are those from people who have been exploited by phony or ruthless immigration consultants. These include "ghost consultants" who take money to assist people but who sign no documents and leave no fingerprints. Promising speedy application approval and family reunification, they prey on vulnerable people, raising hopes and shattering dreams.

When I was Dan Heap's assistant in the early eighties, I was already seeing the harm being done. Canadian immigrants—who sometimes understood neither our system nor our language—were being fleeced by some unscrupulous immigration lawyers and consultants who ripped them off financially and left them subject to deportation.

Enter Victor Malarek, the Canadian journalist and author in whose *Bully* documentary I would briefly appear, and who today is a senior reporter with CTV's *W5*. But back in 1984, he was an investigative reporter with *The Globe and Mail* and he had embarked on a series of articles that would examine the exploitation of illegal immigrants.

Victor had been avidly pursuing the predators and exposing much of the corruption. I shared the same goals, so he and I discussed ways of getting the inside story. We came up with a perfect plan.

We needed an undercover agent—someone who could make appointments with crooked consultants and get them to reveal their fraudulent claims and schemes. Someone we could wire with a body pack so we could capture the revelations on tape. Someone who was credible. Ideal would be a middle-aged Chinese immigrant woman who spoke little English. Someone who was smart, resourceful, courageous. Someone who was aware of the issue and cared about the outcome.

Someone like . . . my mom!

Mom and I would sit at the table in my basement flat in Kensington Market while planning and rehearsing with Victor. It felt like a scene from one of my childhood fantasy games. *Mission: Impossible,* once played out on our rooftop in Happy Valley, was now being plotted in our kitchen and played out in offices across the city—some swanky, and some in sleazy little walk-ups. Victor and I coached and grilled my mother.

"Don't worry," she would say. "Don't worry—I know. I'll get them." My mother loved this. She would be working with me on a project that held out the promise of effecting change. And indeed that promise was met.

My mother's undercover work produced a wealth of material, and Victor used it well. (She and the other actors were never named in the articles.) My mother must have been tempting bait for unscrupulous lawyers unaware that she was attached to a very sharp hook. That's because the advice they sometimes offered for fees as high as $5,000 was available for free from the constituency office where I worked—and often in less time.

Hoping that Victor would have memories of this time to flesh out my own, I invited him for dinner one evening in the spring of 2013. My mother remembered him, of course, and the two co-conspirators greeted each other warmly.

Victor remembers me working for Dan Heap at the time and meeting my mother and me at Heap's office in Toronto. That office was the headquarters for this little operation: wiring people and sending them off to meet with six immigration lawyers. The trick was to let the lawyers lead. Our actors had to stick to the script.

"I'm illegal. What do I do?"

And the answer would come: "Claim refugee status."

"But I'm not a refugee," my mother or the other undercovers would reply.

And the response to that was invariably, "First give me five thousand dollars."

The tapes, Victor recalls, were incredible. One immigration consultant was clean. The other five were dirty.

Of course the stories were scrutinized very carefully by *The Globe and Mail*'s libel lawyers before they were published. And of course lawyers working for the consultants named in the series threatened to sue. One of them called Victor, and the exchange went something like this:

"I'm suing you."

"Go ahead. Have a field day. But your guy said what he said and did what he did."

"You better be able to prove it."

"Listen to this tape." And as Victor retold that story over dinner at my house, he mimed turning on a tape recorder and putting it next to the phone. Then he mimed the lawyer putting down the receiver. "The lawyer never called back."

Victor's exposé ignited outrage and raised awareness, but we saw no action from the governments of Pierre Trudeau, John Turner, Brian Mulroney, Kim Campbell, Jean Chrétien or Paul Martin. Over the years, I pursued the issue, but the abuses continued.

The problem was that immigration consulting was unregulated. Anyone could hang out a shingle and claim to be a consultant, with no oversight. Immigration lawyers were subject to the oversight and discipline of the Canadian Bar Association, but that wasn't the case with consultants. And while there were, and are, many good consultants doing honest work and legitimately helping people, there were many others who were not. And the people they exploited had no protection from the law.

Finally, in 1996, the Standing Committee on Citizenship and Immigration in the Chrétien Liberal government issued a report on consultants who are not lawyers—but there was no follow-up for legislation or oversight.

In 2003, Immigration Minister Denis Coderre announced the establishment of the Canadian Society of Immigration Consultants. This was supposed to be a regulatory body, but there was no ministerial oversight, no requirement that consultants be members, and no real process for stopping members from engaging in fraudulent practices. The body had no teeth.

Along with others, I kept up the call to protect the victims of crooks and charlatans. In 2007, as the NDP's citizenship and immigration spokesperson and as a member of the House of Commons Standing Committee on Citizenship and Immigration, I pushed for action and made it a priority of the committee. I lined up a number of witnesses with compelling stories to tell the committee. I worked hard to ensure that the resulting report was both comprehensive and well done, so the government could proceed quickly.

For some reason, though, calling out for the protection of immigrants wasn't resonating with the Harper government or with Jason Kenney, the immigration minister. So I tried a different approach. I accused the government of being soft on crime against immigrants. With a government that prides itself on being tough on crime, that hit a nerve.

"Soft on crime against immigrants" became a rallying cry and helped galvanize attention. I went across the country, doing talk shows and interviews in both the mainstream media and the ethnic press. I would go to the media on the Hill with the committee report and say: "Here's the road map. Where's the minister? Why are the Conservatives soft on crime against immigrants?"

Finally, the government inched ahead with legislation. Bill C-35—An Act to Amend the Immigration and Refugee Protection Act—created an oversight body and established penalties for crooked consultants.

On June 8, 2010, Jason Kenney noted the long years of work towards this goal in a speech. "I'd like to acknowledge," he said, "the good work of all those on the committee, particularly Olivia Chow, who has been a tireless champion of victims of ghost immigration consultants." The bill finally received royal assent and became law in 2011.

The organization it established, the Immigration Consultants of Canada Regulatory Council, makes it clear that only members in good standing are authorized to act on behalf of immigrants.

Abuses still occur, of course—human smuggling, the sex trade, fraud against vulnerable and desperate people. We hear about it in my constituency office every day, and we must always be vigilant. But at least with C-35, the government of Canada can no longer turn a blind eye. Mom's career as a secret agent paid off.

CHAPTER 16

Lessons Learned

Do not be fooled by hand-over-heart promises to lower taxes—you may well find the trickster's other hand is reaching surreptitiously into your back pocket.

I have always been a penny pincher—at least since I came to Canada when I was thirteen. I had been overindulged and spoiled as a little girl in Hong Kong, but when we immigrated to Canada, times were tough. My parents were frugal, and I soon learned to watch every penny, nickel and dime. To this day I have maintained this approach—in both life and politics.

When I arrived on the political scene, I found that far too often progressives were being unfairly painted as spendthrifts. I also came to realize that there are many politicians on all parts of the political spectrum who simply don't fully understand the complexity of government budgets. From the beginning, I set out to make sure that I would never lose one childcare space, one supportive housing bed or one vote for lack of budget smarts. And let me tell you, there was much to learn.

My time at Metro and Toronto city councils spanned the years 1991 to 2005, and for ten of those years I was on the Budget Committee. I knew budget documents inside out. I knew the importance of a ten-year capital budget and an asset management plan, and how much cash should be spent on them versus how long a debt should be carried. I knew the value of reserve funds for rainy days, and I understood the importance of a balanced operating budget.

Chief of the Budget Committee for some of those years was Tom Jakobek. We had pitched battles during these times. He and I were polar opposites. Tom wanted to do magical accounting tricks, such as off-book financing—asking a private company to buy the computers city hall needed and then lease them to the city. I preferred to be up front with our budget, since leasing from private companies would inevitably cost more in the long run. And if the police needed to build a new division, or sewage pipes needed to be fixed, the city should just get it done instead of asking a private company to do the borrowing, since we paid less interest with the triple-A or double-A credit rating we had at the time. During committee meetings, it was usually me versus Tom, with everyone else in between.

If Tom is remembered at all at city hall today, it's as a strident, attacking right-wing politician who left under a cloud of scandal when the computer leasing deal he had engineered for the city morphed from a $43-million price tag to more than twice that. No charges were ever laid, but Jakobek paid the price at the polls. His run for the mayoralty was a disaster—he got less than 1 per cent of votes.

Moral of the story: beware of politicians who claim to be saving taxpayers' dollars. Jakobek's entire reputation was built on that claim. He was very smart, very quick on his feet. But he admitted to the inquiry that investigated the computer brouhaha that he had lied about certain details, and his political reputation was left in tatters.

~~~
~~~

I dealt with these stressful budget battles in several ways. After a long, tough day arguing over every item of the budget book, line by line, I would run to the gym to work out. I found that adding an extra ten pounds to every exercise was especially effective. So my lateral pull-down would go from seventy pounds to eighty pounds, as would the triceps and the biceps weights. I was practising the no-pain, no-gain theory to reduce my stress levels.

And before going to sleep, I would read seed catalogues. This is one of my favourite pastimes—surrounding myself with pictures of beautiful flowers and imagining when I need to start the seeds and how and where the flowers will be planted in the garden. There is something to be said about being able to imagine beauty and growth after long, tough, pitched battles over budgets.

My bedroom once had three shelves of floral lights, where I started seeds in flats. After the seeds arrived in the mail, I'd pack them into flats and water and spray them daily. And it wasn't just flowers I grew; I got into herbs, Chinese herbs that my mother used in her soups, basil of every kind (Thai, lemon, sweet, purple), as well as heritage seeds. At the end of a long day at work, there was nothing more gratifying than watching these little seedlings sprout leaves.

I understood from all those years examining budgets the enormous amount of city tax dollars that went into policing. Year after year, the money spent on policing was the largest single operating expenditure.

The struggle I had at council was always this: how to find money to, say, do something for children in the city when policing costs were devouring a quarter of the budget. The police union would get what they demanded in their contract negotiation—including an automatic 3 per cent pay raise after seven years of employment, a 6 per cent jump after fifteen years and a 9 per cent increase after twenty-three years of service. With the contract locked in, there was no wiggle room.

The other hurdle I faced was how to overcome the widely prevalent (and quite wrong-headed) notion that those on the right of the political spectrum are the wise holders of the public purse while those on the left simply want to spill the purse's contents. Yet it was often me and others from the progressive side of city council who dared to stand up to the police union and call for restraint in their budget, where salaries and benefits were the runaway items—fully 89 per cent of the total spending.

During the fourteen-year span from 1991 to 2005 that I served as a city councillor, I kept folders detailing all my communications with the Budget Committee, other councillors and citizens engaged in the budget process. Toronto's budget is in the $7-billion to $9-billion range—six provinces in Canada have smaller budgets than that.

Poring over my old files as I wrote this book, I saw patterns emerge. And I was reminded of a lesson learned long ago: be wary of politicians who talk incessantly about fiscal responsibility.

In a public letter to council in 2002, I outlined where I thought cuts could be made as part of a sound, humane and fiscally responsible budget. I went after the fat, not the bone. Reductions, I argued then, should come from administrative costs and not by paring services and programs, which would mean laying off front-line staff. Further, I called for the entertainment, public relations and promotion budgets of Metro's departments, the Toronto Transit Commission and the Toronto Police Service to be reduced by 40 per cent. Exempted were agencies involved in tourism and the arts. I called for the money spent on consultants, conference and business travel, and vehicle and furniture replacement to be reduced by 20 per cent.

I also pushed for more accountability. I wanted city staff to report to the management committee on how money was spent on public relations, city promotion (including advertising) and receptions. And I wanted a performance review process to be implemented so that every department would be assigned specific goals and timetables at the beginning of each budget year, with reviews at year's end. (This was precisely the sort of thing I was doing when I was Children and Youth Advocate for the city: my annual reports and action plans were a way of calibrating where we were and how far we still had to go.)

In 2002, I also argued against across-the-board cuts. Going through the budget line by line is tough going; it is far easier to simply do across-the-board cuts of every department by the same percentage. But to flat-line every department and agency penalizes penny-wise managers.

I was ever alert to budget cuts that affected the very young (in childcare) and the very old (in seniors' homes). My instinct, always, was to protect the vulnerable while going after the most powerful. In 1994, for example, I urged city council to cut the police public affairs budget but to protect funding for Meals on Wheels and the city's service for victims of domestic violence. In 1995, I went after councillor and staff perks such as chauffeur-driven cars and free parking in order to spare programs offering wheelchairs and hearing aids. That same year, I protested the unfairness of cutting 25 per cent from children's services and just 2 per cent from the police budget.

In all my years wrangling budgets, I learned what to do—and what *not* to do.

Do not, for example, be fooled by hand-over-heart promises to lower taxes—you may well find that the trickster's other hand is reaching surreptitiously into your back pocket. While some citizens are mesmerized by all the fanfare about cutting taxes, they don't notice that other costs they face are rising fast, as lost tax revenues are covered by regressive hikes of user fees on public services—including transit fares, ferry rates, parking fines, and costs for community centres and childcare services. I believe it is the height of hypocrisy to be claiming to implement a tax freeze while taking more money from taxpayers in the form of user fees—higher taxes by another name.

After years of budget reductions, 80 per cent of the funding to operate Toronto's transit system—the biggest in Canada—now comes from transit riders. That's the highest percentage in North America. At the same time, the percentage of government subsidies provided to operate transit in Toronto is one of the lowest in North America. As well, there is no predictable long-term capital funding, as federal infrastructure spending is doled out in one- and two-year blocks. Being chronically underfunded and unable to plan ahead for ten or twenty years into the future, the Toronto Transit Commission can't improve or grow. The Federation of Canadian Municipalities has called on the federal government to dramatically increase infrastructure spending to $5.75 billion annually for the next two decades—a $2.5-billion yearly increase from current levels. Unless and until that happens, the TTC will be unable to accommodate growth in ridership, and as a result traffic congestion in the Greater Toronto Area will get worse and worse. We already have the longest daily commute times per person in all of North America. Worse than New York. Worse than LA. One consequence? Gridlock in the GTA is costing the economy $6 billion a year, according to the Toronto Board of Trade.

Another move that looks good on paper but is equally damaging is the practice of downloading costs to those who can least afford it. Soccer clubs, swim teams and childcare centres, for example, are often forced to dramatically hike the fees they charge. That's because during budget crunch time, some municipalities and school boards jack up rental fees for using public playing fields, community centres and ice rinks. The organizations that use these spaces are run by volunteers, who are least likely to complain or even to know who to complain to. They have no time, little access to decision makers and no money to hire lobbyists.

Here's another political trick you should know about: *Replace a reliable financial and accounting system with one that can be manipulated politically*. Soon after the megacity of Toronto was created in 1998, I rang the alarm bell that the financial system was in chaos and open to abuse. I spelled out how the budget chief of the day, Tom Jakobek, working with his chief financial officer, did the following: they gutted Metro Toronto's award-winning finance system that had reliably tracked, documented and presented financial data. The old system had a triple-A credit rating, with healthy reserve funds and a balanced debt ratio between income and size of debt of around 12 per cent.

A few days before council approved the scandalous computer-leasing deal that wasted millions of dollars, I questioned why there was a 175 per cent increase in the computer spending budget in one year. I was brushed off by Jakobek, who, it turns out, was roundly discredited when a Commission of Inquiry looked into the scandal. The self-styled "fiscally responsible" councillors at the table approved the budget without question—costing millions that could have been better spent on vital programs and services.

The inflated computer leasing deal demonstrates another deceptive trick: *Focus on small spending while leaving big, powerful contracts alone.* The City of Toronto nitpicked $10,000 grants to small, non-profit, largely voluntary organizations. These little charities deliver critical social services, such as care for seniors and new immigrants. For their grants to be approved, they must endure several rounds of interviews and relentless grilling by city staff. If they make it through that gauntlet, they then face more of the same from a plethora of council committees. Meanwhile, information technology contracts worth millions of dollars were processed through an obscure tendering system involving bids by various would-be contractors. These contracts were not publicly or politically scrutinized, nor were they all approved by council committees.

Here is another deceptive trick: *Keep the spending opaque, since transparency means accountability.* Why is it so difficult for the public to find out how their tax dollars are spent? In this computer age, it's easy to make the entire budget-making process as participatory and transparent as possible. But to do so would mean that elected representatives—be they the prime minister, the provincial finance minister or the city budget chief—would have to relinquish some of their power and work with citizens to come up with clear directions and priorities regarding how their money should be spent.

When budget information is hidden from ordinary citizens or the media, it's often a sign that something is fundamentally wrong. That was the case in Toronto's computer-spending fiasco. The city's spending on information technology was split into four accounts: the Y2K account ($150 million for the so-called millennium bug—a feared worldwide computer crash that never occurred), the amalgamation transitional account ($108 million), the miscellaneous "non-program" account ($19 million) and the IT department account ($18 million). Such arbitrary fragmentation served only to obfuscate IT expenditures. What's more, staff reports on IT spending consistently landed on the desks of city councillors right before the budget meetings—a manoeuvre designed to limit scrutiny and debate.

This hoodwinking practice is widely used by governments at every level. Several times in my past few years on the House of Commons transport committee, I was unable, as the NDP's transport and infrastructure critic, to haul in the minister to defend the department's billion-dollar budget. Conservative members of that committee routinely vote down any request to examine the department's mammoth spending. Each MP is given, at most, seven minutes to query staff on the budget.

When details on spending are hidden from MPs, it means there is no accountability and the Canadian public is kept in the dark. The mandate of the parliamentary budget officer (according to its own website) "is to provide independent analysis to Parliament on the state of the nation's finances, the government's estimates and trends in the Canadian economy; and upon request from a committee or parliamentarian, to estimate the financial cost of any proposal for matters over which Parliament has jurisdiction." But in November 2012 this same officer, Kevin Page, had to actually take the government to Federal Court to try to find out what the government was spending and what public services were being cut.

This practice should not be tolerated, as it often leads to abuse. Before the G8 summit in 2010, frivolous spending occurred in the Parry Sound–Muskoka riding of Tony Clement, including, most famously, a $100,000 gazebo an hour's drive from where the summit was held. The source of all this spending? A $50-million fund set up to ease traffic jams at border crossings between the US and Canada. The last time I checked, Muskoka is nowhere near the border. One other point: as president of the Treasury Board, Clement is supposed to be in charge of ethics and accountability.

When I was a Toronto city councillor, I devoted an enormous amount of time to engaging citizens so they could have a say in how the city put together a budget. I worked closely with Toronto's Community Social Planning Council and the hundreds of voluntary organizations that deliver critically important services to the city's citizens. Through newsletters, memos, flyers, weekly updates and forums, thousands of residents were kept informed and were able to influence how their hard-earned dollars were being spent.

Another example of what *not* to do? *Take lobbyists' sales pitches at face value.* Lobbyists have a tremendous amount of influence over elected representatives. Companies gladly pay for advocates because the potential dividends are enormous. But we should all remember that lobbyists serve their employers and not taxpayers.

Here's what we *should* do. *Go to the source of the problem.*

In 1994, a proposal was made to cut the *entire* Toronto emergency dental program for people on social assistance. Painful toothaches and abscesses were to be ignored. How this mean-spirited cut would have saved money is beyond me, since these folks would inevitably end up in hospital emergency departments, where fixing a problem would be far costlier. Cutting that program saved the city a tiny amount but left the provincial health care system with a much heftier bill.

It's false economy to cut back on vital services. A better approach is to find ways to end the cycle of poverty by figuring out why people are on assistance in the first place. That's why I pushed to allow refugee claimants to work during the long period of time (often years) their cases were being heard. I also suggested reducing the number of people on social assistance by providing employment and training initiatives, backed up by childcare and transportation support.

Of all the lessons I have learned, this much I know: investing in people to help break the cycle of poverty, to create job opportunities and to improve the quality of life in our society is never a waste. It is the best investment we can make in the future—and it is what we owe each other in a civil society.

CHAPTER 17

Hard Blows

The idea of passing my heart and soul to Olivia to shepherd me to the next phase of my spirit and soul is totally comforting. Held in her arms, I have no fears.
—Jack Layton, in a note written two days before his death

When I look back at the spring and summer of 2011 and the extremes of emotion I felt then, I think of Dickens's *A Tale of Two Cities*: "It was the best of times, it was the worst of times . . . it was the season of Light, it was the season of Darkness, it was the spring of hope, it was the winter of despair."

I find it hard to go back and recall the unbridled joy of election night on May 2 of that year. Under Jack's inspired leadership during the campaign, the NDP had pulled off what the pundits and headline writers were calling the "orange crush"—stunning success for the party in Quebec and gains all across the country that pushed us to unprecedented heights: we won more than a hundred seats and were now Canada's Official Opposition.

Symbols matter hugely when it comes to appealing to voters. Jack had had hip surgery to deal with a fracture just two months before the election, and during the entire campaign he was never seen without a cane. It became a symbol not of weakness or of frailty, but of defiance. A symbol of hope. We can fight the power, Jack's uplifted cane said, we can overcome hurdles—and that we did.

Six weeks after the election, we marked another joyous occasion—the NDP convention in Vancouver to celebrate the party's fiftieth anniversary. Some two thousand people came. Jack's words provoked thunderous applause, and late in the evening, he and I took to the dance floor and we both felt a great wash of love, laughter and joy. The moment was pure magic.

Jack was now leader of the Official Opposition, and with that territory came the Opposition leader's official residence—Stornoway, a graceful old house in Rockcliffe Park in Ottawa. The property features an acre of lovely grounds on a street with magnificent trees in a neighbourhood filled with embassies. Jack and I didn't relish the prospect of a move—we had a perfectly fine apartment just a stone's throw from Parliament Hill. But we also understood that Stornoway is a national asset, an important symbol. And as leader of the Opposition, Jack had a new role to play.

Stornoway came with a staff of three—a housekeeper who had been there for years, a driver and a chef. We decided we wouldn't need a driver or a chef, but we gladly retained the housekeeper—a lovely woman named Expectation Castuera and affectionately called Epi. We didn't have time to move in personally while Parliament was in session, but I packed our clothes in wardrobe boxes at the apartment on Sparks Street and arranged to have them taken to Stornoway.

I selected my favourite colour, a deep yellow, and had the bedroom repainted. The curtains and bedsheets were matched by the National Capital Commission's team. (The NCC administers official residences such as Stornoway, Rideau Hall and 24 Sussex Drive.) Most of the magnificent Canadian paintings already on the walls stayed, since I didn't have time to select any of my favourites from the NCC's collection. Jack particularly liked the piano in the living room, as he loved to play. We had plans to retrofit Stornoway with solar panels, more insulation and triple-pane windows—much as we had our own house in Toronto—so the energy bill would go down dramatically. Jack even approached Canada's best-known contractor, Mike Holmes, to see if he was interested in doing a joint project with us so we could highlight the importance of energy retrofitting. We gave notice to our landlord on Sparks Street and arranged to move after Parliament rose for the summer on June 24.

One tradition at Stornoway is an annual garden party for the media, and we set the date for June 27. It was a fabulous event. NDP staff in Ottawa made the arrangements for the marquee tent and the catering. Jack and I flew in from Toronto—with my mother and with Jack's mom, Doris—to join the festivities that were already under way. Jack loved the party. I remember him sitting at a table with his mom, chatting with the journalists. Craig Oliver, a veteran reporter with CTV, had brought his daughter to the party, and Jack had a lovely chat with them. The party ended with a bang—a huge thunderstorm. Uncharacteristically, Jack went to bed early that evening.

All was not well. Jack had been feeling some pain since the end of the parliamentary session, was limping more heavily and had lost weight. At first, it seemed as if the rigours of the campaign—following his hip surgery and earlier treatment for prostate cancer—had taken their toll and he was simply exhausted.

The day after the garden party, we flew back to Toronto with our mothers, and there followed weeks of tests and more tests. Jack had been diagnosed with prostate cancer in December of 2009, and treatment for that in 2010 had been successful. But now a second and more aggressive cancer was discovered, and this time the prognosis was grim.

Jack announced the news at a press conference on July 25, and people were shocked by the change in his appearance. He was thin and frail, and his voice was hoarse and weak. But his ghastly pallor that day was partly my fault. The green room where we had assembled before the TV appearance was dark, and his assistant, Eiman Zarrug, had already put some pancake makeup on Jack's face—as she often had for his TV appearances. "More makeup," I insisted. Alas, that only made Jack look worse.

During that press conference, with me by his side, Jack announced that he was stepping aside as leader while undergoing treatment for this new cancer. Jack chose not to disclose the type of cancer that was having such a rapid and aggressive impact on him, because he knew from his own experience that it would be deeply distressing to others fighting the same disease if he didn't win his battle. They might lose hope. I supported and respected his decision in this, and I will always honour it.

After the press conference, Jack retreated to our house on Huron Street and our third-floor bedroom, where our roof deck was festooned with flowers. There he would sit under a patio umbrella, receive visitors and read. (We never actually lived at Stornoway. We moved some clothes and belongings in, but slept there for only one night.)

In the meantime, he was getting aggressive therapy. When negotiating the stairs of our three-storey house became difficult, we rearranged the furniture in the living room, putting Jack's mechanized chair by the window, his hospital bed by the door and the couch against the opposite wall. I slept on that couch for weeks. I also installed a set of curtains that divided the living room and afforded Jack some privacy.

~

In one sense, for Jack to die when he did—so close to achieving what he had set out to accomplish—a progressive, NDP government for all Canadians—represented the worst of bad luck. And yet through that extraordinary summer, there were many moments that brought great happiness to Jack and to me—and for that I will always be thankful. One thing I was grateful for was the season—Parliament had recessed for the summer, and so I was able to take the time off and be at home with Jack. I was also grateful that Sarah Layton, too, was able to spend a lot of time with us. The night before the press conference, Sarah received some medical news of her own. Five months pregnant, she had gone into an urgent care clinic after experiencing abdominal pain and was told she would require an appendectomy. To say the least, we were all quite anxious. Sarah recounted the story to an interviewer a few months later.

"It became quite comical. Here is Olivia with my father who was about to announce his news while everyone could see that he was having a particularly bad day. It was so strange to see him then and it was a *bad* day—in looks especially. That's not the image that I have of him in the last month of his life. So Olivia and I are talking briefly—and she kept asking, 'What do you need? Can I bring you anything?' And I'm thinking, Here you are, already taking care of somebody who is going through a quite large event tomorrow and I'm like, 'Leave me, I'll be fine.' I was on the phone with my dad the next morning and he was saying, 'How are you?' but I said, 'No, how are *you*?' We were laughing because it was just so unreal."

Sarah's own surgery meant that she was off work for one entire week and working only half-time the following week. That meant she was able to walk to our place for visits after work, so she gained precious time with her father. She was able to spend a lot of time at our house and sit with him. I made them smoothies while they swapped tales, went through get-well cards and watched movies. Jack wanted to know everything about Sarah's pregnancy.

Sarah has great emotional strength, and when it became clear to her that her father was not going to recover, in a way things became easier for her—not more difficult. "I knew I had to prepare myself emotionally as I was going through this with Dad and the pregnancy at the same time," she said some months later. "Not that I wasn't hopeful and optimistic about everything, but I was trying to be realistic about what the outcome would be. I certainly think that helped me in the last weeks. I would leave every time thinking that if this was the last time I see him, then I'm prepared."

Sarah saw her father as he was—a totally genuine human being. He was the same keen and interested man whether the TV cameras were rolling or not, whether he was mainstreeting or sitting on a couch and watching a movie with the kids and me. As he lay dying in those last days, there was no facade or protective layer that had to be penetrated. Jack was Jack.

Sarah saw her dad so clearly and knew him so well that for her, his death seemed natural—unfortunate, but a natural process. It was just a peaceful moment. Sarah's strength helped immeasurably.

In my teens and early twenties, I'd been obsessed with death as a philosophical concept. Out of this obsession, I became determined to live my life in such a way that when I died, I would die with no regrets. Jack lived his life that way, too, and at the end he felt connected to the universe so vast, so majestic, so beautiful that it didn't seem like an ending at all—just an inevitable part of the cycle of life. Who were we to understand the mysteries? In the timeless words of Ecclesiastes, "There is . . . a time to give birth and a time to die; . . . a time to tear down and a time to build up . . . A time to mourn and a time to dance." We had our time to dance together. And we shared a belief that if we live our lives to the fullest, then no matter when we die—in Jack's case at the moment of his greatest accomplishment—there should be no fear. And, at the end, Jack had no fear of death. We faced it together, not with anger, but with love.

Mike Layton smiles now when he recalls how conversation in the last days with his dad would switch from the mundane to the profound. Mike was at our house one time when Jack was chatting with one of his cousins, and they spent about fifteen minutes recalling how their grandfather had taught them to shuck an oyster—and just where, by the way, *was* that oyster knife?—for Jack's grandfather had willed the tool to him. Mike was then dispatched to hunt through our kitchen drawers and find it.

More deeply moving for Mike was a story Jack told then about the historical debt that the Layton clan owed the Mi'kmaqs. Mike holds back tears as he recounts the story: "We were going through some family history, going way, way back, pre-Confederation when some of our ancestors were in trouble in the wilderness—but they were saved and supported by the Mi'kmaqs. I don't know why this story has such a big effect on me."

Mike was clearly touched by the aboriginal presence at his father's funeral, by the eagle feather that was presented to me by Assembly of First Nations national chief Shawn Atleo, and by the healing blanket sent to the family from Northern Ontario via MP Carol Hughes. Grand Chief Patrick Madhabee from Aundeck Omni Kaning First Nation (and the Union of Ontario Indians) had loaned the healing blanket, which they had used in a ceremony at their lodge in North Bay to send Jack's spirit off on his journey.

All these details were indelibly imprinted on Jack's son.

Mike adored his father and was incredibly proud of him. As a university student, he often asked, "Hey, Dad, if you get a chance, can we chat?" Jack always found the chance, and he helped Mike connect the dots between the theory and the practice of politics—even offering his own highlighted copy of works by Aristotle. Jack was the very best of mentors. Pretty soon, Mike knew the inside story on how to achieve political change ("inside baseball" was his own metaphor) better than some of his political science professors.

Mike saw his dad as "a policy wonk," but one who could make the complex comprehensible—to the media and to a seven-year-old. "You can make stuff dance," Mike once said to Jack, and I think he meant that his father could make others buy into his vision because that vision was so grand, so generous to all and so elegantly simple to grasp.

Mike always grasped the vision, even as a child. I remember when, back in the mid-eighties, an unofficial activist for the disabled named Victor began to show up at city hall. In a wheelchair, untidy and barely comprehensible, Victor would get extremely frustrated when misunderstood, so Jack would help by acting as his translator whenever he appeared before council. One time, when Mike was five, Victor went to see Jack at his home, and Mike greeted Victor with a hug before running off to play. Victor was moved to tears—he told Jack he had never had a hug from a child.

Like father, like son.

We had to restrict visitors by the end, but still a steady stream of people were coming to the door bearing food so we wouldn't have to cook. Bryan Dale, Jack's NDP riding association president, delivered fresh home-cooked meals weekly; so did my sister-in-law Carol, with her delicious chicken pot pies. My good friend Tania Liu took me out on long runs to keep me healthy and positive. My wonderful staff, led by Susan Kwong, took care of the office so I didn't have to worry about my work.

And all during Jack's final weeks, a steady flow of e-mails came in from the world outside the house on Huron. On August 8, Jack received a touching note from Laureen Harper, the prime minister's wife. Under the subject line "A big juicy steak . . . ," she wrote: "Good afternoon Jack and Olivia, I am sorry I didn't email you earlier to offer our best wishes (I know you talked to my husband). I was away hiking in the Yukon and lived days without any media. Just wanted to offer up a nice steak when you get back to Ottawa cooked by me. You are in our hearts and prayers (my heart, Stephen's prayers)."

During Jack's last weeks, we often watched a movie in the late afternoon or evening. We tried for funny movies, such as *A Fish Called Wanda* and *Best in Show*.

But we were also looking for funny yet meaningful and uplifting movies. I e-mailed Sarah Polley, the Canadian filmmaker, actor and director, wondering if she had any recommendations. We had known Sarah a long time as a passionate fellow campaigner during protests against poverty and homelessness (in fact she had lost a tooth during one demo), and she had dropped in countless times during my election campaigns to volunteer on the phones for hours at a time.

Two days after I sent that e-mail, Sarah arrived at our door bearing a giant basket containing dozens of DVDs along with four pages of notes that explained the choices she'd made after polling directors from the Hot Docs film festival, the Toronto International Film Festival and the National Film Board. In the basket were classics (*Citizen Kane* and the entire boxed set of Woody Allen films) and many Canadian films. We were able to watch a lot of them together, and I enjoy them still. It was a wonderful gift.

During those weeks, while we did all we could to address Jack's cancer, many well-wishers also tried to help. Boxes would arrive at our door containing ginseng or alternative medicines. One man banged very loudly on the door at one in the morning, but because I didn't know him, I didn't answer the door. He continued banging until one of the stained glass windows (each depicting three tall tulips) broke.

Not long after, our long-time friends Paul Copeland (a human rights lawyer) and his wife, Pattie Walker (a prominent stained glass artist), dropped by to cook a splendid meal of red snapper for Jack and me. They noticed plywood where the stained glass panel had been broken. Pattie would succumb to cancer herself in December of 2012, but before she died she crafted a beautiful piece of stained glass featuring red and blue flowers to replace the broken pane. I think of Pattie and Jack whenever I open the door.

The man who did the damage was well intentioned. He left a long letter explaining that he had travelled through a rainstorm all the way to Stornoway, hoping to find Jack there. The alternative medicine he was offering involved magnetic fields, and he seemed genuinely convinced this would work. Like so many others, he was distressed to see a man he admired being taken away at the very pinnacle of a career in public service.

As I faced the prospect of losing my soulmate and life partner, I was deeply touched by the fact that my sense of loss was so widely shared, even by people who had never met Jack.

While always optimistic, Jack knew when his time had come. Whatever hours remained to him, he was determined to spend them with those he loved. Like so many who must deal with grave illness at the end of their lives, Jack had a grim choice: take medication and painkillers that would make him drowsy or unconscious, or choose lucidity at the expense of pain. He chose lucidity so he could spend precious minutes and hours with the ones he cherished. Thankfully, a pain specialist stepped in and alleviated much of the pain in later days.

Among those he cherished were his friends and political colleagues Brian Topp and Anne McGrath, who had been helping Jack with his last letter—to be released to the country at the time of his death. They joined us the day before Jack died, and spent about four hours working on the letter with Jack—reading out loud, making suggestions and absorbing Jack's wishes. I helped type up the successive drafts, and Jack knew when it was right. As I look back, I think that letter was perhaps Jack's greatest achievement. And it was Jack to the core.

Precisely one thousand words long, the letter begins by acknowledging the incredible thoughtfulness of people from all across the country: "Tens of thousands of Canadians have written to me in recent weeks to wish me well. I want to thank each and every one of you for your thoughtful, inspiring and often beautiful notes, cards and gifts. Your spirit and love have lit up my home, my spirit, and my determination. Unfortunately my treatment has not worked out as I hoped. So I am giving this letter to my partner Olivia to share with you in the circumstance in which I cannot continue."

Jack offered some practical advice for the New Democratic Party of Canada, and some encouraging words to the caucus, to Quebecers and to young people in the country. And he offered this counsel to anyone with cancer: "You must not lose your own hope. Treatments and therapies have never been better in the face of this disease. You have every reason to be optimistic, determined, and focused on the future. My only other advice is to cherish every moment with those you love at every stage of your journey, as I have done this summer."

He ended on this note: "My friends, love is better than anger. Hope is better than fear. Optimism is better than despair. So let us be loving, hopeful and optimistic. And we'll change the world."

~~~
~~~

The day Jack died had started like any other that month. I made him a big breakfast that included a large bowl of cereal and a mango smoothie with protein mix—much more than he could possibly eat. His assistant, Eiman, came over and they did about an hour of signing thank-you cards to well-wishers, often adding a personal note. Then he had lunch, followed by a snooze.

Sunday traditions were observed. Jack's brothers, Rob and David, came for a visit along with their mother, Doris, who had made a key lime pie—a dessert that Jack adored—and a shepherd's pie.

The last movie Jack watched was *Return of the Jedi*. He took it in with his childhood sweetheart, Sally—Sarah and Mike's mother—with the volume cranked up. I remember that detail fondly. It called to mind a snorkelling vacation one time with Jack and me retreating to the hotel, where we watched the entire *Star Wars* trilogy in one go. Inside the man was still a boy who could delight in the frivolous as a break from more serious adult pursuits.

By now, Jack was no longer reading his last book—*A Secular Age* by his former mentor and McGill professor, the political philosopher Charles Taylor. One of Taylor's abiding interests is the connection between the spiritual and the secular, a connection that resonated deeply with Jack.

On the evening before Jack died, we all dined happily on Doris's shepherd's pie. We then got him up on his feet because he was having trouble breathing, owing to a buildup of fluid in his lungs. I pulled his gold-coloured robe, the one with the embroidered dragon, closer around his neck and tried to make him as comfortable as I could. Once he was back in bed, I put my hand on his cheek. My Jack was still a very good-looking guy. His hair was white now and sparse at the top, and he had lost a lot of weight from an already lean frame, but there was still a spark in his eyes. He was still beautiful, still vibrant, still radiating love and happiness and the energy and goodness that had attracted me from the very beginning, a quarter of a century before.

By late evening, he was still conscious and aware, but he could not speak and he could only mouth "thanks" for any kindness. We could tell by his breathing that he was getting weaker. So I got on the phone, called the entire family and said, "Everyone, just get here." I called his palliative care nurse and doctor, and they immediately made their way to our home.

We were there at his side—Sarah and Mike, his brothers Rob and David and their spouses, Carol and Sandra, my mother and our friend Bob Gallagher.

Jack's mother had gone home, but she called around eleven, and her voice came over the speakerphone. "You've had a great life, Jack," she told him. "It's time to close your eyes and sleep now, son."

We smiled and laughed and sang songs in those last hours. Songs by musicians Jack loved—Creedence Clearwater Revival, Van Morrison, Cat Stevens. Jack's sister, Nancy, couldn't be there, but at one point she was on the phone, joining in. Hugh Campbell, Sarah's husband, had brought his iPad on which he had recorded their daughter Beatrice singing her ABCs.

There were tears. Of course there were tears, but there was also acceptance. The moment had come. We took turns sleeping and watching over Jack as he hung on. We took turns holding his hand. We knew the end was near. At 4:45 a.m., on August 22, 2011, surrounded by the people he loved, Jack took his last breath.

Sarah has always joked that when I am stressed or upset, I make lists and keep busy. After spending the first day alternating between weeping every time I watched the news coverage of Jack's death and dealing with calls from friends and relatives, I went into overdrive to plan the details of Jack's funeral.

The prime minister had graciously offered a state funeral (a rare honour normally used to commemorate former prime ministers and governors general, though cabinet may use its discretion to pay tribute to eminent Canadians). We thus needed to plan the details of Jack's journey to Parliament Hill and then to Toronto's city hall for lying in state, and then the funeral itself.

There were key decisions to make around this whole time: all the details that went with planning the funeral and selecting Jack's final resting places, the choice of music (playing John Lennon's "Imagine" and Jack's grandfather's creation, "Dominion March," on the bells of the Peace Tower at Parliament Hill), and the timing of the many occasions for greeting, hugging and providing comfort to those who came to share in the mourning.

I spent one entire week making sure the funeral would be perfect.

On August 24, Jack's flag-draped casket was driven, escorted by the Toronto Police Service, to Ottawa, where it was met by an RCMP honour guard before lying in state for two days in the lobby of the House of Commons. Then, after a fifteen-gun salute, the cortège departed for Toronto City Hall, where mourners again had a chance to pay their respects. Finally, on August 27, the casket was transported from city hall to Roy Thomson Hall with a mounted police escort. I remember walking behind the coffin on an already hot, sunny morning with Sarah and Mike, Beatrice and the rest of the family behind me. This was my last walk with Jack.

Bob Gallagher was such a great friend through this whole time. He was with me most of the time, helping me and others to organize the funeral, including amassing the invitation list—a colossal undertaking in itself. Everything about the funeral had to be thoroughly planned, from the multi-faith component (including a nod to atheists) to the music.

Kathleen Monk, the NDP's director of strategic communications, took charge of the funeral at Roy Thomson Hall. The music director of Metropolitan Community Church of Toronto, Diane Leah, worked with me to choose the music. Nancy Tong, a filmmaker and my best friend, flew in with an award-winning filmmaker from her home in New York to help NDP video artists Ben Dickerson and Aaron Floresco create the documentary that was aired at the funeral. Together that team of four stayed up all night to craft a powerful visual narrative of Jack's life. At ten the following morning, Nancy showed it to me, and I breathed a sigh of relief.

The choice of music was absolutely critical because music sets the tone and mood of such an event. *Requiem for 9/11*, by American composer Wilson Gault Somers, was played as mourners walked into Roy Thomson Hall. Members of the Toronto Symphony Orchestra played Samuel Barber's *Adagio for Strings*, followed by the Pifa from Handel's *Messiah*. Christopher Dawes, the organist, played an Oscar Peterson composition, "Hymn to Freedom." Van Morrison's "Into the Mystic" was played, of course, as was Moe Koffman's "The Magnificent Cat"—a tune that Jack used to whistle all the time. (This choice offered a rare moment of levity: when I had said I wanted this piece of music, one of my staff thought I had said "Magnificat"—as in Bach's canticle by the same name. After several days of futilely searching for a Moe Koffman version of the *Magnificat*, the staffer finally came to me, and we both laughed about the wild goose chase she had been on.)

And Jack's old friend Steven Page, of course, sang Leonard Cohen's "Hallelujah." Steven had been a front man with the Barenaked Ladies before a fall from grace (a charge of cocaine use), but Jack very much wanted him there. This was an act of inclusion that was vintage Jack. And Steven repaid that faith in him with a stirring rendition of that song.

I have looked at footage of the broadcast of the state funeral several times—to hear the beautiful blessing by Shawn Atleo. To hear the words of Karl Bélanger and Anne McGrath, the magnificent oration of Stephen Lewis, the deeply spiritual and inspirational sermon of Brent Hawkes, Jack's pastor. I watched with pride the incredible courage of Sarah and Mike, who stood and talked so warmly and openly about their beloved dad—giving comfort to so many. Near the end of the funeral, I wanted Jack's spirit and legacy to carry on. And I could feel spirits soar when Julie Michels and the choir sang "Get Together" by the Youngbloods, calling on us all to love one another.

The same thing happened when Lorraine Segato sang "Rise Up." That song has special resonance. Lorraine had performed it at our wedding and again in 2003 when Jack ran for the leadership of the NDP. Jack had a political show on Toronto cable TV, and it always opened with "Rise Up." For a time, whenever anyone called NDP headquarters, that was the music that welcomed them.

I wanted the funeral of Jack Layton to be perfectly paced, and I thought long and hard about the order of things. There was a mournful and sombre beginning, with the Requiem. The video was meant to have emotional punch—and it did. The eulogies struck notes of celebration, of a life well lived. And as the casket left the stage at the end, the tempo of the music really picked up. I wanted people to mourn, as I mourned, but I also wanted them to think about Jack's legacy, and by it, to be moved to act. People in the hall, or watching on big screens outside, or watching at home: I wanted them all, as those final upbeat notes were played, to be thinking of what they could do to make the world a better place.

I can watch the funeral on video now, and I can see it as others saw it. But during that week and at the funeral, my only focus was to make sure collectively that we perfectly captured and celebrated Jack's life. I fussed over how many seats would be made available for the public and whether people who couldn't get into Roy Thomson Hall would be able to participate fully. All the time I was keenly aware that Jack would have wanted an open and celebratory event that would inspire change.

All through the funeral, I fought to maintain control—talking silently to myself. Will everything go as planned? Hold yourself together. Know that love conquers death and our love will never die. Do not break down. Jack is the focus of attention, not me. That's what I was thinking.

Four days before Jack died, we had taken him to Princess Margaret Hospital for some treatment, and while there we both chatted with a psychiatrist. He was very helpful, putting to us questions designed to get us talking. Later, after Jack's death, I saw this doctor again, and he remarked on my powers of dissociation—the ability to focus on what I want to focus on and not what's going on around me. The psychiatrist wondered if I had developed it during the intense years of my childhood. At that funeral, I was drawing on every ounce of that strength.

When Sarah Layton went to the lectern to speak, Beatrice began to fuss—uh-oh, Mom was gone—and her father was having trouble handling her. But Sally was there, thankfully. Her nonna, as Beatrice calls her, took her and walked her on a side aisle.

The funeral was everything I hoped it would be. I am so thankful to Reverend Brent Hawkes, Kathleen Monk and Jack's NDP family for doing the lion's share of organizing. And to Diane Leah, who had worked with me on choosing the songs, the arrangements, the choir, the tempo.

Amid the tragedy, there was one moment that was both comic and poignant. I couldn't fully appreciate it at the time, but it makes me smile now. As I was standing beside the flag-draped casket in the foyer outside the House of Commons with Sarah and Mike, I heard my mother's voice—scolding someone, in Cantonese. She was saying, "You should have done what I told you. You should have drunk all my soup."

There was my mother staring at a beautiful black-and-white photographic portrait of Jack. She was rapping the glass with her finger and the photograph was shaking and almost fell from the easel. Cooking for people has always been my mother's way of expressing love. By berating Jack, she was revealing the depths of her grief.

After the ceremony, after the reception, after our family had followed the hearse to the crematorium—we returned to our house on Huron. The scene of so many gatherings and parties, family times and political times in the past was the destination at the end of the day. About forty of us were there that night—the great extended Layton clan, all four generations, from Beatrice to Doris, plus a few close family friends.

Nancy Tong had flown in from Manhattan. Kiloran German had come from Lunenburg, Nova Scotia. My old friend Wing Ah Fung came from Hong Kong and stayed for a few days, even though she was allergic to the cats. My cousin Ingrid and my niece Althea arrived from California. In the week after the funeral, Nancy, Kiloran and Ah Fung stayed on. Together they helped me mourn. They helped me clean the house and pack up Jack's effects, and took care of the meals. Bob Gallagher, Susan Kwong, Nathan Rotman, Joe Cressy, Kathy Le and others took over the cataloguing of the thousands of e-mails, cards, flowers, candles. They took care of so many logistics, and they took care of me.

These friends had somehow managed to pull things together for a gathering at Huron after the funeral. A nearby restaurant delivered food, including those delicious Portuguese custard tarts that Jack loved, and the counter was laden with wine. The house on Huron was a most welcome haven of privacy after the public outpouring.

The Laytons did what Laytons do at times like these: they sang. After food and drink, hugs and tears, the guitars inevitably were picked up, the *Rise Up Singing* books were passed around, and the singing began. Jack's brother Rob remembers that we sang "Blowin' in the Wind," "This Land Is Your Land," "The House of the Rising Sun." It was joyous. People were belting it out. We sang loud enough to cover for the one voice that was now missing.

A few days after the funeral, Nancy took me to a cottage three hours from Toronto, a drive she remembers as one of the longest she had ever experienced. I had just had a tooth pulled in order to enable a tooth implant, so my face was half swollen and I could not talk, and my wound would not stop bleeding. And Nancy was very worried about my state of mind. I have no clear memories of either the journey or the time we spent at the cottage.

What Nancy recalls is that once we got to this beautiful and peaceful cottage by a small lake, I had a meltdown, a blessedly brief one.

When I could, Nancy says, I read. I was already obsessed with reading about the experiences of other widows—Joyce Carol Oates (*A Widow's Story*) and Joan Didion (*The Year of Magical Thinking*).

Nancy is the most grounded person I know, and she was like an anchor then. I do remember that she helped me breathe and learn to meditate. We sat on the dock, and she helped me feel the air in my body, feel the rhythm and get back in touch with myself. As I breathed in and out and was absorbed in the process, my mind went free and I felt Jack breathing beside me. And I felt a sense of peace.

I also wanted to go swimming in the lake, but I have always been fearful about swimming in dark water where I can't see the bottom. Jack had always patiently encouraged me to not be afraid, and I was confident when I swam with him. Now I had to prove to myself that I could do it alone. So I swam a great deal. This cottage trip, just two short days, gave me some space and helped me get in touch with my emotions. I was given a space for rest and was nursed through Nancy's good friendship and cooking, for which I am forever grateful.

My cell phone rang several times during that time at the cottage. The publisher of Random House Canada, Anne Collins, asked if I would assist her in putting together an e-book on Jack called *Hope Is Better Than Fear: Paying Jack Layton Forward*. The book would gather essays on some of the issues that Jack championed in his life: homelessness, feminism, civic engagement, the environment and the experience of First Nations people. Net proceeds from sales would go to aboriginal youth initiatives that I earmarked.

I also had to prepare for interviews—the first a one-on-one with Peter Mansbridge for CBC-TV's *The National*. A seasoned filmmaker and interviewer, Nancy helped me rehearse.

That interview was conducted on September 5, in the rain, on the Toronto Islands, where Jack and I had been married so many years before. One of the things I talked about was Jack's amazing ability to see the goodness in every single human being. He would see their flaws but refuse to let them be a deterrence. He had an incredible optimism about the capacity of people to be good, to be loving—even people who were not naturally that way inclined.

The next day I was interviewed by Anna Maria Tremonti, host of CBC Radio's *The Current*. I really appreciated her line of questioning, her sensitivity and her care. Maybe, too, it was the intimacy of radio versus the bright lights of television, but I found myself opening up and returning to that theme of goodness. I told Anna Maria that the waves of applause that rose as I walked in the wake of the casket enveloped me like a blanket, and that this was not about Jack or me but about them. The outpouring of love was stunning to witness.

I also said that time spent with a dying loved one need not necessarily be a negative experience, that it can be a great blessing, and so it was for me.

Jack and I both believed at our very cores that whereas the Conservatives were offering a Darwinian view of the world and urging Canadians to be fearful and angry, we were offering a counter to that—love, hope, optimism. That message really touched a chord, and I wanted to see it echoed and expanded.

Jack and I saw that message as a cultural shift in the works, a move away from that old approach that sought to pit people against each other. This was about the power of goodness to lift a community or a society to a place where everyone is more generous with each other. I wanted to create a cultural and spiritual space where this could happen and where individuals could connect with the goodness inside them. So everything I did then and since has been to circle around that spiritual aspect, that goal of tapping into goodness—which I believe is a form of the divine.

In the days after Jack's death, every one of the several hundred paving squares at Nathan Phillips Square, every inch of the concrete walls, was marked by chalk. I stole away for a few moments and rode my bike over to see for myself—and it was breathtaking. Drawings, messages, notes of thanks and affection in English, French, Spanish, Chinese, Italian, Farsi. One of my favourites: "If you don't know Layton, you don't know Jack." Another read: "To Jack, to Canada, to Change." In the square people had left flowers and wreaths, balloons and Canadian flags. Someone had even left a small white chalk-filled pail and a sign in black that read: "Chalk 4 Jack."

The rain would wash away the chalk messages in a few days' time, but almost immediately the square was covered again with fresh messages. The following year, on the anniversary of Jack's death, more messages in chalk were left in the square. And a website called dearjack.ca continues to draw notes from people who still miss Jack Layton. He is remembered.

Through the years, Jack and I spent a lot of time on the Toronto Islands, often house-sitting many of the Islanders' homes with our kids. Both Jack and I had a long history of fighting for the rights of Islanders. The fight went back to 1981, when Metro Toronto tried to take ownership of the lands—including the homes that Islanders had either bought or built themselves.

After Jack died, grateful Islanders put together a gem of a book called *Islanders Remembering Jack*, and it's full of wonderful stories and beautiful photographs. One story recalls the time that Jack volunteered as auctioneer at the Toronto Island Public School's annual Dream Auction one summer. When all the lots had been sold, someone offered to bid on Jack's jeans—so he took them off and got $500 for them. He did get to wear them home. "I do remember the cute butt!" Islander Diana Rowland writes in the book.

The bronze plaque fixed to a stone by the linden tree we planted on our wedding day soon grew over again after Jack unveiled it that day. The plaque read:

To commemorate the marriage of
OLIVIA CHOW and JACK LAYTON
Celebrated 88-07-9
A gift to keep our Toronto a
healthier City!

Best Wishes for a lifetime full of
Love, Happiness and Peace
Blair & Virginia Stephenson

This is the story behind the tree and the plaque. When Jack first became a city councillor, Virginia and Blair Stephenson were living in a rundown apartment building in his ward. He helped them form a residents' association, and the landlord finally agreed to fix up the building. The tree was their gesture of thanks.

After Jack died, Virginia drove all the way from her home in Ohio to find the plaque, which had become overgrown. This was no easy task, and several Islanders joined her, but no luck. Then someone came up with a bright idea—try a metal detector. After several false alarms (tin cans and other metal detritus in the soil), the plaque was finally unearthed from under three inches of vegetation. Today, a circle of fresh flowers encircles the linden tree, and the plaque—just a few feet away from a bench that honours the memory of our dear friend Dan Leckie—is once more readable.

Bill Freeman describes all this in a piece titled "The Quest" in *Islanders Remembering Jack*. He writes: "Legend has it that Jack had two trees planted somewhere in the area. It is said that he had the idea that the trees would be placed in such a way that when they were mature a hammock could be strung between them and people could swing in the hammock thinking of Dan, the task of building a caring, vital city and anything else that came to mind."

All true. The tree we planted for Dan Leckie was an oak—a slow-growing tree but a strong one. A tree that would endure for a long time.

I was at that spot in the summer of 2013 and I can report that the trees are better than thirty feet tall. And a third tree we planted there, a jack pine—where some of Jack's ashes are spread—is even taller.

When you look at that tree from the land facing the water, the tree has a decidedly, quite playful, leftward lean.

In March of 2013, Brent Hawkes, the minister at Metropolitan Community Church of Toronto—commonly called simply MCC—sat down with me and talked about his friendship with Jack and with me.

Brent Hawkes is a gay married minister who officiated at Jack's state funeral and at the interment of Jack's ashes and who blessed the bronze bust I did of Jack for his headstone. He also helped Jack and me, on our anniversary, renew our vows to each other at MCC. And he would officiate at the wedding of Mike Layton and his bride, Brett Tryon, in 2012—just three days after the first anniversary of his father's death. Brent understood Jack's passion for the underdog and the vulnerable as the one thing that had drawn him to the issue of gay rights, just as it had drawn him to the issues of homelessness or women's equality.

"And at your wedding," Brent reminded me, "you and Jack lifted up the issue of gay marriage." He recalled how our friend John Campey had spoken at our wedding and expressed his fervent hope that one day, same-sex marriage would be a reality and gays and lesbians could celebrate their weddings as joyously as we had ours. When the first gay marriages were celebrated at MCC on January 14, 2001, Jack and I were there to lend our support. Brent had been assaulted by a woman in the church just before that wedding. And at the wedding, he wore a bulletproof vest because he had been the target of death threats and bomb threats; he was accompanied by bodyguards, and he took a roundabout route to the church. (Later, Brent made light of the steps he had had to take: "That morning, I met my bodyguards: ten of the meanest lesbians you've ever seen.") Meanwhile, both the Ontario and federal governments were fighting the marriages in court. On the tenth anniversary of the first gay marriages, the two original couples came back to the church to renew their vows, with Brent presiding. Jack and I were among many couples who did the same.

The Globe and Mail once asked Jack to name his top ten favourite spots in Toronto, and MCC was one of them. Jack had a political activist-to-activist friendship with Brent Hawkes, but he also saw Brent as his spiritual counsellor. So the political became more and more personal over time.

When Jack got sick that second time, we invited Brent to help us plan the funeral. This is what Brent remembers saying to Jack: "'Are you sure you want me to do this? You could get bishops, you could get heads of denominations to do this.' 'You know,' Jack said, 'you're my pastor and MCC is my church.' So then to be invited in that journey over the next short while and to talk about the details of the service, but also to talk about dying and death and then to do the funeral was an amazing moment, an opportunity and far beyond what we thought. In fact, in the earlier planning, all of us thought too small. I don't think we could have predicted, because something happened. Jack's death touched a chord on so many different levels. At the funeral, I said that Jack gave so many gifts in life and in death."

Brent continued, "I got e-mails from significant leaders of different non-profits saying that they were so pleased to see the spirituality in the service. They hadn't expected it. But what they didn't know was that Jack was a very spiritual person. Which is why I quoted him at his funeral: 'I believe how I live my life every day is my act of worship.'"

Brent told me that there were times during his last meetings with Jack, while they talked about death and dying and the planning of the funeral, that Jack broke down in tears. One time was when Jack told Brent he had dreamed of Moses in the wilderness, seeing the Promised Land, but not being able to go on.

Jack cried, too, after Brent asked him what message he had for me. "The idea of passing my heart and soul to Olivia to shepherd me to the next phase of my spirit and soul is totally comforting," Jack said. "Held in her arms, I have no fears." Two days before dying, Jack put those words in writing.

Brent talked to me about how others were inspired by the love between Jack and me and by the strength and wisdom that came out of that partnership. He gave this example: "We were talking about who would read the scriptures and the idea of having scriptures from various traditions, and when it came to someone to read the Muslim scripture—who should it be? And Jack was saying, 'Well, there's a mosque in the riding and maybe the head of the mosque.' And you said, 'But, Jack, why wouldn't you have Tasleem Riaz?' And Jack said, 'Well, I would worry, because in the Muslim tradition it's not done. A woman does not read the scriptures in a public setting, and some people might take offence to that and I don't want to offend anybody.'"

As Brent and I recalled the conversation, I remembered saying, "But, Jack, she's your good friend." To which Brent said, "Isn't this the time to move the goal post? Isn't this the time to move things forward?" Tasleem did indeed read at the funeral from the Qur'an.

In the days following Jack's death, a makeshift shrine formed on the sidewalk leading up to our front door. Candles and flowers were left, and someone painted on the concrete the words, "Alive in Our Hearts." It's there yet.

We left a basket on the wicker couch on our porch so people could drop off cards. The cards came in great numbers, and I was reminded of what I had told Anna Maria Tremonti in our interview: how Canadians, though occasionally cynical, are essentially kind and generous. The goodness is there, and that outpouring of love told me that I was not alone.

CHAPTER 18

Back on My Feet

It was magical and wondrous witnessing the birth of the baby. Solace is beautiful and full of life, and she came at a time when we were still very much grieving Jack's loss. The name Solace brings me comfort and calm and reminds me of the sun.

On the morning of August 23, 2011, I experienced a panic attack. Jack had passed away the morning before. The memory of his last breath was still raw and vivid. Yet there was something almost unbelievable about it, as if I were floating above a play, watching the characters descend into tragedy.

Maybe it was the sudden change in routine that caused my chest to tighten, my heartbeat to quicken. For the past month, Jack had been the focus of every waking moment of my life. We had reached a precious state where we were able to live in the moment, and be thankful for it, until his last breath. Now, I no longer had to wake up wondering how he was doing or having to administer the pain medication and oversee all the other duties that are part of palliative care.

Eventually, I pulled myself out of the spin. I experienced a few more such attacks in the months that followed, but they gradually subsided. For the most part, it's easier now. Time does heal.

In the weeks, months and now years since Jack died, I have, of course, been in the public eye, and many people have commented on how strong I seem to be. I have been able to throw myself into my work, which I love and which gives me great satisfaction. Focusing on others has helped me hold myself together.

In the summer of 2013, I received an e-mail from my old friend Jane Bertrand, who had fought in the trenches with me on many early learning and childcare battles in the past. Jane's touching note reminded me that words have the power to heal.

"Hello Olivia," Jane wrote. "Larry Corea, my husband, died on May 27th this year. Cancer. Sixty-three years old. We had been together forty-one years and still liked and loved each other a lot. He did his best to launch me into life without him by focusing on a quote from Gabriel Garcia Marquez—'Don't cry that it is over, smile that it happened.' Death sucks. Cancer sucks. But I do smile through the tears. I am sending you this email to thank you for the interviews you did shortly after Jack died. Your words of wisdom have been most helpful to me and I have returned to them often. Take care. Jane."

I am deeply grateful that I have been able to provide a level of comfort to others and to help others accept. And I am deeply grateful for the overwhelming outpouring of support, for me and our family, from millions of Canadians. This has helped, and so have my faith and my philosophy. It seems as if all my life I had been preparing for this time, this difficult time. My early obsession with death and suffering, my interest in gods and goddesses and relations between them and us mortals. I know and accept that, in the end, we all die.

One of my favourite passages in the Bible is from the Book of Job in the Old Testament. I love it for its descriptions of nature, the sun rising, the water, the waves. Consider this passage:

> *But now ask the beasts, and let them teach you;*
> *And the birds of the heavens, and let them tell you.*
> *Or speak to the earth, and let it teach you;*
> *And let the fish of the sea declare to you.*
> *Who among all these does not know*
> *That the hand of the Lord has done this,*
> *In whose hand is the life of every living thing,*
> *And the breath of all mankind.*

Job was a righteous man who believed in God and who loved his family. But God decided to test Job's faith. He was afflicted with terrible skin sores, his ten children died, he lost his wealth and he was cast out. Job was faced with choices: blame himself (he must have done something bad to deserve all this), blame his friends (who likewise thought he had done something heinous, else why his gross misfortune) or blame God (whom he rails against for a time as an unjust God).

But in the end, Job comes to accept the mystery of life, and that acceptance becomes the foundation of his faith. Job comes to understand that God's goodness and human suffering coexist.

I never prayed that Jack would be healed. I accepted that suffering is a part of life. Since Jack's death, I have tried to preserve his legacy and the eternal values he stood for, but also to get on with my own life. And I have constantly reminded myself to feel grateful for all the time I had been given with this man I loved.

In the wake of Jack's death, it was the small stuff that got to me.

Making coffee, for example. For the longest time, I didn't know how to make coffee because Jack had always made it. I stared at the coffee maker and couldn't figure out how to program it to brew coffee at a set time in the morning.

I would go to a new city and get lost because I had always counted on Jack to set the direction. He always seemed to know where north was, even in the pre-GPS days. And it was always Jack who would buy the wine when there was company for dinner.

Making coffee, navigating, choosing wine: these are mundane matters, but life is full of them, and when you spend half your life relying on another person to do these mundane things, how do you go on without being lost and sad?

The other day, I found Jack's business card in the tag on the luggage that I have been using, and that little discovery hit me hard. What does one do with all these cards, all these pieces of ID after a loved one has disappeared? During our lives, we are identified by the identity cards we carry. In Jack's case, these included the special passport he carried as an MP, his Aeroplan card (because he flew so much), plus his bank and credit cards. After Jack's death, none of these mattered anymore. All that mattered was what he had accomplished in life and the people he touched and the memories he left behind.

After Jack died, I tried to remove all the reminders. But as the daughter of immigrants, I had been taught not to waste anything. (My mother has collected large numbers of plastic bags and they are on every floor to reduce our need to buy garbage bags.) So I started using up all of Jack's old stationery, notebooks and computer flash cards. I would tear out used pages and keep the notebooks. But the problem with all this frugality is that Jack's notes and handwriting resurface. I would be reminded anew that he is not around anymore, and that would hit me emotionally.

Immediately after Jack's death, I asked Sarah and Mike to take away many of his clothes and personal things that would remind me of him. And my friends Kiloran German and Ah Fung bundled up Jack's books, papers and many political mementoes to donate to the library and archives at Ryerson University. I thought if I wasn't surrounded by his stuff (and he had lots of stuff), it would be easier for me emotionally. But I soon realized that life is not that simple. Two years after Jack's death, I regularly have people coming up to me offering condolences, often with tears in their eyes. So instead of trying to eliminate Jack all around me, I have been attempting another approach: see Jack's objects and images as just that—a snapshot of him in a certain moment in time. And yes, those are precious moments to be relived on occasion. But I would not want to be trapped in them. I remind myself that by giving away or recycling his possessions, pages of his writing or photos of him, I am not betraying him or denying his existence. Jack's legacy is not the physical objects he left behind.

So while it is tremendously sad for a minute or two when Jack's presence comes back to remind me of our life together, I no longer seek to avoid these moments, but nor do I seek them out. I let them come to me naturally, and I am learning to live with them in the moment and then move on to matters at hand.

Jack often joked about how he would be a total basket case without me, and that since I was supposed to be the emotionally stronger one, it was better for him to leave this world first. Well, he got his wish. Jack didn't have to live without me and bear the sorrow and loss I am enduring. In the long run it is better this way. Or am I rationalizing?

When I was a teenager, I had a romantic notion of sorrow, of a life dominated and dictated by blue and greys, by loneliness and suffering and sadness. I believed then that such feelings were grand and noble and connected somehow to beauty and the creation of great works of art. I was reading novels from English and European literature in which the tragic heroine is left behind; suffering, it struck me, seemed so sweet, so innocent. But I had not yet lived a life full of blessings and joy with a loving partner. Little did I know how sorrow gnaws at the bone, how it creeps up at the most unexpected place, how devastating and soul destroying it can be.

Yet there are beautiful moments when I look up and wonder if Jack's spirit is there in that vast blue sky. When I look at a sunset and marvel at the beauty, I think of the thousands of sunsets Jack and I watched. I sense in the setting sun, as with the stars, his spirit.

From the Mountain River in the High Arctic, I wrote this note to Jack's mother, Doris Layton, on July 18, 2012:

Dear Mom,
I am writing to you on the day Jack was born 62 years ago.

While feeling his absence tremendously, at times almost unbearably so, I also celebrate his life and his love to all of us.

Jack's walk on this earth is a blessing, especially so to those close to him. You have raised him with such love, encouragement and affection, he was able to give it back thousands fold to all those around him.

In my dreams, I tried phoning him but he wasn't able to give me his new number! So while I wasn't able to talk to him or connect directly, I feel his spirit in the mountains, the river and the waves, the clouds and the majesty around me here on the Mountain River.

This is a place where I can properly grieve, properly remember the beautiful times we had together, and when I come through the other side after the sorrow is so overwhelming and unbearable, I can begin to heal and renew.

Olivia

Early in 2013, I had another vivid dream. I dreamed of Jack coming close to me. I lived in a beautiful place and believed that we had an unlimited amount of time together. In the dream there was another woman, probably representing death, and I wanted her to leave so I could spend more time alone with Jack. We were so much enjoying each other's company. But this other woman wasn't leaving, and I am not sure she understood what I was saying.

At that moment I woke up—and in my head was a clear image of Jack. The emotions I felt were very intense but not necessarily sad, because his presence was so strong and the image of him so vivid. Still, the realization set in that I would never be able to talk to him again. The dream presented a stark reminder that Jack was gone forever and I would never again be able to reach him, to seek his advice, to share in the joy of daily living.

A few months later, in the summer of 2013, I had another dream. I dreamed that after Jack had died, he called me on the cell phone from "the other side" and he said he wanted lunch, a smoked meat sandwich. Perhaps Montreal smoked meat—he loved the smoked meat sandwiches at Schwartz's Deli in Montreal. I could tell that he was sick, his voice was hoarse, and he was packing up his office, knowing he would not be back. We lost the connection, so I started calling him back. He came on the phone after I tried to reach him several times, and finally I was able to chat with him. I was trying to connect with him about saving some files of significance. And he said yes, he would save the files. And then he said he had time, so could we do lunch and would I bring him smoked meat? Then I woke up, startled and sad.

Still, maybe this was progress. After two years, Jack's spirit finally connected—through smoked meat!

~

I returned to life on Parliament Hill just weeks after the funeral—for the first time without Jack. In September of 2011, I stood in Parliament to respond to tributes made to Jack by the prime minister and all the party leaders. And I said, "It was easy to be hopeful and optimistic when Jack was around. The hard part is now."

Every time I walk past the eternal flame in front of the Parliament Buildings, I remember how excited Jack was to show me all of his favourite spots on the Hill. We would watch the sun set behind the Hill, and Jack taught me that one of the best spots to view the setting sun is from behind the Supreme Court building. We would run and bike along the Rideau Canal in the summer and skate on it in the winter. Now I try the same routes but I often seem to lose my way.

The hallway of the Centre Block of the Parliament Buildings also brings back memories. I remember Jack giving me roses one Valentine's Day and me holding the roses—the two of us working with an *Ottawa Sun* photographer to perfect a kiss with the stained glass window illuminated behind us. That photo stayed in our Ottawa apartment until Jack's passing.

Here is the challenge: How do I turn those beautiful memories into just that—memories? How do I cherish the beauty of it all, and not be sad or depressed that it's over? I issue to myself a constant reminder to enjoy those moments and not to dwell on the fact that they have passed and can never be repeated. Stay in the moment, Olivia. Stay in the moment.

So this is what it's like to live alone. How long will it take for me to learn how to live by myself, I wonder. I am a flexible and adaptable person, so it can be done. And yes, I will learn to enjoy it one day.

I will learn how creativity comes not just when brainstorming with someone who shares the same passion. Creativity can manifest itself when one is alone. I knew that when I was a teenager, when I was in art school and when I was a sculptor. I now need to get back into that space.

There is the mind to train, and then there is the body.

During the first week of October 2011, I worked myself into a frenzy. In my role as the Opposition transport and infrastructure critic, I was determined to make progress with my pursuit of a national transit strategy for Canada—something I think is vitally important for all our cities and communities. I met with mayors and municipal councillors and transit advocates in seven provinces and territories to muster support for a national plan that I believed would result in fast, reliable, accessible public transit. And the vast majority of those I met invariably signed on, seeking leadership from and partnership with the federal government.

I also wanted to ensure that the polling numbers stayed strong as the NDP sought a new permanent leader—so we could build on the gains we had made under Jack's leadership.

And I wanted to connect in any way I could with all the people who had shown such support after Jack's death. I crossed the country, attending many vigils and memorials in honour of Jack—ranging from an Irish wake in a Calgary library attended by a few hundred to a full-fledged memorial of more than a thousand people in Vancouver. These vigils were beautiful, but they often showed videos featuring music and images of Jack, which were hard for me to bear.

So I kept busy, but I neglected my health. In October, I missed my flu shot and came down with the flu, but recovered quickly (or so I thought) and went back to work. But the cough lingered and grew worse.

There were nights when I heard Jack's laboured breathing as I myself was trying to breathe in the middle of a coughing fit. Was that his breathing I heard, or mine? Sleep, imagination, reality: my brain could not decipher which was which. The more I coughed, the more difficult it was for me to sleep, and the weaker I grew. But I didn't want to stop working. I wanted to carry on, doing the work in the House of Commons that could no longer be done by Jack.

I went to my family doctor in Toronto, but since I am basically very fit, he thought there was really no reason to worry about a lingering cough. "It will go away soon enough," he said. "Here is some cough medicine that will help you sleep through the night."

Several weeks later, I was wheezing and getting no better. I couldn't get off the train when I arrived in Ottawa and had to be conveyed in a wheelchair to the taxi. The next day I went downstairs to the nurse stationed in the House of Commons. She listened to my lungs and sent me to a doctor in Ottawa. He diagnosed a nasal infection and gave me a puffer and some antibiotics. But I was beginning to feel even weaker.

Two days later, I went to the NDP's annual Christmas party—the first one where we had a staff that exceeded six hundred, the biggest holiday party in the history of the party on Parliament Hill. I was determined not to miss it. I did an hour-long interview with Tobi Cohen of Postmedia about how I was coping with Jack's death, and off I went to the party.

Except I could hardly stand. My friends fussed over me, bringing me food and drinks, but all I wanted to do was lie down. After interim leader Nycole Turmel delivered her speech, I went straight home, but I had difficulty walking the five-minute stretch back to my apartment.

Somehow I made it—but only with the help of my wonderful staff. By now I knew something was very wrong, so I called my family doctor again (bless his heart, he had given me his cell number), and he told me to go to the emergency department of the closest hospital. He didn't want me to fly home the next day because I was having such difficulty breathing. Perhaps I had a blood clot.

So my entire staff spent their holiday party at the Ottawa Hospital. We were the best-dressed lot in emergency that night!

At the hospital, doctors finally came up with a diagnosis: pneumonia. But I had to get back to Toronto the next day because the Toronto Islanders had assembled an art show in honour of Jack. There were to be beautiful paintings, sculptures and installations, along with that stunning book, *Islanders Remembering Jack*, with moving stories about how Jack had touched the lives of Islanders, describing our loving and long relationship with them. A copy was to be presented to me, and I was determined to attend that event.

So I was loaded up with antibiotics and boarded the train. But then I broke out with hives. I couldn't breathe. I was dizzy and could not swallow because my throat was constricting: the antibiotics had triggered a serious allergic reaction. Luckily, I had an antihistamine with me and I managed to start breathing again. But that was one of the worst five hours I had ever spent travelling in my life.

My body was still puffed up and my eyes half-shut because of swelling. Somehow, I made it to the Islands party, and I enjoyed a beautiful evening.

During the Christmas holiday season I slowly regained my strength and I went back to work in January.

The next year, around the same time, I was really enjoying the NDP's holiday party. This time I was healthy—or so I thought. My Toronto staff came to Ottawa, and after the performance the year before at the hospital, I wanted to make sure they had a great evening. And we all did.

A day after the party, on a Thursday morning back in Toronto, I woke up early to do a radio interview. I stared at the mirror: the left side of my face was paralyzed. I couldn't move any of my muscles. I had difficulty pronouncing my *p* and *b* sounds because the left side of my mouth was not moving.

Still, I did the radio interview, hoping listeners understood what I was saying. I went to see my doctor immediately afterwards, and he told me I had shingles in my left ear and the infection had destroyed the facial nerves. He prescribed a week of steroids and antiviral drugs.

My affliction had a fancy name: Ramsay Hunt syndrome. The pain I had been experiencing in my left ear went away a few days later as I finished my medication. Now there was nothing more to do but wait for the facial nerves to grow back. Since I couldn't blink, the contact lenses had to go and out came the glasses. And since I couldn't speak properly, so much for giving speeches at public events.

I tried to continue with normal daily living and I tried not to drool when I was drinking and eating. I also massively researched shingles. Different doctors offered different advice. One suggested electro-stimulation so my facial muscles would not atrophy. Others advised against that lest the nerves grow back in the wrong place—I could be smiling, but simultaneously trigger the nerve near the eye and tears would flow. (How ironic, I could see some saying: a politician crying crocodile tears.) Or I could be blinking and that could trigger a sneer. Great, I thought. Just what a political figure needs: I would appear to be sneering at constituents when I was actually empathetic.

I was told to do hourly massages on my face and regular facial exercises. Oh sure, let me pause during my question to the minister in the House of Commons as I massage this funny face of mine.

In any case, I carried on after the holidays, and my ability to speak recovered quickly. But I had never looked at my face in the mirror this much in my entire life as I faithfully did my facial exercises: lift my eyebrow, frown without moving my cheek muscles, and smile evenly on both sides of my mouth. And I tried hard to stop the sneering—

especially when facing the Conservatives across the aisle in the House. I reassured friends who were concerned, saying that I couldn't see my face (as I was behind it), so it really wasn't so much a problem for me as it was for those who had to look at me. I also told everyone who would listen to get a shingles vaccination if they were around my age.

Almost a year has passed since, most of my nerves have grown back, and I am back to smiling—even though my smile is a bit crooked. I can close my left eye now without having to tape it shut at night. And I can even wink if I keep up with my facial exercises. Still, I have to apply drops in my left eye every few hours since the nerves that produce tears are dead.

There is a moral to this story: stop working when your body tells you to, and go to the doctor earlier rather than later.

I developed various mechanisms to cope with my grief: I learned to meditate and to breathe deeply. I used the power of routines and duty (make the bed, clean the house, check the BlackBerry) when overwhelmed with sadness. I would acknowledge these sad moments and allow them to pass. I was determined to overcome these moments of darkness, to sleep and function without the aid of medication.

The strategies worked. I was able to find the strength to go through the state funeral, the many emotional tributes large and small that followed. I found the courage and inner fortitude to give many interviews and speeches about Jack's death. I watched the very emotional biopic, *Jack*, several times in public.

There were two personal, creative journeys that I wanted to take. One was to create a bronze bust of Jack, for his headstone. The other was to tell my story with this book.

It took almost a year after his passing for me to find the creative energy to complete the sculpture, which I created in clay before it was cast in bronze. It was especially difficult when I posted on a wall at home hundreds of photos of Jack smiling as I sought to mould the clay to capture his likeness, his spirit, his joyful smile.

Art has always been a solitary pursuit for me, but I had never felt this alone. During the twenty-six years I had known Jack, he had always been there—when I fell asleep, when I got up in the night, when I woke in the morning. And even when he wasn't physically there, we were always in touch by phone. During all the time we were together as a couple, I don't think I ever went to sleep without having said goodnight and without Jack having said he loved me. It was often late at night when we were alone together—talking over the events of the day, what was on our minds, what was bothering us, what we planned for the next day. We'd laugh, relax, and offer each other mutual support.

So many times in the months following his death, I would be at my desk in our third-floor bedroom, working on a press release or a speech or a strategic plan, talking it through out loud, and my instinct was to turn and say, as I had so many times before, "What do you think, Jack?"

All that Jack and I shared together I now face alone. I deliberately return to many of the activities we loved, to remember the wonderful times together, but also as a way to move forward on my own. So I went back to canoeing in beautiful Arctic waters, I went back to snorkelling in tropical waters.

I do, though, find it hard to observe, without Jack at my side, a pair of queen angelfishes swimming in coral reefs. Gorgeous blue-green fish that grow up to a foot and a half in length, they were our favourites. We loved the look of them and we loved that they always swam in pairs.

I sense Jack's spirit and his love when I'm watching sunsets, calm seas, majestic mountains, full moons and bright stars, while hearing the laughter of family, while eating delicious food. Such beauty is eternal while life is not. I am still waiting for the day when I can be reminded of him (which I am constantly, especially when I am on holiday) without feeling sadness—so that all that's left are the beautiful loving memories. When this time will come, I don't know. But I know it will come one day.

I have always intellectually understood the power of death and emptiness, and I have always appreciated the empty space in art, the void and tragedies in literature and the minor chords in music. To *experience* emptiness is another matter. Still, I am at my most creative when I am forced to reflect and come to terms with solitude. All part of life's blessings.

On January 5, 2012, at 2:15 a.m., Sarah Layton gave birth to her second child, a sister for Beatrice. I was there to witness the happy event, along with Sarah's husband, Hugh Campbell, and her mother, Sally Roy.

It was magical and wondrous witnessing the birth of this baby. Solace Layton Campbell is beautiful and full of life. I have no doubt she will grow up intelligent and creative. And she was well named, for she came at a time when we were still very much grieving Jack's loss. The name Solace, which Hugh had suggested, brings me comfort and calm and reminds me of the sun. A new year, a new birth, a new life to celebrate. At the moment she was born, Solace lived up to her name. She has indeed been a solace to us all.

Sarah was pregnant before Jack died, and he was very excited at the prospect. When the family gathered at the hospital waiting for labour to progress, we looked at photos of Jack on my BlackBerry and we reminisced. One of the photos we admired was of Jack holding Beatrice, Solace's sister, right after she was born in 2009. I have a similar photo on the wall of my living room.

I remember when Sarah conveyed to Jack the news that she was pregnant with Beatrice. "You are going to be Grandpa Jack," she said, and he just started blubbering. This was election night in 2008, so Sarah had chosen her moment well. Jack was the crier in the family; I was the rational, let's-get-on-with-things type.

A birth is a joyous event. You can't be sad when a baby is coming. I had a bottle of champagne on standby to celebrate once Solace was out of the hospital.

In the eulogy Sarah delivered at her father's funeral, she talked about how Jack would take Beatrice on long walks and how he always made time for family. Sarah addressed her father: "You've been a city councillor, the deputy mayor of Toronto, the honourable member for Toronto-Danforth, the leader of Her Majesty's Loyal Opposition. But most of all, I will remember you as Grandpa Jack—fun-loving, smiling, with all the time in the world, having a tea party on the floor with Beatrice."

In a family video shot in 2009, Jack described what becoming a grandfather meant to him. "There is nothing more exciting, thrilling and precious than holding a grandchild in your arms, and then how fast they grow and how fast it changes, and before you know it, they're getting heavy to hold in your arms. You're looking in their eyes, and they're looking at you. And when you're singing a song to them and when they're laughing and playing with you and you feel that hand going around that finger and squeezing—these are the intimacies you really can't put into words. I knew it was going to be great. I now know why grandparents all walk around smiling."

In a piece she wrote for the *Toronto Star*, Sarah looked to the future while lamenting that her father was not there to witness the birth of her second daughter. "How I wish," she wrote, "that he could have been there when my daughter Solace was born . . . He was so open with his love and hopes for her big sister Beatrice and he was already dreaming of what the future would hold for his new granddaughter that was on the way, with her ultrasound picture by his bedside in his final days.

"When I look into her young blue eyes, I see the same excitement of what's to come that glistened in his. I hope that when his grandchildren grow up they are inspired to be as passionate as he was in their life's work."

Stephen Lewis, in his eloquent eulogy, also talked about Beatrice. "Inevitably," he said of Jack's last letter, "we fastened on those last memorable lines about hope, optimism and love. But the letter was, at its heart, a manifesto for social democracy. And if there was one word that might sum up Jack Layton's unabashed social democratic message, it would be generosity. He wanted, in the simplest and most visceral terms, a more generous Canada . . .

"From time to time, Jack and I would meet in the corridors of my foundation, where his supernaturally competent daughter Sarah works, and we would invariably speak of our grandchildren. You cannot imagine—I guess you saw it in the video—the radiating joy that glowed from Jack as he talked of Sarah's daughter, his granddaughter Beatrice, and when he said as he often said that he wanted to create a better world for Beatrice and all the other Beatrices to inherit, you instantly knew of one of his strongest and most compelling motivations."

What Jack wanted, what I want, is an engaged society. Anything with the words "community-based" in front of it is bound to be good. With engaged citizens, you get better decisions. When there is common purpose, a deadline and a good facilitator, democracy works fine. Lately I see a drift towards less participation—in part because families have less money, less time, more debt. Together, this means that there's less time to participate. Some people in power want that, but it's not healthy.

As I watch Beatrice and Solace grow, I silently rededicate and recommit my efforts to creating a world, a country and a city that have children at their heart. A world full of love, full of peace and joy. A world that is hopeful.

After my experience of losing someone so close, I came to realize that community organizations wanted to learn more from me about palliative care. I would accept their invitations whenever I could, for I believed there was value in others hearing about my experience. Still, these talks were difficult to deliver, and I had to rehearse the speeches so I could learn to control my emotions.

One such conference, held in Saskatchewan in June of 2013, was called, aptly I thought, Out of the Shadows: Extending the Boundaries of Palliative Care. I liked the name, for it hinted at some of the good things we are doing around death and dying and how we might do this better.

At these public gatherings, I talked not just about death but about life—and how Sarah Layton, for example, had received help in the community when she was pregnant with both Beatrice and Solace, in addition to the love and support of family and friends. And of course Sarah had help from the health care system. When her baby was almost ready to arrive, Sarah had nurses to assist her. And she had her doctor to help control the pain, to coach her, to help with the birth. This support network made the whole experience so much smoother, enjoyable and inspirational. And, of course, a lot less painful.

Just as we all come into the world, we all must leave. The journey is different for everyone, but the destination is constant. And just as a new baby ideally has support from the community, so too should someone on that last journey. Solace came into the world surrounded by people who deeply love her. Jack left this world in precisely the same circumstance.

He was blessed with excellent palliative care. We had nurses to provide personal care and support in our home, we had doctors to help control pain and to prepare us for the final hours—we had compassionate and caring people in our corner. Not only did we have a palliative care doctor, who broadly managed Jack's case, but we also had a pain care specialist, who brought with her an astonishing tool kit (as she called it) to manage pain in all its various forms and locales. A few days after the public announcement of his cancer, Jack Skyped into a caucus meeting to greet his second family, the more than one hundred NDP members of Parliament, and this specialist was able to offer him a pain control cocktail that left him energized, lucid and pain free.

What a miraculous gift. The gift of specialized medical care. Jack's death was virtually without pain, and it was certainly without trepidation or fear. His family experienced neither guilt nor regret, and made decisions in full accordance with Jack's will.

We were lucky—financially and professionally. I was able to set aside all my other obligations in the last month to help with Jack's care. Our children and many of our family and friends live nearby, so we could take turns being with Jack around the clock. I had backup when I was tired or needed a swim or a run. I was able to access information so Jack and I could understand this journey.

In the biopic *Jack*, there is a scene—this actually happened—during Jack's last hospital stay where he is talking to a member of his cancer care team. He was always engaged with all of them and always made a point of writing down their names. That scene ends when the Olivia character tells the Jack character that it's time to take him home for that final journey.

Our home is a place where we were able to take care of Jack in comfort. In the front garden we planted flowers—phlox, a butterfly bush, bright coneflowers, climbing roses—that bloomed where he could see them, and the bees and butterflies drawn to them, from his vantage by the window. And of course we were lucky to have palliative support from the medical community, nurses and caregivers. We had spiritual guidance from Reverend Hawkes, and we had psychosocial support when we needed it. And because of palliative support in death, we were able to celebrate Jack Layton's life and to rejoice in his spirit. We were so fortunate to have those days at home.

Sadly, Jack's experience is not at all universal in Canada. In this land where universal health care is part of our national identity, too many Canadians embark on their final journey without the kind of comprehensive care and support that Jack received. Too many families lack the knowledge and the power to feel they are in control of a loved one's final journey.

Control is a key word here. When you die in a hospital, even one equipped with a palliative care unit, you are nevertheless in the care of strangers—no matter how compassionate those nurses and doctors might be. Hospitals run on schedules. At home, you are spared that. You sleep in your own familiar bed, you are surrounded by loved ones and you eat comfort food that they themselves have prepared. This is how it should be.

Palliative care is critically important—not just for the patient but for the entire family. But until we have comprehensive, accessible and universal palliative care provided though our health care system, volunteers and front-line staff must fill this crucial role.

I was moved when I saw that a focus of the Saskatchewan conference was to extend the boundaries of palliative care to marginalized and stigmatized populations. No one should be left behind. This became so evident to Jack and me, years ago, in the middle of the AIDS epidemic in Toronto. So many young people were shunned by their own families and even by the health care system.

That's when I began to realize the importance of palliative care. Whether through a visit, a prescription or a sponge bath, these caregivers provide a helping hand and hold a hand in time of need. They listen sympathetically to an outpouring of loss and grief, and they help families cope and focus on the love, not the fears. What an amazing gift they give. To do what they do requires great courage—and great humanity.

Healing in the wake of grief comes in so many forms. Here is another: the healing power of nature.

I often wish that all Canadians—and especially young people—could have the chance to experience this majestic land of ours. To experience the wilderness and the awesome power of nature. I wish all could know the grandeur, the sense of the infinite—because all that power, and all that glory, does bring peace.

In 2010, Jack and I marked his sixtieth birthday by going on an amazing whitewater trip in the Arctic. One year later, we went through a historic election, and Jack became leader of the Opposition . . . and then he began his last battle with cancer.

In the summer of 2012, almost precisely a year after Jack's death, I went back to the Arctic for a journey down the Mountain River. I paddled the white waters, I watched the sunsets, I saw the stars—and I pondered life without Jack. I thought once more of the story of Job, of his contemplation of the mysteries of nature and the universe and his ability to accept those mysteries. I did experience sadness, but there was peace, too.

In August of 2013, I went back to the Dumoine River, site of the first whitewater canoe trip I ever took with Jack as my partner—this time with Mike, his son. And I experienced something quite different. Instead of the sorrow I had felt on my wilderness trip the summer before, I cried tears of joy when I saw Mike's excitement as he shot a rapid perfectly. I felt a surge of pride when I saw the look of determination and courage on his face as he tackled yet another Class III rapids. The last time Mike had done a whitewater trip was twenty years before, when he was a teenager.

I smiled when I heard his cries of amazement at night as he gazed at the millions of stars, just as his father had done so many years ago. Quite by accident, Mike had brought on the trip a sky-blue shirt much like one his father had worn on this same river—same make, same material.

The great circle was turning, ever turning, and I took comfort in it while marvelling at it. As I so often do on these trips, I felt a strong connection to nature—something so strong and powerful, so pure and beautiful and good. And I found peace. That's what I know. Whatever you do, however you see yourself, whatever your passions, it's important to take the time to explore the vastness and mystery around us. Take the time to reflect, to listen, and to be inspired. And, as I have in these pages, take the time to share your story with others.

CHAPTER 19

A Better Life for Beatrice and Solace

If you can imagine something, you can achieve it. One wish leads to another. That's not wishful thinking. That's pragmatic. That changes the world. And that's why politics, which can be so frustrating, can also be so rewarding.

One-and-a-half-year-old Solace and four-year-old Beatrice have discovered that the floor-to-ceiling drapes in the Regatta Room at the Westin Harbour Castle hotel are perfect for hide-and-seek and playing tag. The two are in sundresses, and Beatrice, especially, is giggling as the game revs up. There is no sweeter sound in the world than a child shrieking with pure delight.

"Who needs toys?" someone says to their mother, Sarah Layton.

"You're right," she replies, and jokes about ordering such curtains for home.

We are at this hotel by Toronto's waterfront shortly before the unveiling of a bronze statue to honour Jack's memory at a ceremony marking the official opening of the Jack Layton Ferry Terminal, gateway to the Toronto Islands—a favourite destination for our family. At the ceremony, I said that being in this place—the starting point of so many wonderful journeys—brought back a flood of joyous memories. When I was a child, a newcomer from Hong Kong in 1970, I went with my parents to the Islands and there learned to ride a bike.

That same year, another newcomer to Toronto also went cycling on the Islands. He was a university student from Hudson, Quebec. His name was Jack Layton. Eighteen years later, Jack and I were married on the Islands, and twenty-four years after that, his son, Mike, was married there. The Toronto Islands hold a very special place in the history of our family.

And on this August morning in 2013, the whole Layton clan is here, including Jack's mother, Doris. As is my mother, with one arm in a cast following a fall, using her other hand to direct her helper.

Had my granddaughters paused in their game to look through the hotel windows, they would have seen not fifty metres away a blue cloth draped over a bronze that would be unveiled in less than an hour. On that hot, mostly sunny day, the forecasted rain holding off nicely, a crowd one thousand strong had already gathered. And the TV cameras, a dozen or more, had arrayed themselves behind a bank of benches with every lens pointed at the blue bolt of cloth. If Beatrice and Solace had gone outside and peeked under the cloth to see the bronze, Beatrice might have recognized the man on the back seat of a tandem bicycle. Grandpa Jack.

If Beatrice and Solace and every child in this country are to have a better life in the years ahead, we should let that bronze statue be our guide. The tandem bicycle is a powerful symbol of co-operation and trust and of the advantages to be gained from working together.

"The great thing about the tandem bicycle," I said at the unveiling, "is that it's faster than a regular bike—because when you're together you're stronger, you're faster, you move forward, just like a community. Together you support each other, just like a community."

Mike Layton spoke that day, too, and he remembered the family dropping Sarah off at summer camp one year before father and son cycled from Haliburton back to Toronto—a 230-kilometre distance peppered with challenging climbs (the Haliburton Hills are aptly named). Mike remembers seeing the odometer on the tandem bicycle hit sixty kilometres an hour on some of those exhilarating downhill stretches. Mike called the bronze tandem bike "a great symbol . . . That's how my father lived his life. He worked hard, he co-operated with others in his job, and he had fun through it all."

The more I thought about that bronze, and how it came to be, the more it struck me: this is how to get things done. Everybody pedalling hard in the same direction towards a common goal, sharing the work, and the work made joyous as a result.

The bronze was unveiled on August 22, 2013, precisely two years after Jack died, and it was the result of an amazing collective effort. First, someone had an idea. In the wake of Jack's death, Toronto Islanders Doryne Peace and Bill Freeman called a meeting, at which another Islander—Maya Toman—suggested a sculpture of Jack on a tandem bike as a lasting way to honour his memory. There was consensus: this was a good idea. Maybe a bronze sculpture?

Bronze is a notoriously expensive undertaking, but wheels were set in motion. A committee was formed, led by the city councillor for the ward, Pam McConnell. She was a long-time friend and colleague; both Jack and I had served with her on city council for years. The committee worked to expedite matters at city hall and to negotiate all the bureaucratic hurdles. The city donated the land adjacent to the ferry terminal, and city council approved renaming the terminal as the Jack Layton Ferry Terminal.

But we needed funds to make the bronze a reality. Through a

good friend, Sandra Clifford, I took the idea to the Ontario Federation of Labour, which wholeheartedly embraced it. Many union members had been looking for a way to commemorate Jack. On the day of the unveiling, OFL president Sid Ryan said it was the easiest fundraising he had ever done in his life. Several dozen unions and labour groups, with the help of Ken Neumann, and scores of individuals cobbled together the $350,000 required, and Toronto Island sculptor David Pellettier was brought in to create the statue. MST Bronze provided the engineering, landscaping and casting work. The team generously included me in the creative process—as a sculptor myself, I was able to work with my hands to ensure that Jack's smile was just as I remembered it.

After the statue was unveiled, Beatrice had first honours, as Sarah climbed onto the front seat and held her daughter on her lap. That is exactly what the statue was designed for—participation and fun. In the decades ahead, as parents playfully lift their children onto that front seat, I hope they will reflect on the real meaning of *Jack's Got Your Back*—as this memorial is called.

I said at the unveiling that the bronze will endure long past the time that all of us are gone, and that in the distant future, newcomers to Canada who have never heard of Jack Layton will come to this spot. They will see the statue of this happy, joyful man on a tandem bicycle. A man dedicated to equality, justice and the environment. And it will make them smile.

In an ideal world, and certainly the world that Jack and I envisioned, we have each other's backs. We work together as community members and as Canadians; we co-operate with each other.

Five days after the unveiling, a writer and professor of history at Carleton University named Matthew McKean wrote a piece in the *Hill Times*, the independent weekly that covers Parliament. The article, clearly triggered by the unveiling, astutely examined what the outpouring of affection for Jack in the wake of his death says about us as Canadians.

> *Today, as the challenges posed by globalization and global conflicts, environmental decay, declining patriotism, political disengagement, failing public services, crumbling cities and the disaffected populations within them increasingly give way to skepticism, distrust, sometimes out-and-out revolt, collective memory (in this case, the collective response to Jack Layton's death) can likewise be called upon to console Canadians, to renew confidence in Canada and its leaders, and, of course, to shore up and redefine new political identities.*
>
> *Memory has always played a key role in the shaping of political culture . . . What we see through the collective response to Jack Layton's death is the construction or reconstruction of a singular, uniquely Canadian political identity. The various meanings we confer upon Jack Layton through the processes of commemorating him are not only about the man, but also about the values and qualities we'd dearly like to see in our elected officials.*
>
> *By choosing to remember and memorialize Jack Layton, Canadians commemorate peace, civility, religious and cultural inclusiveness, optimism, the arts, social and environmental change, political dialogue, improved public services, improved cities, and an improved country. Canadians continue the process, in other words, of polishing the myth and remembering the politician we one day hope to have.*
>
> *In this way, the reconstructive ritual of collective memory was and remains an act of evoking or calling to mind, if not restoring, to politics and the social fabric what so many Canadians would agree has long been lost and forgotten.*

Amen.

Shaping the collective memory of Jack Layton has been my top priority since I knew he was going to die. But it's also been an extraordinary team effort: I think of Brian Topp's and Anne McGrath's assistance in drafting the last letter, Kathleen Monk's organizational efforts for the funeral, the tribute at Nathan Phillips Square in 2012 and the dearjack.ca memorial website, the naming of the ferry terminal and the bronze, the creation of the Jack Layton Chair at Ryerson University and the numerous scholarships and awards established in his name.

This has been a massive effort—a labour of love with one simple aim: to keep the legacy of Jack Layton alive. The past two years and more of my life have been dedicated to capturing the spirit of who he was and keeping that spirit intact. A perfect example of that legacy in action is the still very active dearjack website, with all its messages expressing affection for the man and detailing what this or that person has done to advance the greater good. "This man's life deeply touched me," reads a typical note to the website, "and I'm doing something to honour his memory." I think of the lecture series at Ryerson University and of the Federation of Canadian Municipalities fellowship awards in Jack's name. And I think of that 2012 NDP leadership convention where so many attendees wore T-shirts that read, "I Am the Layton Legacy."

Even Jack's ties have been called into service. Jack owned hundreds of ties, and after his death I took the best of them and offered them at charity auctions. The yellow tie he wore during the leaders' debates in 2011 fetched $1,000; his favourite one went for $5,000. The beneficiaries were typically non-profit organizations. On the back of each tie was his signature, the hand-designed creation of Jack's mother. Those ties are out there, circulating, just as Jack's books are circulating in the library at Ryerson University, where he once taught.

And it occurs to me that once I finish this book, a chapter in my life will come to an end.

Jack believed, as I do, that we all owe a responsibility to the next generation and the next. That is what brought us into public life. Just days after the unveiling of the bronze, a three-year-old child drowned in the city of Toronto. His mother had gone to the bathroom and he ventured into the swimming pool. All it took was three minutes. Drowning is a silent killer. This boy, like the other almost five hundred children who drown every year in this country, probably couldn't swim. That boy's death affected me deeply.

I go swimming with Beatrice and Solace, and as I watch them enjoying the water, I wonder: In a country so rich in lakes and rivers, how can we have so many people drowning? In the past decade, close to two thousand Canadians died by drowning.

Jack and I introduced Beatrice to swimming when she was less than one year old. We passed her back and forth, up and under the water, as we played together. Jack, remember, had been a competitive swimmer when he was young, and he and I agreed that we should start the grandchildren swimming early in life. Sarah and I enrolled them in swimming lessons and we all spent many joyous hours splashing and playing together.

We know that children from one to four are most at risk of drowning, and nine out of ten of them can't swim. Why can't we as a society offer free swimming lessons to these little children and their parents? The earlier they learn, the less fear children have. Think of the fun these children would have if they grew up with no fear of water. Think of the lives that could be saved when we have a nation of swimmers. Think of the health care costs we as a society could save if all Canadians swam more.

So many studies have recommended more exercise for children to reduce obesity rates. Yet for some parents, swimming classes are just too expensive. Or the parents can't swim and are thus unable to teach their children. Often as I walk past mostly empty pools and beaches, I wonder: Why can't the government partner with the Canadian Red Cross and offer free swimming classes in community centres and pools every summer, when most of the drownings occur?

And while I am thinking about my grandchildren, what about after-school activities, affordable childcare and a healthy breakfast and lunch in school?

A few months before the unveiling of the bronze, the Toronto Environmental Alliance celebrated twenty-five years of advocacy (A Greener City for All is its motto) by hosting a fundraising dinner at the grand old now funky-modern Gladstone Hotel on Queen Street West. This hotel is often the site of readings and literary events, but this night it had drawn a who's who of the politically and environmentally engaged. A friend of mine described standing in a streetcar en route to the event and listening to two young women deep in a conversation about youth drop-in centres.

Sure enough, the two women—a staffer at city hall and an urban affairs consultant—showed up at the dinner. There were half a dozen Toronto city councillors, MPs and MPPs, including Thomas Mulcair, the leader of the federal New Democratic Party, who was in town to champion a push for more federal support of cities such as Toronto. There was Julia Langer, the director of the Toronto Atmospheric Fund and former director of the World Wildlife Fund with whom I had canoed on the Nahanni River. There were people from most environmental organizations, such as Greenpeace and Environmental

Defence, as well as lawyers and financiers interested in creating green jobs and a sustainable future.

After the dinner, I was on a panel with two people I greatly admire: Michele Landsberg, the well-known journalist and an officer of the Order of Canada, and David Crombie, a former Conservative cabinet minister and Toronto mayor (his "tiny, perfect" appellation came up that night as it so often does). Moderating the panel was Hamutal Dotan, editor of the torontoist website and a commentator on city hall matters for CBC Radio's *Metro Morning* program. One of her questions concerned how best to reach out to voters and taxpayers when many of them are struggling to put food on the table from one day to the next.

"Challenge people," I told the audience, "to think not just about tomorrow but about twenty-five years from now. My granddaughter Beatrice will be twenty-eight then. Will we have clean air and water for her? We have to think about the future and envision how that future might and should look. But at the same time, we have to be practical. In some subsidized buildings in the city, the heat supply is electric. These seniors can't afford to pay for both heating and groceries. They have to turn off the heat in order to eat. We used to have an ecoENERGY program at the federal level; we should bring it back and massively expand it so these buildings can be retrofitted. You save in the pocket and you think about the future. That's how to engage people."

That night I wore a yellow blazer—because yellow is the colour of the sun, of joy and hope. Yellow because it's an uplifting colour that counterbalances all the black I wear. And yellow to remember the yellow tie that I made sure Jack wore during the leaders' debates in 2011.

When he offered his thoughts on engaging citizens, David Crombie stressed the importance of giving strength to the progressive movement, and then he looked at me and said, "You have to get behind a good mayoralty candidate dressed in yellow." Everyone laughed.

Hamutal Dotan asked some smart questions of the panel, and one was this: What's the hardest thing to do in the world of advocacy? Michele Landsberg said, "Galvanizing people so they believe they can work together. We have forgotten the thrill of working together. We have all forgotten that. It's deeply rewarding. Now it's each for himself, herself. Our municipal culture is so ugly." Michele paused and looked at me. "You, Olivia, were such a genius at getting things through all party lines—on women and kids. I'd like to see it happen again."

David Crombie agreed. "We need that sense of hope," he said. "We need to articulate what the city should be."

What he said next really resonated with me. "If I had a magic wand," he said, "I'd turn schools into community centres. Community schools are neighbourhood anchors. In rural areas, schools are the *only* community anchors." He went on to describe how seventy-two swimming pools in the city had been on the chopping block again, but neighbourhoods raised money to save sixty-eight of them.

I was the last speaker on the question about advocacy. "Overcoming cynicism," I told the audience, "that's the hardest thing." And I told them my story about starting the model school we called Rosedale Heights when I was a school trustee and Jack was a councillor, how we assembled a team and introduced after-school activities and brought in mothers and grandmothers and started a breakfast program. "It all started," I said, "with a vision. Bring Back the Don started that way, the Healthy City movement started that way. We need to articulate a vision, but it has to be a practical vision. You, too, the vision should say, can become a trustee or councillor or serve in some other way. People should be able to see that they can participate, they should be able to see themselves reflected in that vision, our vision."

~

Articulating a progressive vision is always a challenge. It is so much easier to embrace the status quo—and to fight progress by summoning up a fear of change. But at heart, I think we all yearn for progress—and for the hopes and dreams of the next generation. And that is what keeps me going. That has always been my quest.

Years ago, in 2004, I celebrated twenty years of public service, and friends and colleagues held a gala ceremony in my honour. I came across my speech from that occasion when clearing through some files recently. That night I said what I would say again—"Thank you." Those two simple words.

I could spend the next twenty years saying thank you, and it still wouldn't be enough. Politicians can never say thank you enough. We ask so much of people, demand so much. We ask for support, for money, for the time and talents of volunteers. And we ask for that ultimate leap of faith. We ask for votes. We ask for trust.

And of course, we selfishly ask for your unselfishness. Your dedication to change. Your citizenship, your *engaged* citizenship. Being involved with politics and activism can seem like a thankless task. And yet for me, it has been a source of great joy. It has been a great privilege.

Someone once asked me how I keep so positive and hopeful. In almost thirty years in office, I have recorded my share of wins and defeats. I made some mistakes and I made some progress—and then I look around and I see there is still child poverty. There is still violence against women. There is still pollution and gridlock. Injustice, inequality, bigotry, war, ignorance, disease and despair. Around our country, around the world.

Some might ask, what's the point? What difference will we make? But then I look ahead and I imagine how great things could be in another three decades, not how terrible.

If you can imagine something, you can achieve it. One wish leads to another. That's not wishful thinking. That's pragmatic. That changes the world. And that's why politics, which can be so frustrating, can also be so rewarding.

At the opening of the Jack Layton Ferry Terminal, I thought back to the hopes and fears I had as a child, as a newcomer to Toronto. I thought of Beatrice and Solace today. And I thought about all the things we still have to achieve.

And I recalled a passage in Isaiah that I had Jack's good friend Professor Myer Siemiatycki read at Jack's funeral:

If you give of yourself to the hungry,
Fulfilling the needs of the poor—
Then shall your light shine in darkness,
And your darkness shall be like the noon.
Then shall you be like a garden given water,
Like a wellspring whose waters never fail,
And you shall lay foundations for the coming generation.

As I enjoy my friends and my city, as I work on issues that are so important to me, as I help my parents and spend time with my grandchildren, as I connect and reconnect with people who have been part of my story and as I reflect back, I realize something. I have been blessed with amazing opportunities and a life filled with moments of great and surpassing joy. There has been darkness, but mostly light. An extraordinary journey has taken me from the heart of Hong Kong to the heart of Toronto. It has been a journey of the heart, and the journey continues.

ACKNOWLEDGEMENTS

After Jack died and I faced a life alone, without my personal and political partner, my soulmate and the love of my life, I worked to keep his memory, legacy and spirit alive. But I also came to realize that moving forward in the future, and working towards all the goals I shared with Jack, would mean telling some of my own stories. At the same time, many people who were touched by Jack's death and by my loss reached out to me, and wanted to know more about me and my life.

My friend Brad Honywill sent me a note one day to say that a book would be a good idea. He even got me excited enough that we put a few stories down on paper. Joe Cressy and Bob Gallagher thought the project a tad ambitious, but I was encouraged to put more thoughts together. I wasn't terribly confident that a book was in order until I had a drink with another old friend, Victor Malarek, who encouraged me to tell my stories. After the Easter weekend, I began writing vignettes, from my time with Jack, from my childhood, of dreams I have had, of events—and an outline emerged. Much was a stream of consciousness, but it was a wonderful exploration.

Then in came literary agent Bruce Westwood, who introduced me to Iris Tupholme of HarperCollins Canada. I want to thank them sincerely for making this book possible.

But for this book project of mine, I needed a great deal of help and professional assistance. I also needed a plan. With a demanding career as an MP, and many personal and political commitments, I had limited time to conduct research I would require to accurately recount all the key events in my life and career. My real forte is organizing and strategizing, as I have for countless political campaigns in the past. So I pulled together a team and set a process in place.

Helping me pull it all together was Lawrence Scanlan, a seasoned journalist and bestselling author from Kingston, Ontario. He waded through mountains of material—electronic folders of my files from my time as a school trustee, city councillor and MP. Old articles and reports. Transcripts of interviews with myself, Layton family members and close political colleagues. Larry spent many months working round the clock, enduring my late-night e-mails. Without his assistance, this book would not have been possible.

He also took notes at a series of dinners I arranged, mostly at my house on Huron Street, where I drew together groups I had worked with in the past, and we recalled and recounted the events that had shaped us and that we had shaped.

With these dinners and phone interviews, we gained vital input for the book, but also the pleasure of reconnecting and sharing memories with people who had played a major role in my life. And food—glorious food! I want to thank friends and colleagues Dr. Joseph Wong, Winnie Ng, Sean Meagher, John Campey, Katheryne Schulz, Tim McCaskell, Paul Copeland, Howard Morton, Anna Willats, Ryan Teschner, Will Chang, Ken Setterington, Martha Friendly, Dr. Charles Pascal, Kerry McCuaig, Fiona Nelson, Laurel Rothman, Debbie Field,

Anne McGrath, Brian Topp and Libby Davies. And thank you to writers Judy Steed and Michele Landsberg for your encouragement.

I received tremendous support from friends who reviewed drafts, provided input and critiques, and helped me talk and think things through, with cottage visits, swims and late-night talks over a glass of wine. Four who were key to the process were my dear friends Bob Gallagher, Joe Cressy, Nancy Tong and Kiloran German. A gifted writer, Kiloran relentlessly challenged me to explore the emotional side of my journey and helped me find ways to express it.

As I revisited my journey, family time was most important—Sarah and Hugh and Beatrice and Solace, Mike Layton and Brett, Doris. Dim sum with my father. Many long talks with my mother at our kitchen table at home. A wonderful visit with my brother Andre, who gave me insight into his childhood, and mine, in Hong Kong. I am grateful beyond words to all of these dear people.

I am thankful to the CBC for generously providing the transcripts and material from the Jack Layton interviews. And to Laszlo Barna of Pier 21 Films for providing me with all the research and interviews done for the Jack Layton biopic. And last but not least, I am very grateful for the support of the HarperCollins editorial team, with a special thank you to Shaun Oakey for his wonderful touch in copy editing the book.

When I celebrated twenty years in politics, close to a decade ago, I remarked at the time that I owed so many people so many thanks and could never say thank you enough. I can't do it with words. My way of saying thanks is to take action.

INDEX

Note: All locations are in Toronto, Ontario, unless otherwise noted.